1989

Power and Politics in
Early Medieval Britain and Ireland

Power and Politics in
Early Medieval Britain and Ireland

STEPHEN T. DRISCOLL

and

MARGARET R. NIEKE

Editors

Edinburgh University Press

© 1988
Edinburgh University Press
22 George Square, Edinburgh

Set in Linoterm Plantin
by Speedspools, Edinburgh
and printed in Great Britain by
Redwood Burn Limited
Trowbridge

British Library Cataloguing in Publication Data
Power and politics in early Britain and Ireland
    1. Monarchy, British — History — Sources
    2. Great Britain — Kings and rulers —
    Sources   3. Great Britain — History —
    Anglo-Saxon period, 449-1066 — Sources
    I. Driscoll, S. T.   II. Nieke, M. R.
    321.1'4   JN131

ISBN 0 85224 520 3

Contents

Stephen T. Driscoll and Margaret R. Nieke
Introduction: reworking historical archaeology   1

Margaret R. Nieke and Holly B. Duncan
Dalriada: the establishment and maintenance of an
   Early Historic kingdom in northern Britain   6

Leslie Alcock
The activities of potentates in Celtic Britain, AD 500–800:
   a positivist approach   22
Appendix: Enclosed places AD 500–800, by Elizabeth A. Alcock

Richard B. Warner
The archaeology of Early Historic Irish kingship   47

Rosemary Cramp
Northumbria: the archaeological evidence   69

Richard Hodges and John Moreland
Power and exchange in Middle Saxon England   79

Michael R. Spearman
Early Scottish towns: their origins and economy   96

Christopher J. Arnold
Territories and leadership: frameworks for the study of
   emergent polities in early Anglo-Saxon southern England   111

Genevieve Fisher
Style and sociopolitical organisation: a preliminary
   study from early Anglo-Saxon England   128

J. D. Richards
Style and symbol: explaining variability in Anglo-Saxon
   cremation burials   145

Stephen T. Driscoll
The relationship between history and archaeology:
   artefacts, documents and power   162

Works referred to in the text   188
List of contributors   208
Index   209

STEPHEN T. DRISCOLL and
MARGARET R. NIEKE

Introduction :
reworking historical archaeology

Too often historical archaeologists see artefacts through the fragile veil of surviving documentary sources without critically assessing how this influences their vision of the past. Whether it be Schliemann viewing Hissarlik through Homer's eyes, the broch digger's contemplation of the *Tain,* or any excavator drawing upon contemporary historical literature, the relationship is the same: the text intercedes. Thus at the heart of the practice of historical archaeology lies an ambivalent relationship between the archaeologist and the artefact. On the one hand, we expect richer, deeper interpretations from historical archaeologists than we do from prehistorians, yet such interpretative efforts are not likely to satisfy the criteria historians establish for historical knowledge: archaeological events are imprecisely dated and the identification of an individual's actions nearly impossible. So it would seem that artefacts provide the archaeologist with material for composing glosses on the historian's text. This marginal activity is the result of accepting traditional history and its definition of the archaeologist's role. Neither of these things ought to go unchallenged, especially if archaeologists are to make meaningful contributions to historical knowledge.

In collecting these paper we hope to encourage archaeologists to recognise their assets and to embrace the difficulties presented by the task of integrating historical and archaeological knowledge. These difficulties, as they pertain to the early medieval period, form the subject of this book. As is evident from their papers, the contributors, while not by any means following a single approach, do share an awareness of the theoretical and methodological issues involved in historical archaeology. For the most part the papers avoid abstract argument, but consider the problems of working with artefacts and documents through the discussion of specific groups of archaeological material. This is by design, for we feel that any consideration of historical archaeology should adhere to the undisputed strength of the discipline: the ability to discover new information about the past through excavation and analysis. Lurking within any discussion of the practice of historical archaeology there is the question of how valuable even these discoveries are to the study of history. Does archaeology make a meaningful contribution to the study of the Middle Ages?

We believe that medieval archaeology has matured to the point where to refute in detail Peter Sawyer's dictum, that archaeology is an expensive way of telling us what we already know, would be superfluous if not regressive. But if the importance of archaeology is beyond question, the nature of its contribution remains an open issue. Judging from written histories, archaeology produces knowledge of particular past living and working conditions, but little more. The traditional task of filling in the detail to a picture sketched from documents remains the principal activity of medieval archaeologists. Sadly this remains true even when conscientious efforts are made to integrate archaeological data into historical discussion, as for instance in *The Anglo-Saxons* (Campbell 1982). Here the archaeology is highlighted in short picture essays, which, although internally coherent, are isolated from the main text. The physical layout of the book serves as a graphic metaphor for the peripheral status of archaeology within historical endeavour. Surely a discipline which can attract historical attention, while eluding meaningful interpretation, requires reworking.

Some of the many reasons for the present state of play are touched upon in these essays. Here it is necessary to recognise that a major reason for the peripheral status of archaeology lies in the failure of archaeologists themselves to exploit the potential of their material. This failure can to some extent be blamed upon a defective view of history – one which is uncritically elitist. If as archaeologists we perceive history as the exploits of named individuals, then archaeology can only provide the occasional footnote and colourful detail. The contributors to this volume have a more sophisticated view of history and a more critical approach to the past. They are interested in employing archaeological material to write about the evolution of society, the growth of political institutions and the development of ideas, in short the essence of social history.

It is perhaps unfair to categorise these writers, especially since we noted above that there is no firm consensus of approach displayed in their contributions. However, two major influences may be discerned within this collection of papers. The first reflects a belief that the prime source of knowledge about past society is drawn from documents and maintains that any social model must be informed by a familiarity with the historical literature. As a theoretical perspective it is internal, since it emphasises the contemporary account as the basis of interpretation. The second influence, the New Archaeology, in some of its various guises, appears in a number of these papers. The willingness to employ constructs whch lack direct documentation gives the New Archaeology its external theoretical quality. This second influence need not conflict with the first; ideally they should complement one another. Both influences are positive in that they implicitly argue that the true task of the archaeologist is to contribute to the understanding of specific social processes using material evidence. This means looking to documentary sources not for labels or landmarks but for *context*: using writing to grasp the values and meanings ascribed to the material world by past society.

The first tradition can be traced back at least as far as Collingwood. In particular Collingwood's desire in *Roman Britain and the English Settlements* (1936) to explain the development and collapse of Roman Britain, as distinct from its military conquest, serves as an example for blending archaeology and documents into history. Even if his findings have been superseded, Collingwood's treatment of the subject-matter guaranteed that subsequent students of the early Middle Ages would become familiar with his work, while his status as a philosopher of history provides the approach with added credibility. Essential for the practice of historical archaeology in the tradition of Collingwood is an intimate knowledge of the documentary record, which provides the interpretative framework for the material record. Instances where archaeological interpretation goes far beyond identification and labelling in an effort to achieve some degree of historical synthesis are exceptional. Influential exceptions have been Rosemary Cramp's *Beowulf and Archaeology* (1957), Hugh Hencken's Lagore crannog excavation report (1950), and Leslie Alcock's *Dinas Powys* (1963). The last example is significant precisely because it is *not* in itself a documented site, but is one which none the less has had some of its lost history restored through the analysis of artefacts and judicious use of documentation.

In this collection, Professor Alcock's paper attempts to push the documentary approach to its inferential limits in order to generalise about the fortified centres of political power in the Celtic west. Professor Cramp sets out what she believes are the aspects of Early Northumbrian politics which can be most usefully examined archaeologically, as well as defining those which should be left to the historians. Richard Warner discusses how, with the use of the documentary record, the material evidence for royal residences may be extracted from a complex archaeological record and demonstrates its importance for an understanding of the changing political landscape of early historic Ireland. Michael Spearman outlines the case against accepting David I as the principal force behind the foundation of Scottish towns and provides an example of using archaeology to gain a critical insight into the documentary record.

If the documentary approach is taken to its logical extreme, it becomes subject to the criticism that those members of society who did not express themselves through writing are systematically excluded. Permitting documents to authorise or define the legitimate subjects of study imposes severe limitations on research, especially in the poorly documented early medieval period (see Driscoll in this volume). Any extension of research beyond the confines of the documented past must acknowledge the New Archaeology as a source of analytical techniques and of ideas designed to control the theoretical constructs drawn from outside the documentary record. The prominent use of computer aided statistical methods in the papers by Viva Fisher and Julian Richards on Anglo-Saxon mortuary practice serves to illustrate directly how items of material culture were drawn upon to define both individual and group identities. These sophisticated analytical techniques work because they are grounded on specific theories about the relationships between material culture and society and thus contribute to our understanding of politics on the community level, something which has been lost entirely to documentary historians. Similarly, on a larger scale, Christopher Arnold's paper suggests how changing burial practices may reflect the development of regional politics in early south-eastern England.

The idea that material culture plays an active role in the construction and maintenance of social relations is a strongly flowing undercurrent in many of these contributions. That this interest in the social implications of material culture should be the most common indicator of New Archaeology signifies the importance of the shift in emphasis from systems theory to social theory. The challenge of recognising the political aspects of material culture use has been met through the deployment of fairly precise concepts of power and ideology. For instance, the paper by Margaret Nieke and Holly Duncan suggests that the fostering of specialist craft production at centralised fortified strongholds was an essential component of Scottic political strategy. Similarly Richard Hodges and John Moreland argue that the appropriation of continental architectural forms for Anglo-Saxon churches was part of a deliberate attempt by the ruling class to acquire religious legitimacy. Archaeological resources contribute information vital to these two discussions of power and ideology, showing that such topics can no longer be regarded as the exclusive domain of historians. These papers and the collection as a whole are evidence of the maturity of early medieval archaeology and indicate that the division of the past into strictly bounded domains of history and archaeology needs reconsideration.

We hope that one result of the new vigour shown here will be to enhance the credibility of medieval archaeology within the discipline and within historic studies in general. It has been mooted frequently that medieval archaeology could in theory serve as the testing ground for archaeological thought because of its relationship with another source of knowledge, history. This presumes a degree of interpretative independence which is neither desirable nor possible. Historical archaeology should be in the vanguard of archaeological practice, because the richness of our material should permit a level of interpretation which cannot be matched by our prehistoric colleagues. It is precisely our access to contemporary values and beliefs through documents which enables us to produce interpretations which are subtler, more specific, more historical and thus more human and, perhaps, even more interesting. After all, the relationship between the archaeologist and the data resembles far more closely that of the historian than that of the anthropologist. The apparent failure of medieval archaeology to realise the potential of its data should not be taken as a cause for despair and isolation, rather it should be acknowledged as the major challenge confronting all historical archaeology.

The ideas which led to this book were at first only snatches of lunchtime conversation between the editors and John Barrett. The eventual outcome of these discussions was a conference held in Glasgow in February 1984 entitled *Early Historical Archaeology: Emergent Political Groups and Kingship*. This was organised by the Glasgow University Archaeology Society, whose turn it was to host the joint Glasgow and Edinburgh students' societies conference. The chosen topic, the politics of early medieval kingship, was selected for several reasons. It is a popular topic, one which is of importance to both archaeologists and historians and one of those (rare) issues which is of interest to both Celtic and Anglo-Saxon scholars. Behind this choice lay the intention of providing a focus for discussion which could reveal distinctions in the sorts of past created by historians and archaeologists. The desire to expose the true nature of the relationship between history and archaeology through direct confrontation can now be seen to have been optimistic if not downright naive. The papers in this volume make it clear that the disciplines are too cunningly intermeshed to have been untangled in the course of a single day. Four of the papers, those by C. Arnold, R. Cramp, M. R. Nieke and H. B. Duncan, and R. Warner form part of this volume. The remaining papers have been solicited in order to expand the scope of the debate.

The conference and this volume would not have been possible without the help of several members of the Glasgow University Archaeology Society. In particular we must thank Irene Cullen, Neil Curtis, Iain Banks and Miriam Macdonald. We must also thank other postgraduate students, Nicholas Aitchison, Duncan Campbell, Alan Leslie, Colin Richards and Ross Samson, who have all cheerfully suffered our editorial work over the past few months. Special thanks are also extended to John Barrett for his encouragement and ready advice. We are grateful to Patrick Wormald and Leslie Alcock for chairing the conference, and to Professor Francis J. Byrne, James Campbell, Michael Clanchy and Wendy Davies for their oral contributions. Thanks are also due to Leslie Alcock for much help with publication matters. Financial support for the conference was generously provided by the Glasgow Archaeological Society and the Department of Archaeology, University of Glasgow.

Glasgow, April 1985.

Dalriada : the establishment and maintenance of an Early Historic kingdom in northern Britain

According to documentary sources the kingdom of Dalriada was founded in Argyll by Fergus Mór Mac Erc around AD 500. The rulers of this kingdom were not natives of Britain but immigrants from north-eastern Ireland. The early history of the kingdom, the establishment of Christianity, the eventual take-over of Pictland and the Norse incursions are all essential themes of early Scottish history.

The aim of this chapter is to present an integrated view of the history and archaeology of this kingdom, strands of evidence which formerly have been treated in isolation. Our study illustrates the potential for research within the area as well as highlighting problems inherent in former approaches to the material.

If we believe the historical sources, the territory held by the kings of Dalriada was extensive, covering areas of both mainland and islands (figure 1). The map provided here is based upon one presented by Bannerman (1974) and was produced as a result of analysis of the available documentary sources; mainly the *Senchus Fer nAlban* (a History of the Men of Scotland) and the *Life of Columba* by Adomnan. Both were originally compiled in the seventh century (Bannerman 1974; Anderson and Anderson 1961). This map also illustrates the tripartite division of the area recorded in the sources. According to genealogies, each of these divisions was held by a separate lineage or *Cenél*. The main *Cenéla* were the *Cenél nGabráin*, the *Cenél Loairn* and the *Cenél nOengusa*. Each of these was supposed ultimately to have descended from Fergus Mór or one of his brothers. Throughout most of the history of Dalriada a single king, drawn from one of these groups, ruled over the whole kingdom.

Because a variety of documentary sources which provide information about the kingdom and its history survive, Dalriada has received a fair amount of attention both from historians and archaeologists. The former have engaged in detailed examinations of the written evidence which is now fairly well understood. The latter have mainly been concerned to verify the recorded migration by identifying Irish traits within the visible material culture of the area. The stress placed upon the culture-historical approach, which attributes a specific and identifiable material culture to a distinct group of people, can now be seen to constrain archaeological studies. It is an approach which has been shown to be too simplistic; the work of Hodder and others, for example, has illustrated the complexities of material culture and its workings within society (1982a, 1982b). It is no longer adequate to see artefacts as passive reflections of human action. Instead, acceptance of the active nature of material culture is necessary

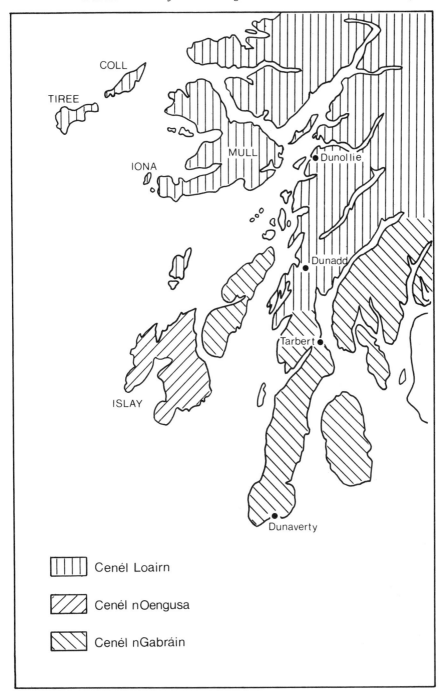

COLL

TIREE

MULL

IONA

●Dunollie

Dunadd

Tarbert ●

ISLAY

●
Dunaverty

⊞ Cenél Loairn

⊟ Cenél nOengusa

⊠ Cenél nGabráin

Figure I. The Early Historic kingdom of Dalradia.

for an understanding of its importance in creating, structuring and maintaining patterns of social relationship. In this chapter an attempt will be made to examine the surviving material culture of the area, in particular placing it within its social, political, economic and historical context. Emphasis will be placed upon an analysis of how it may have articulated, or been used to articulate, past social relationships.

At the outset it is of importance to question the nature of the Scottic migration to northern Britain, and examine how the immigrants were able to control such a large territorial extent. These issues are important for any consideration of the material culture since, as we will show, it was active in the formulation and maintenance of these patterns of control.

The conventional view of the Dalriadic establishment is that the kingdom was founded rapidly and without recorded conflict in about AD 500. Such a view, however, does not withstand critical examination. This version of events implies a swift imposition of an external power over the pre-existing population. The little evidence we have about the prehistoric native inhabitants of Argyll suggests that they had a fairly complex society. This is indicated by their ability to organise the construction of massive defended hillforts and other defended settlements (cf. RCAHMS 1971, 1975, 1980, 1984). What must be considered here is how the Dalriadic kings were able to establish control over this population.

This establishment must depend in part upon the existence of prior social links between the two areas. North-east Ireland and northern Britain should not be seen as distinct areas. It seems that movement between the two was commonplace from an early date. The close proximity of Argyll to northern Ireland probably led to the establishment of a variety of contacts and ties between these two areas in particular. This contact may have involved, amongst other things, the establishment of marriage alliances between senior households. A consequence of this would have been the development of a population which already had Irish connections, a situation which could have existed long before AD 500.

Various documentary references survive which could be used to support the view that contacts existed across the North Channel before AD 500. Tacitus, for example, records a meeting in northern Britain between Agricola and an Irish prince who had been forced to seek refuge there (Tacitus 24). Neither the exact location of the meeting nor the temporary residence of the prince is noted. However, the passage does illustrate the movement of an aristocrat between the two areas in the first century AD.

In the fourth century several classical authors note attacks on the northern frontiers of Roman Britain by, among others, the Scots and the Picts (Mann 1971). Most Romanists argue that at this time the Scots were still residing in Ireland (cf. Richmond 1955, 1963; Frere 1974, 390; Breeze and Dobson 1976, 220). There seems little reason, though, why this was necessarily the case. We cannot discount the possibility that the *Scotti* referred to were already settled in northern Britain. Taken together these references bracket the Scots and the Picts together. One interpretation of this would be that some form of association existed between them. This would have been more easily achieved if the *Scotti* were resident in Britain.

In addition to classical references there are a number of Irish traditions which credit various prehistoric legendary figures with exploits in *Alba*. In the past these have frequently been alluded to in discussions of an early Irish presence in northern Britain (cf. Watson 1926). It must be remembered here that *Alba* was, initially at least, a name used to refer to the whole of Britain, and not just Scotland (Kinsella 1969, 257). In some instances, however, more specific locations are given. Labhraidh Loingsearch, for example, is recorded as having made expeditions against Skye, Tiree and the Orkneys, while in the tale of Deirdre and the sons of Uisneach refuge is sought in *Alba* from Conchobar, king of Ulaid. According to this tale the sons of Uisneach settled in *Alba* for sixteen years and took possession of an area which extended northwards from Mann. Later versions connect them specifically with the areas of Cowal and Lorn (Watson 1926, 214). The major problem which must be faced in the analysis of these sources is that they were first written down in the eighth century or later (Hughes 1972, 175) and most survive only in medieval manuscripts. The question of the extent to which they record an earlier Iron Age past is questionable. Current opinion tends to favour the view that they were the product of a Christian society, perhaps even the product of ecclesiastical *literati*, and hence do not provide a good 'window on the Iron Age' (Mallory 1981 contra Jackson 1964). Like genealogies, their contents may be largely deliberate creations designed to justify current patterns of social relationship. Hence references to ancient links between Ireland and northern Britain may be legends specifically created to justify later Irish claims to authority over areas of Britain.

The name of the kingdom – Dalriada – lends credence to the view of an Irish presence in Argyll prior to AD 500. This can be translated as the *portion of Riada*, not the *portion of Fergus Mór* as might be expected. Riada was specifically associated with Scottish Dalriada by Bede who attributes the establishment of the kingdom to him (*HE* 1, 1). This origin legend was probably drawn from his sources in the Pictish royal house, and the Iona community (Duncan 1981). Irish genealogists have argued that Riada was a pseudo-historical figure who lived ten generations prior to Fergus Mór (cf. Bannerman 1974, 123). Whether he actually existed or not is questionable, and perhaps he is better seen as an eponymous hero around whom many folktales were woven.

If a population which saw itself as of Irish descent, or which had close Irish connections existed in Argyll prior to AD 500, then the recorded migration at this time may be seen as a further step in a political process which had begun much earlier. Indeed the documentary sources may actually contain an origin myth deliberately created to explain a continuing process.

It is our contention that the documentation records a small-scale dynastic transfer to northern Britain rather than a mass folk migration. An explanation for this can be sought in the internal politics of north-eastern Ireland at this

time. The power and position of the Irish Dalriadic dynasty was being threat-
ened by the growing strength and geographical expansion of the Uí Néill
dynasty (Byrne 1965). This was a contributory factor in the Dalriadic migration, the prior connections with the west of Scotland providing the basis for
transference to Argyll. Byrne has indicated that this was not an isolated
instance of dynastic transfer (1971, 1973).

The infiltration and eventual take-over of a pre-existing system rather than
domination by military conquest may be indicated by a reconsiderain of
genealogical information which survives. Here it must be remembered that
genealogies were compiled in order to explain and justify contemporary patterns of social relationship rather than to record accurately the past (Dumville
1977a). Seen in this light the conventional view that the kingdom was divided
amongst the brothers and descendants of Fergus Mór becomes questionable.
Instead, the tripartite division of the kingdom is better viewed as a later,
deliberate manipulation of the evidence to justify the rule of a single king over
the whole territory. This is of importance since it implies that the division had
ancient origins, and that the Dalriadic kings were able to establish control over
not one but three groups of people. This is a point which has not been made
before and which has obvious implications not only for any study of Dalriada,
but also for the preceding prehistoric period. Analysis of the subsequent
history of the kingdom indicates that the three groups maintained some form
of independent identity throughout its history. Hence the achievement of the
Dalriadic kings appears all the more remarkable.

An important key to understanding the political achievements of the early
Dalriadic kings is provided by an analysis of the early Christian Church within
the kingdom. Soon after the creation of the monastic community of Iona in the
mid-sixth century we see the beginnings of a close involvement between kings
and ecclesiastics. A good example of this is St Columba's involvement in the
ordination of Aedán as king (*VC* 107a). Indeed Iona was to develop as a
protagonist of the idea of the divine nature of kingship (Byrne 1973). The
relationship between the Church and the kings was of a symbiotic nature.
From the point of view of the former, the establishment of links with the royal
lineage must have strengthened the position of the Church within society.
From the point of view of the rulers association with new religious and ritual
practices would have been of importance for their own prestige and position.
In addition to this the Church also introduced literacy. The ability to exploit
such a new and important system of knowledge and means of communication
must have strengthened the position of the rulers of Dalriada, both within the
kingdom and in northern Britain as a whole.

The close relationship which developed between the rulers of Dalriada and
the Church may be reflected in the location of monastic communities within
the kingdom. Most of these are located on islands, for example on Iona, Tiree
and the Garvellachs. These lay on the fringes of Dalriadic territory, the main
centres of which lay on the mainland in the territory of the *Cenél nGabráin* and
the *Cenél Loairn*. Hence the islands were peripheral and are likely to have been

the areas in which royal control was weakest. In allowing the establishment of monastic communities in these areas the kings were acknowledging this weakness, and deliberately using the Church to control such areas for them. Once established, these communities would have been more inclined to support the Christian kings of Dalriada than their neighbours in Pictland who were not converted to Christianity for some years.

The concept of a small-scale migration and the likely existence of an Irish population in the area prior to AD 500 must be taken into account in any consideration of the material culture of the area. It may, for example, be incorrect to attempt to identify new aspects of the material culture around AD 500 if the patterns of social interaction suggest pre-existing links between Ireland and northern Britain. Also, such newcomers may not have brought distinctive artefacts with them and may, initially at least, have adopted many aspects of the local material culture. The ability to manipulate and use the material culture of the area in the same way as native communities may have been an important means of gaining local respectability and acceptance, hence lessening the risk of conflict.

As the kings strengthened their hold on the kingdom, they probably devised a more tangible means of expressing their power and position by taking control of certain aspects of the local material culture. To consider this in greater detail we must turn to those sites within Dalriada with royal associations, in an attempt to analyse the role of these and the activities which were occurring within them.

As a result of the analysis of place-names mentioned in annalistic sources, it has been possible to identify tentatively four major defended sites within Argyll: Dunollie, Dunadd, Tarbert Lochfyne and Dunaverty (figure 1). These have been equated with the documentary references to *Dun Ollaigh, Dun Att, Tairpert Boittir* and *Aberte* respectively (Bannerman 1974; Alcock 1981a). Of these, the locations of the first two are the most secure. References to attacks, burnings and sieges at these sites indicate their importance and have been taken to imply royal status. All would appear to have been stone-walled enclosures located on craggy rock outcrops.

The following discussion will draw mainly upon evidence from the site of Dunadd in Mid Argyll since it has been subjected to several excavations (Christison 1905; Craw 1930; Lane 1980, 1981) and hence is the site about which we have the most knowledge.

In our view, the primary function of such sites was as a centre at which tribute owed to the king by the surrounding population could be taken for royal collection and consumption. Clientship was a basic underpinning of society at this time (Gerriets 1983). This involved the establishment of reciprocal relationships between individuals of different social position. A client was offered a fief, which usually took the form of stock, as well as physical protection. In return for this, renders of agricultural produce and labour service were made. Relations of clientship provided a measure of economic and social security for lower grades of society and helped define and maintain the status and position of persons of higher social status. In the case of kings, the ability to maintain numerous clients was an important measure of status, clientship being a medium through which the relationships of power were negotiated. To work, however, such a relationship had to be seen to operate, hence tribute owed to the kings had to be visibly collected and consumed. The most efficient means of achieving this would have been through the establishment of a series of centres throughout the territories held. The defended sites mentioned above would have served such a role well. That more than one such site existed reflects the nature of the terrain of the kingdom which is dominated by highland and water, both of which impair easy communication. Sea transport was of major importance in linking the various areas of the kingdom, as is well illustrated by the naval assessments contained within the *Senchus Fer nAlban* which indicate the size of warfleet a king could expect to raise from the population (Bannerman 1974). Use of boats to move around the kingdom, however, was dependent upon access to the vessels, and also good weather conditions. We do not know how the former was organised, while the latter could not always be relied upon in an area open to Atlantic storms. Because of these factors, it would not have been realistic for kings to expect distant clients happily to transport their tribute to a single royal centre. This would have been particularly true if, as seems likely, the tribute was raised in the form of agricultural produce. If this was the case, alternative arrangements would have been needed to ensure that payment was made and that this essential link between the king and subjects was maintained.

One answer to this problem would have been the establishment of a series of royal centres around Dalriada between which the king could progress. A similar situation may have led to the development of peripatetic kingship elsewhere in the British Isles. An example of this is found in Anglo-Saxon Northumbria where the journeyings of the kings are recorded in documentary sources (Alcock 1982b). The establishment of an efficient system of progress around Dalriada may have been a major contributory factor in the success of the Dalriadic kings.

With these thoughts in mind, the defended sites discussed earlier would have been inadequate to serve the needs of the whole kingdom. In particular we must question what happened to the tribute owed by island communities, many of which lie at some distance from these sites. Of course, it seems probable that other sites existed for which no documentary record survives. In the case of Islay it has been argued elsewhere that the fortified site of Dun Nosbridge, located in the centre of the island, was well suited to fulfil such a role (Nieke 1983). In the case of Mull and Tiree the rights of tribute may have been granted by the kings to the various monastic communities which developed there. Such royal grants of the products of land to the Church appear common throughout the early medieval period, certainly in Wales (Davies 1978).

During royal progresses these defended sites were probably used as residential centres by the kings and their followers. We should then envisage the

occurrence of feasting and other social activities. The former was of importance as a means whereby the leader could display his largesse to the local
population, and hence impress his status upon them. As gathering-points for
the local population they also provided centres at which other administrative
and perhaps legal functions could be performed.

The artefactual evidence from Dunadd also reveals that a variety of other
activities were taking place there. In particular there was a concentration of
craftworking activity. A range of iron tools indicate wood and leather working
(Duncan 1982), while iron working is indicated by a sizeable quantity of bog
iron-ore and other debris. Of particular significance to the present discussion,
however, is the working of fine metals – bronze, silver and gold – indicated by
crucible fragments, waste metal and most importantly by a vast quantity of
clay mould debris from jewellery casting. The range of artefacts being produced included pins, discs and other decorated metalwork, but the major
product appears to have been penannular brooches.

Some of these activities could have originated as a result of the role of the
site as a centre for the collection of tribute. The numerous rotary querns, of
which over fifty examples are known (Christison 1905), must indicate the
processing of cereal grains. The latter would have reached the site as rendered
tribute. The leather being worked could have been a by-product of meat
renders. As well as being used for clothing, shoes and various items of
domestic equipment, it was commonly used to produce military equipment
such as shields, tents, blade-sheaths and possibly armour. The production of
items for military use would have been necessary to supply the warband which
accompanied the king. Indeed, amongst other artefacts from the site are shield
bosses, fragments of spearheads and a sword (Duncan 1982). These also serve
to indicate the status of the site, since as a general rule weapons are rarely
found on settlement sites. While on the theme of military activity at the site, it
may have been a gathering point for the large armies which the *Senchus Fer
nAlban* indicates could be raised in the kingdom (Bannerman 1974).

While an explanation for the processing of agricultural products at the site
can be offered, the fine metalworking is not so easily explained. One problem
is that the raw or reworked materials upon which the industry was based seem
unlikely to have been the product of tribute. Hence some alternative explanation must be considered. The clue to this may be the site's royal status.
Kingship in this period was not a stable office. The history of Dalriada was
marked by frequent struggles to gain supremacy, either between lineages or
indeed within individual lineages (Anderson 1980). Aggression both within
and without the kingdom was one of the major elements in maintaining a
king's power and position. However, in addition to this, his ability to mobilise
wealth and control the production and distribution of certain craft products
played a central and critical role. Ethnographic studies indicate that hierarchical status can be obtained and maintained through privileged access to valued
items and control of their distribution through society (Hodder 1982a, 150).
In this light, the control of craft activity can be seen as important to the

Dalriadic kings for the enhancement of their own power and position. Parallels for such control of craft working can be sited from elsewhere in Europe. The Emperor Charlemagne, for example, gathered his Rhineland potters together in craft villages (Hodges 1982, 163). Concentrating groups of craft workers together in this manner was beneficial to their skills, leading to the development of higher standards. This became possible as supportive networks of specialists developed, each of which could concentrate on a specific aspect of their work rather than having to go through all the processes of artefact production. This would have been of particular importance at Dunadd where the production of fine metalworking involved a range of skills including metal casting, engraving and inlay work.

At Dunadd the concentration on the manufacture of a variety of styles of penannular brooch may hint at the particular importance of this form of decorative jewellery. Indeed it is possible that these brooches were used to display social position and in particular close links with the royal lineage of the kingdom. Possession of them would have been unlikely to confer social status in and of themselves, instead their display was a means of symbolising relationships which were already clearly established by other means, mainly kinship links and patterns of clientship. Indeed the Irish Brehon laws indicate that a silver brooch was one of the customary insignia of a chief (Small et al. 1973, 105; Henry 1965, 102). These laws were compiled in the seventh and eighth centuries AD (Hughes 1972, 43) and thus are highly relevant to the period under consideration here. It is surely significant to this argument that the figure of Christ on a late ninth to tenth century high cross from Monasterboice is seen wearing a penannular brooch (Henry 1967, pl.79). If the brooches are seen as a symbol of social position, then this may indicate the high status of ecclesiastical figures within Early Historic society. Indeed Irish legal tracts tell us that this was the case in Ireland. It may also indicate that as well as symbolising relationships within secular society such brooches also evoked religious connotations. What we may be witnessing here is the deliberate adoption and use by the Church of an item of material culture originally created and used within a pagan milieu. Of course this material culture was most familiar to the early ecclesiastics. However, the exploitation of material culture in this manner by the new religious authority was probably of major importance in legitimising the position of the new institution within traditional pagan society.

While many of the artefacts at Dunadd are assumed to be of local origin, some were the product of external trade contact. Imported objects include numerous fragments of imported pottery. In particular, there is E-ware which originated in either northern or western Gaul (Peacock and Thomas 1967; Campbell 1984; Peacock 1984; Hodges 1984). Fragments of glass of Merovingian type also occur. These seem to have reached the site in a broken form as cullet for use as inlays in the fine metalwork being produced, and perhaps also in the manufacture of glass beads. Not all the beads, however, were necessarily made at Dunadd, indeed some were the product of continental contact.

Examples include a drum-shaped tricolour Frankish bead and others may be of either Frankish or Scandinavian origin (personal communication, M. Guido).

In addition to the pottery and glass, continental origins can be argued for other artefacts. A bronze gilt disc decorated with interlace found during the 1929 excavations (Craw 1930, fig.4) is most closely paralleled by a bronze gilt disc from Rhenen, Holland (Glazema and Ypey 1956, pl.24).

Some of the imported artefacts discussed above could have arrived as adjuncts to cargoes of more perishable items. The presence of imported pottery, for example, may reflect the importation of wine in casks from Gaul (Alcock 1983). The origins of this trade probably relate to the use of wine by ecclesiastics for liturgical purposes. However, it was probably also used within secular society, being important for instance in the feasting activities mentioned earlier.

We would argue that specific reasons could be offered for the presence of this imported material at Dunadd. It should be seen as the product of external contact which was deliberately instigated and controlled by the kings. These imported artefacts serve to illustrate that the outlook of the Dalriadic kings was not parochial, but extended over several areas outside their immediate kingdom. The development of contact with the continent must owe much to the close relationship the rulers developed with the Church. It is clear that from an early date Irish Christian missions were being successfully established in several areas on the continent, most particularly in Gaul. The major impetus to the development of this contact came from north-eastern Ireland. Columbanus, a monk from Bangor, moved to the continent where he established monastic houses at Annegray, Luxeuil and Bobbio before his death in AD 615 (Hughes 1966, 57). Bangor lay within the territory of the Dál Fiatach who were close neighbours of the Dalriada in Ireland and were fellow members of the Ulaid.

These imported artefacts were presumably the product of some form of trade or gift exchange system with the continent. Items of jewellery which could be displayed, or cargoes of wine which could be drunk could have been the product of gift exchange. The broken glass, however, seems unlikely to have been a gift, and hence we must see it as the product of some more formalised system of trade with the continent. The Scottish products which made up the return cargoes could have included white furs which were unobtainable in warmer southern climes. More likely, however, are cargoes based upon the products being collected and controlled by the kings. A good example of this would have been animal hides. We know that these could be traded over long distances since Hodges notes references to Irish monks in the Loire Valley in the seventh century trading in leather (1982, 127). Wool may have been another export. The importance of the latter is well attested in the medieval period although the precise origins of it are unclear.

While imported products were reaching Dunadd we would not envisage the site as a port of trade or emporium similar to those discussed recently by

Hodges (1982). The total amount of imported material at Dunadd is small, and the site may not have been directly accessible by sea. The primary importance of the site lies in its role within the kingdom, linking the kings with the rest of the population.

To summarise our view of Dunadd, it was one of a number of major defended centres at which local tribute could be collected and consumed by the kings, who probably resided there during their progresses. The kings also instigated craft production within the sites, as well as channelling continental trade and exchange through them. Control of these activities and the products thereof was important for the development and maintenance of royal power and position.

While the activities discussed above may have been occurring at each of the royal fortified sites of Dalriada, there is evidence to suggest that Dunadd held a prominent position. In previous discussions of the site it has frequently been referred to as the capital of Scottish Dalriada. As Lane has indicated, this is based upon certain interpretations of available documentary evidence and also on particular archaeological features of the site (1984). There are many problems with this identification, the most basic of which is that the concept of a 'capital' site as we would know it is anachronistic at the time of which we speak. The site may, however, have been associated with inauguration rituals. This suggestion is based upon the discovery of a series of impressions carved into a sheet of living rock near the summit of the site which includes that of a footprint. Various accounts of medieval Irish and Scottish inauguration rituals which involved the placing of the royal foot in such a depression have survived (Martin 1703, 240–1; Hamilton 1968, 151–6; Hayes-McCoy 1970). The aim of this ritual was to mark the unity of the king and his kingdom. The precise origins of the ceremony are unknown, but a similar footprint stone has been noted at the fortified site of Clickhimin in Shetland which may date as early as the third to first centuries BC (Hamilton 1968). It was the presence of this stone at Dunadd which led several early scholars to refer to the site as a capital.

Within Dalriada a similar footprint stone is known from the so-called St Columba's Chapel in southern Kintyre (RCAHMS 1971), a site which lies adjacent to the possible royal fortification at Dunaverty. This may originally have been of importance as an inauguration site for the leaders of the *Cenél nGabráin* who held Kintyre as the major part of their territories. Until the late seventh century kings of the whole of Dalriada were drawn from this group. The location of this stone at an ecclesiastical site may reflect the involvement of the Church in such rituals; King Aedán, whom Columba ordained as king, was a member of the *Cenél nGabráin*. Subsequently the importance of this site may have been eclipsed by the rise to power of the *Cenél Loairn* who held lands further north in Argyll. The precise boundary between the territorial holdings of these two groups has not been firmly established. It would, however, appear to have been located in the area of northern Knapdale or southern Mid Argyll (Bannerman 1974).

The *Cenél nGabráin* and the *Cenél Loairn* were the two most important groups within Dalriada, and indeed the recorded history of the kingdom is really the history of these two lineages, the *Cenél nOengusa* apparently not having been closely involved in recorded political events. Because of Dunadd's central location between the *Cenél nGabráin* and the *Cenél Loairn* it would have been well suited to develop as an inter-*Cenéla* meeting point. Hence, it would have been an ideal location for inauguration of kings drawn from either group.

While sites like Dunadd were major centres within Dalriada, they represent only the top of a hierarchy of sites which were in use. In addition, a range of other defended sites including duns and crannogs were occupied (Nieke 1983, 1984). The former were defended homesteads, in many cases probably totally roofed over. They were inhabited by small social groups, possibly nuclear family units. The dating of such sites is still a matter of debate. They may have had origins in the Iron Age, but if so their use continued. Of the eleven sites in Argyll which have been partially or totally excavated, five have produced clear signs of occupation in the Early Historic period.

The artefactual evidence recovered from these sites includes groups of glass beads which can be paralleled on Early Historic sites in Ireland, sherds of E-ware pottery and penannular brooches. If our suppositions about Dunadd are correct, and the production of and access to these types of artefact were being controlled by the kings, then their occurrence at sites other than the royal centres indicates contact between the inhabitants of the latter sites and the kings. The former were likely to have been persons of considerable social position who would have had close connections with the rulers. This view can be supported by the nature of the duns themselves, which are massively constructed and hence seemingly the product of some form of labour mobilisation. Persons of high social position would have had numerous clients from whom to exact labour services for construction work. The use of prestigious dominant locations within the landscape for such sites would also indicate the status of their inhabitants.

The penannular brooch from Kildonan dun in Kintyre (Fairhurst 1939) is a crucial piece of evidence in support of our present argument. Comparison of this brooch with a mould from the recent excavations at Dunadd suggests that it may have originated in the Dunadd workshop (figure 2). This illustrates not only the role Dunadd played in the royal control of production and distribution of metalwork, but also, if our hypothesis about penannular brooches symbolising a high social position is correct, strengthens our contention that the occupants of Kildonan enjoyed an elevated social position.

Crannogs appear to have been similar settlement units to duns. Within Dalriada the best evidence for Early Historic occupation of a crannog comes from the site of Loch Glashan in Mid Argyll (Scott and Scott 1960, 1961). As well as producing a mass of finely worked wood and leather, several sherds of E-ware and a bronze penannular brooch are indicative of occupation by persons of relatively high social standing.

While at least some of the duns and crannogs of Argyll were occupied at the

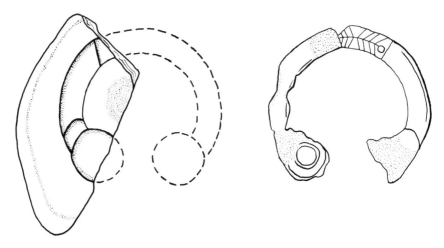

Figure 2. The Dunadd-Kildonan connection. The mould fragment (*left*) from Dunadd may have been used to cast the bronze brooch from Kildonan Dun, Kintyre (*right*). Scale 3:2.

same time as Dunadd, it is highly unlikely that they represent the totality of the settlement pattern of this period. The settlement sites of the mass of the population have still to be identified. The location of the latter sites is imperative for further studies of Dalriada for two reasons. Firstly, until these sites are identified and examined we will not have the total picture of the contemporary social structure. Secondly, any detailed analysis of the workings of material culture within the kingdom will be biased towards wealthier sites and therefore inaccurate. To attempt to resolve this problem of missing elements of the settlement pattern a series of questions must be examined. To begin with, further investigation of dun and crannog sites would be of use. Normally these are seen as isolated settlements within the landscape. Recently, though, it has become clear that this need not necessarily be the case. Fieldwork in Argyll has located some dun sites which appear to be associated with structural remains and building platforms. The best, and also the most complex, example of this is the site of Ardanstur on Loch Melford where two duns are located in close proximity. Around one lie several walled terraces which may be contemporary with the main dun enclosure. Around the other are several oval platforms and scoops which would have provided ideal stances for circular structures (Barrett, Hill and Nieke in preparation). Of course excavation would be necessary to test the hypothesis that these terraces and platforms were contemporary with the main dun. The argument that dun sites were inhabited by persons of relatively high social status could provide support for the view that other settlements may have developed around them. Earlier in the present work the importance of clientship was noted. We would envisage each dun or crannog dweller having dependent clients who may have settled near the residence of their overlord for physical protection.

A related question is to what extent, and when, nucleated settlements began to develop around church sites. This problem as not been examined in Scotland. In addition, the origins of many of the deserted settlements which exist throughout the Highlands have never been satisfactorily examined. The majority of these sites are normally dismissed as of 'relatively recent date'. However, at many sites, structural remains and remnant building platforms imply a complex settlement history which extended over a considerable period of time. Alcock and Alcock have discussed the possibility that some of these sites may have Norse origins (1980). It is equally possible that some pre-dated the Norse arrival.

Discussion so far in this chapter has concentrated on the period up to the mid-ninth century, a period during which the Dalriadic kings established and maintained an extensive kingdom. The period was not without incident; the lineages in control of the kingdom were to change, and conflict is recorded within and without the kingdom. In some instances the Dalriadic kings were successful, in others not. A good example of the latter occurred in the early eighth century when the Picts were able to invade the kingdom, ravaging various areas and capturing Dunadd; some would argue that this was followed by a period of Pictish overlordship of Dalriada. The main period of change, however, occurred in the ninth century.

In AD 843 King Cinaed Mac Ailpín (Kenneth Mac Alpín) of Dalriada was able to effect a union of Pictland and Dalriada, thereby creating a large territorial unit which formed the basis for the creation of medieval Scotland. The manner in which this unification occurred is poorly documented. The annals which were being recorded in the monastery at Iona end around AD 740, their compilation perhaps being disturbed by the Norse raiders.

It has been argued that it is unlikely that Cinaed inherited his Pictish position (Anderson 1982) and hence some form of military conquest must be envisaged. Whatever the details, Cinaed appears to have rapidly established a permanent position in the east, and documentary sources tell how he 'led the Scots from Argyll into the land of the Picts' (Anderson 1980, 247, 267). He appears to have moved the main royal centre to the east, probably at first to Forteviot in Strathearn (Alcock 1982b). Examination of the impact of this movement on Pictland lies outside the scope of the present chapter, but it is important to consider its effect on Dalriada.

This massive expansion in the area of interest of the Dalriadic kings must have stretched the mechanisms of control then in use. Indeed Cinaed may have appreciated and tried to deal with this problem from the outset. Annalistic sources indicate that in AD 843 Godfraith, chief of Airgialla came over to Dalriada from Ireland at the bidding of Cinaed (Anderson 1922, 284). When Godfraith died ten years later it was recorded that he held the title 'Lord of the Hebrides' (Anderson 1922, 284). The areas most weakened by Cinaed's movement to the east were likely to have been on the periphery of the kingdom where royal control was probably always at its weakest. Earlier it was argued that this same problem led Dalriadic kings to encourage the establishment of monastic communities in these areas. This system of control, however, may have been weakening in the early ninth century as a result of Norse raiding, much of which appears to have been directed against these religious communities.

A system of deputised control may also have been instituted on the mainland, and it is perhaps in this period that we should see the rise to prominence of lineages such as the Macsweens, the Lamonts, Maclachland and Macgilchrists who were important local leaders in the medieval period (Duncan and Brown 1957; Barrow 1981). That Dalriadic power did not collapse on the mainland is implied by the paucity of evidence for Norse settlement and activity in the area. This must surely suggest that the area was not readily open to Norse infiltration, rather than that it held no interest for them.

The picture of ninth century events, however, is not one of total continuity. At Dunadd, for example, the most intensive period of craft activity dates to the early ninth century, when many of the penannular brooches may have been made (Lane 1984). After this, activity at the site appears to have come to an end. If earlier hypotheses about the role of Dunadd are correct, then this would seem to have major implications for any study of the events of this period, implying a disjunction of the kings from the population. The evidence for continuity indicated above, however, forms the basis for the suggestion that perhaps now royal deputies took on the role of tribute collection for the king.

It would seem unlikely that the ninth century was marked by mass migrations from Dalriada into Pictland. Cinaed was probably accompanied by his personal *comitatus* or warband. Once this group had settled there they would have provided the basis for the development of further links. The creation of more extensive systems of marital alliance would be a good example of the latter.

It is unlikely that the kings abandoned Dalriada altogether since, apart from anything else, this would have removed them from the social context which helped to define and maintain their position. Indeed, we know that close links with Iona at least, where several subsequent kings were said to be buried, were maintained. By analogy, after the original dynastic transfer from Ireland to northern Britain, contact was maintained with Irish Dalriada for many years.

In conclusion, the achievements of the Dalradic kings of northern Britain were great. Not only were they able to establish an extensive kingdom in the west, but also, in the ninth century they gained control over neighbouring Pictland. The initial Dalriadic establishment was the result of the successful infiltration and take-over of several pre-existing political groups. During their period of control the kings may have sought deliberately to control the production, distribution and circulation of a range of items of material culture, thereby strengthening their own power and position within the area. The establishment of widespread relationships of clientage was also of importance for royal power. Furthermore, a series of defended sites was created to function as centres for the collection of tribute owed to the kings.

In this study particular concern has been placed on an analysis of the importance of various items of material culture within the area. It is our contention that this material can only meaningfully be understood within the specific context of its production and use.

Acknowledgements

This chapter would not have been written without the help and encouragement of several individuals. Professor L. Alcock, J. C. Barrett and S. T. Driscoll provided much assistance with the production of the original conference paper and Dr A. Lane kindly permitted us to cite evidence from his recent excavations of Dunadd prior to publication. We would also like to thank N. B. Aitchison, R. Samson and I. P. Duncan for their helpful comments on the various drafts of this paper and A. McGhie (for figure 1). Of course, final responsibility for the ideas conveyed in this paper lie with the authors.

The activities of potentates in Celtic
Britain, A D 500–800 : a positivist approach

Prolegomena

Recent studies of the written sources for Celtic Britain in the early medieval period are characterised by a predominantly reductionist approach. A useful contrast may be provided by the archaeological evidence, with all its concreteness, immediacy and contemporaneity. In this study, therefore, the material evidence observed by the archaeologist is first surveyed. It is then asserted that certain inferences flow ineluctably from the empirical evidence, and these are further explored.[1]

Thus far, my approach would conform to the reductionism of one school of archaeologists currently active in the early medieval period. Their claim is that the integrity of archaeology as an academic discipline can only be maintained by studying it, even in a historical period, in total separation from the written sources. In other words, they wish to treat the archaeology of the fifth to eighth centuries in Britain as though it were prehistoric, or more correctly preliterate.[2]

This attitude is expressly rejected here, first, and at the most general level, because in our attempts to observe and to understand the past it is absurd to deny ourselves the assistance of any single part of the evidence. At a more particular level, much of our chronology in western Britain is ultimately dependent on written sources in the Mediterranean which provide dates for imported pottery and thence, by inference, for Insular sites. Moreover, historical sources still provide the only reliable guide to the discovery and interpretation of the major settlements of the period, at least in northern Britain (Alcock 1981a, 1981b). Finally, the pretensions of the prehistorian to write about social and economic matters are largely dependent on logically-questionable analogies with modern hunter-gatherers, or quasi-neolithic agriculturalists, in areas remote from western Europe. If we are to interpret early medieval archaeology in economic and social terms, as we should surely endeavour to do, then it is foolish to deny ourselves the evidence of written sources that were both contemporary and generated within the societies whose archaeology we study; and which, moreover, constitute an essential element in the culture of those societies. In the third section of this chapter, therefore, some relevant written evidence is used to fill out the picture which we derive from the material remains.

Before embarking on a survey of the archaeology, however, another reason for archaeologists' reluctance to use historical sources in our period and area must be discounted. This is the belief that Dumville's (1977) paper, 'Sub-Roman Britain: history and legend' was a blanket condemnation of the documents of early medieval Britain as 'unreliable'. It is not: for as its author makes clear, it is addressed solely 'to the problems of the political history of fifth- and sixth-century Britain'. To this end, it discusses a carefully prescribed list of four groups of documents. One group of these, indeed, comprises 'the genuine works of St Patrick' and Gildas' *De excidio Britanniae*; contemporary sources which, on the most critical appraisal, provide reliable information about aspects of the mid-fifth and early-sixth centuries respectively. Moreover, Dumville is not concerned with evidence for the narrative history of the seventh and later centuries, or for social and economic organisation. These are the kinds of evidence which will be deployed below, in terms wholly acceptable to most historians active in the period.

The Archaeological Evidence

The most conspicuous archaeological monuments of our period and area are enclosed places – stone-walled, embanked or palisaded – set frequently on hill-tops, promontories or cliff-edges. Conventionally, most of them would be categorised as hillforts; but this shorthand classification has undertones of military purpose which cannot be taken for granted at this stage of the enquiry. To them we will add settlements enclosed by swamps or open water: artificial crannogs, or naturally defended islands (see map and list of sites with summary references, Appendix, pp.40–6).

These enclosed places exhibit great variety in their size and situation, in the structure and layout of the enclosing work, and in the evidence for their chronology. To take this last point first: some have readily datable artefacts stratified in relation to the enclosing bank or wall, or radiocarbon age-estimates from structural timbers. These would include the walled headland of Dunollie, the embanked promontory of Tintagel, the timber-laced banks at Green Castle, Clatchard Craig, Dumbarton or Dundurn, or the double palisade of Kirk Hill. In other cases, occupation in the sixth through eighth centuries is demonstrated by artefacts from the interior of the enclosure, as at Cadbury-Congresbury, phase 4 at Dinas Powys, (hereafter Dinas Powys 4), or phase 11 at Cadbury-Camelot (hereafter Cadbury 11), all in south-western Britain; or at phase 2 of the broch-complex at Burrian, Orkney. In yet other cases, such as Doon Hill A or Yeavering Post-Roman I, stratified relationships allow us to infer that particular phases of a multi-period site were of British rather than Anglian construction. Finally, a pre-Anglian, British foundation can be postulated for Dunbar and Bamburgh on the basis of their original British names, Dynbaer and Din Guoaroy.

Where the stratigraphical and chronological evidence is adequate, it reveals that these sites have a varied structural and occupational history. Some, such as Dunollie, Dundurn, Clatchard Craig or Tintagel, appear to have been newly founded in the late-fifth century or later. Others represent the re-occupation of a long abandoned fort of the Pre-Roman Iron Age: Craig Phadraig,

Cadbury 11 and Castle Dore would be good examples, with the notable difference that at Dore there was little refurbishment of the earlier rampart, whereas Cadbury 11 was marked by rampart-building on a massive scale. At Cadbury-Congresbury and Trethurgy occupation was continuous from the late-Roman period into the sixth century.

In terms of plan, a univallate or bivallate wall, bank or palisade is the most common. This may, however, have been imposed upon a pre-existing multivallate system as at Cadbury 11. The most elaborate layout is seen at Burghead, where four lines of wall cut off a headland, which is then divided into upper and lower enclosures; all this is carried out in stone-revetted rubble laced with nailed timber beams. A few sites have a lofty enclosed nucleus, surrounded by subordinate enclosures. Dunadd and Dundurn are certain examples in at least one phase of their development; and Ruberslaw; Dalmahoy; King's Seat, Dunkeld and Bryneuryn, Dinarth must all be rated as possibles. For lack of adequate excavation, it is not at present possible to say whether the structural division into nucleus and dependent enclosures may be related to the functional and social distinctions between *Burg* – or *Fürstenburg* – and *Vorburg* which have been widely recognised on broadly contemporary sites in north-west Europe (Uslar 1964; Herrman 1981).

In size, the enclosures range from the exceptionally large Cadbury-Camelot at about 7 hectares, to a cluster around 0.15 ha, which includes Dinas Powys 4 and Chûn. Smaller again in area is a group of enclosed places with an interior area of 0.0375 ha or less. Some of these are included here because of the strength and sophistication of the enclosing work, often combined with a naturally defensive position on a rocky hillock or coastal stack. Moreover, such sites have yielded prestige items such as imported pottery, glass or jewellery. These include a number of duns, and also the small crannog in Loch Glashan.[3]

In addition to the enclosed places themselves, some major buildings can be attributed to the sixth to eighth centuries on the basis of associated finds or stratified sequences. Conspicuous among these is the circular house, rather larger than Hall A at Doon Hill, which was built on a crannog at Buiston. To this can be added Doon Hill A itself, probably the hall of Cadbury 11, and possibly one or even two halls at Castle Dore. Minor halls, and other buildings of an essentially domestic or residential character are recorded at Cadbury-Congresbury and Dinas Powys 4.

Altogether an impressive collection of enclosed places, of varied size and character, is listed in the Appendix. In distributional terms, they extend from Land's End throughout south-west England, Wales and the Marches, to northern Britain as far as the Great Glen, and beyond to the Northern and Western Isles. Given this geographical range, it is worth saying that over-whelmingly they are sited on the coast or beside navigable rivers and estuaries; very rarely are they more than 2.5 km distant from water. Many stand immediately beside sheltered havens or natural harbours.

Before we attempt to draw inferences from this information, some further empirical observations may be put forward. Very many sites produce exotic pottery, which may have been imported as kitchen and table ware in order to make good a local deficiency (Class E); or perhaps for Christian rituals (Class A); or as containers for Mediterranean wine (Class B); or as incidental to the importation of wine in cask from Bordeaux (Class D) (Thomas 1981). Given the quantity and distributional range of Class B sherds it can be inferred that the drinking of wine from the Mediterranean – as well as in uncertain quantities from Gaul – was an important activity in many enclosed places.

Metalworking was also very important. The smelting and smithing of iron is demonstrated by the occasional discovery of ores and slags, and it can be widely inferred from the known range of iron weapons, tools and objects of domestic use. With very rare exceptions, the working of bronze, glass and gold, to produce high quality jewellery, has only been recorded in our period in secular enclosed places.[4] The evidence for jewel-making comprises scrap metal; scrap glass from Anglo-Saxon or Germanic sources; coloured glass rods, including millefiori, probably from the east Mediterranean; moulds, motif-sketches and crucibles; and industrial hearths and ovens. All this is evidence for craftsmen at work within the enclosure, but actual finished products are notably rare.

Another skilled craft, attested by its finished products, was the making of antler and bone pins and combs. Leatherworking is inferred from iron awls, heavy needles, and stone polishers; and its products are seen for instance in a punch-decorated shoe from Dundurn. The spinning of wool may be inferred from clay, bone and stone whorls (which may however be flywheels for bow drills). Evidence for weaving is provided by weaving-combs, which are so plentiful at Broch of Burrian as to suggest a textile factory. Unfortunately the ground conditions at most sites rule out the preservation of actual textiles, whether of wool or linen.

Some information is available on the agricultural contribution to diet and economy. In the nature of the evidence, this is weighted in favour of stock-raising, but there is no reason to believe that this reflects the original balance of importance (Alcock 1971; 1973, 231–2). Where preservation is good, animal bones occur in great quantities, representing the principal domesticates: cattle, dog (rare), horse (rare), pig, sheep/goat. This alphabetical listing does not reflect relative importance, which varies from site to site. There is, however, no archaeological evidence that cattle had any special prestige in Britain. Among wild animals, deer may be represented by bones and teeth from slaughtered beasts, as well as by shed antlers; but they are never abundant.

As for arable farming, plough parts are only rarely found, but the occurrence of rotary querns and baking plates or griddles indicates the role of porridge and bread in the diet. Dunadd has evidence for the cultivation of wheat, barley and oats and the collection of hazelnuts, and Dundurn has yielded a few grains of barley and oats.

To these economic indications we should add that none of the enclosed places saw the minting, or even the use of coins. Indeed, except for a contemporary forgery of a gold Anglo-Saxon coin from Buiston, currency is entirely absent from Celtic Britain in the sixth to eighth centuries.

Finally, this sketch of the recorded evidence must include observations at Dunadd and Dundurn. Both sites were built on craggy knolls, with walled summit bosses overlooking a complex of subordinate enclosures. At Dunadd, a terrace of living rock, immediately overlooked from the summit, bears a group of carvings and engravings: a hemispherical basin, one deeply carved footprint and a second lightly pecked one, an outline of a boar, and an untranslatable ogam inscription, allegedly in Pictish (Jackson 1965). At Dundurn, the summit boss rises at its western end in a natural projection which has been sculpted into the form of a seat. At both sites the carved zone is visible from many parts of the main enclosure, as well as from the surrounding plain. These are observations: possible explanations must await a discussion of the purposes and persons for whom enclosed places were built.

From this summary of archaeological observations, I turn first to those implications which arise ineluctably from the record. The builders of enclosed places, or those who commissioned their construction, had access to the labour-services of masons skilled in dry-stone work; and in the case of timber-reinforced walls or palisades, to the labour of skilled carpenters as well. Moreover, the layout of many enclosures and their relation to the terrain implies the skills of architects or military engineers. Other necessary services included the felling and rough hewing of timber; the quarrying or gathering of building stone; the carrying of stone and timber, often laboriously up a hillside; and the smithing, at Burghead and Dundurn, of thousands of iron nails. Managerial competence is implied in the organisation of both materials and services. No less evident are the skills of architect, carpenter and wood-cutter, and the carrying and labour services, which are implied by the hall of Doon Hill A, the probable hall of Cadbury 11, or the crannog substructure and great circular building at Buiston.

These building activities necessarily imply the removal of able-bodied persons from the agricultural pursuits of food production, at least temporarily. This in turn necessitates the existence of a food surplus to feed the builders. This may have been an agricultural surplus produced within the immediate area of the enclosed place, or one produced in a wider territory which was subordinate to it, or it may have been the result of plundering an external surplus-producing territory. The archaeological evidence that is currently available cannot help us to decide between these possibilities. Nor can it reveal the status of the builders: were they free men, or semi-free, or slaves? Was there, indeed, a class of professional enclosure-builders, permanently withdrawn from food production? This seems likely at the planning and organisational levels.

Whatever the case of enclosure-builders, it may be postulated that the jewellers, and probably the blacksmiths as well, were permanently engaged in their craft. The archaeological case for this is based on the high level of technical knowledge, and the artistic aptitudes that are displayed in the fine metalwork: especially in the jewelled brooches and the hanging bowls with enamelled escutcheons. So some craftsmen were necessarily consumers of an agricultural surplus. Other crafts, however, may have been carried out on a part-time basis by persons whose main economic role lay in farming.[5]

A surplus would also have been required to exchange for imported pottery, wine and the raw materials of the jeweller. It may be that some exotic items were obtained not by trade but by gift exchange (Grierson 1959): some of the wine, some of the fine red-slipped dishes, some outstanding metalwork like an embossed helmet from Dumfriesshire (de Paor 1961). This would not, of course, remove the need for surpluses somewhere in the system, to provide the reciprocal gift. But it is difficult to believe in gift exchange involving domestic pottery from some unknown source in Francia, still less scrap metal (as at Dinas Powys) or scrap glass (cullet) which occurs very widely on sites with evidence of jewel-making. Items like these must be seen as the fruits of commerce, albeit in a coinless economy.

The inferences which have been deployed thus far follow from the evidence. Other inferences are more speculative, but they arise from the attempt to answer questions which are in themselves inescapable. These are: what was the purpose of the enclosed places; and by whom and for whom were they built? It will appear later that written sources are of great assistance in settling these questions, but for the moment answers will be attempted on archaeological grounds alone.

For a start, the location of many of the sites seems inconvenient for the occupants: on hills, rocky knolls or promontories that are tedious, if not actually difficult, of access. The intention may have been to deter unwelcome visitors, at some sacrifice of the inhabitants' own convenience. Again, the strength of the enclosing wall or palisade, taken in conjunction with the difficulty of access, seems to rule out a primary function as cattle enclosures. In effect, both location and enclosing work argue for a defensive function: protection against something more than wild animals, or a band of thieves which might, however, be indistinguishable from a cattle- or slave-raiding expedition.[6] In short, our enclosed places were fortifications.

Even so, and without making a parade of anthropological or historical analogies, it is evident that a fortification may have a variety of roles, which are not necessarily mutually exclusive. These may be purely negative, as a secure place of refuge, a fastness, too strong to be attacked. There may be a wider involvement, so that a fortification is recognised as a place which may or must be attacked in the pursuit of politico-military aims; or which serves to control a territory. This last role has administrative implications which transcend the military field. Moreover, even the most formidable of fortifications normally has a domestic or residential role as well. Finally, these objective functions are frequently reinforced by symbolism, in which both the siting and the structure itself play a part.[7]

Can the archaeological evidence on its own enable us to distinguish between the secure fastness and the fort with a more active military role? In southern Britain there is no evidence on this point, but in the north, Dumbarton, Dundurn, Mote of Mark and Green Castle were all certainly destroyed by fire. One of the two palisades at Kirk Hill was also burned, as was the hall of Doon Hill A. Even without the confirmation of the written word it is perverse to regard all these burned fortifications as merely the outcome of accidental fires. It may reasonably be inferred that the forts were involved in military activities: raids and devastations which included in their objectives the destruction of fortifications and their internal buildings.

Moreover, a strategic purpose may be suggested for some fortifications. Dundurn is located where a major pass through the southern Highlands debouches into the fertile lands of southern Pictland. Dunollie, overlooking the sheltered Oban bay, is an excellent base for naval activity along the coasts and among the islands of the Dalriadic thalassocracy. Dunadd controls an important portage across the Kintyre peninsula. Before the river Clyde was artificially deepened, it was only navigable by sea-going vessels as high as Dumbarton. These are no more than hints; and it would be equally possible to suggest that economic, rather than military strategies determined the significance of these, and other, coastal sites.

The second question – for whom were the fortifications built? – may be resolved into the alternatives: were they built for a more or less egalitarian peasant community; or for a lord, a potentate, who might indeed represent the community in a symbolic manner, but who had special responsibilities and privileges within it? Can such a question be settled on the basis of the archaeological evidence alone, without recourse to anthropological analogies or to contemporary written sources? I believe that it may be answered with reasonable assurance, though it is difficult to clear one's mind entirely of the historical evidence.

First, the evidence of large and costly buildings: the hall of Doon Hill A, the probable hall of Cadbury 11, and the large house at Buiston. There is, of course, no difficulty in finding anthropological records of large buildings which served communal purposes in farming societies which had little social ranking. But the Cadbury hall was conspicuously a place where imported wine was drunk (Alcock 1982a, 374–5). Moreover, the Buiston crannog yielded weapons, gold and bronze jewellery, imported pottery and evidence for metal-working, which all argue for wealth and status. Both buildings may more reasonably be attributed to potentates than to peasants.

Furthermore, we have seen that the forts often produce abundant evidence for prestige objects and prestige activities, notably the drinking of imported wine and the making of high class jewellery. The richness of such evidence may appear, on a necessarily subjective appraisal, to be out of all proportion to the relatively small area of the enclosure. This is particularly true by comparison with the forts of the Pre-Roman Iron Age in southern Britain. In the case of Mote of Mark it may indeed be that this tiny fort was eventually taken over completely as a jewel-making establishment, but in this it would be exceptional. Moreover, the layout of nuclear forts, such as Dunadd and Dundurn, of itself suggests a hierarchical structure reflecting a hierarchical society, with the citadel reserved for a potentate. Finally, the distinctive summit features of Dunadd and Dundurn appear to be intended for inauguration rituals: ceremonies which, at Dunadd, involved the placing of a foot in the soil of the territory, and at Dundurn the seating of the person to be inaugurated on a prominent rock. It cannot be doubted that these were ceremonies in which the principal actor was a potentate.[8]

From the archaeological evidence alone, then, we can infer that the fortifications of Celtic Britain in the sixth through eighth centuries were the seats of potentates of varied rank, power and wealth. It must be admitted that among the small fortified homesteads of the west – the duns and lesser crannogs – the concept of a potentate becomes somewhat diluted. But the analogy – not to be pressed too far – of the sixteenth-century society of the Anglo-Scottish border reminds us how low the term 'laird' may sink; and how essential a strong place may be, in troubled times, for the protection of a laird, his land and his kin (Dixon 1979).

Apart from their fortifications, one other group of archaeological remains is particularly relevant to the activities of potentates, and also forms a link with conventional written sources: namely, the carved and inscribed monuments. Potentates utilised the services of craftsmen who were literate in arcane symbolism, whether that of the Roman script in various forms, or the ogam stroke alphabet, or the Pictish symbols which, alone among the three, remain illegible to modern scholars. Other, lesser, social classes also had access to the stone-carvers; men whose descendants might call them *medicus*, 'doctor', or claim a relationship with a civil official, *magistratus*. So, pre-eminently, did ecclesiastics.

The inscribed stones are as important as conventional written documents in showing us that a potentate might be known in Latin as *rex*, and that his sons might be described as *principes*. The memorial to Caelestis Monedorix, 'the mountain king', hints that one British title might be *rix*. Moreover, the inscriptions furnish important evidence for a continued respect for *romanitas* among the post-Roman Britons. Latinate personal names occur alongside both British and Irish names. Voteporix, king of Demetia, claims the Roman military title of Protector, while Cadfan of Venedotia was described on his memorial as *rex sapientis(s)imus opinatis(s)imus omnium regum*: 'the wisest and most renowned of all kings', a high-flown title which may have a Byzantine inspiration (Nash-Williams 1950 for Wales; Macalister 1945 for other areas).

Given the known locations of such memorials to kings and princes, it might be thought that we have here clues to the whereabouts of the power centres from which they ruled. Unfortunately this is not so. We have no evidence for the principal seats, whether or not they were enclosed places, of Voteporix or Monedorix. For Cadfan's dynasty we have documentary evidence to locate one of its centres at Aberffraw, some 2 km from the church of Llangadwaladr where Cadfan's memorial is now located; and from Aberffraw itself we have ambiguous evidence for a post-Roman fortification. As for the domicile of the two princes or chiefs named on the Yarrowkirk stone, no fortification has been recorded along the 20 km reach of Yarrow Water, despite the suitability of the valley for both habitation and cultivation. The memorials to kings and princes hint at the former existence of power centres which remain obstinately unrecoverable by the archaeologist.

In some compensation, the Pictish cross-slabs provide glimpses of the life of those potentates who alone had the wealth to commission such richly carved works (Allen and Anderson 1903). It has been argued that the scenes on the reverse of the cross-slabs are derived as much from copy-books or other illustrated sources as from actual Pictish life (Henderson 1967, 141–57); and it is certain that centaurs and camels had no place in the natural fauna of Pictavia. None the less, the scenes must have been approved by the patrons, and meaningful for them. This applies especially to the popular scenes of the chase. Whatever allegorical meaning these may have had for churchmen, for secular patrons they meant exactly what they depict, the pursuit of stags with horse, hound and spear. They remind us of the prestige attached to horses and horsemanship. The breeding, training and upkeep of horses for the chase and, as we shall see, for warfare created further demands for an agricultural surplus.

In addition to their spear, some Pictish horsemen carry a targe, so these must therefore be warriors. The commitment of potentates to warfare is epitomised in the unique story-telling slab in Aberlemno churchyard (Allen and Anderson 1903, Part III, 209–14). When all allowance has been made for allegory,[9] and for external artistic influences, perhaps from some Northumbrian illustrated work like the Frank's casket, the fact remains that the carving was commissioned by some wealthy Pict in the early eighth century. In three registers, it depicts the conflict between a helmeted horseman, probably a king, on the one side, and both mounted and foot soldiery on the other. The outcome of the conflict is that the helmeted warrior lies dead, food for ravens. The helmet could be based on an eighth-century Northumbrian example, like that recently discovered in York. It is not entirely fanciful to see the story told here as that of the conflict between Pictland and Northumbria, culminating in the death of King Ecgfrith at Dunnichen/Nectansmere in 685.[10] But even if this historical interpretation is rejected, we have at Aberlemno as vivid and immediate an insight into the kingly business of warfare as can be gleaned from all the annals and heroic poetry.

Archaeology and Documents – a Synthesis

In the Prolegomena to this chapter it was proposed that the third section should examine some relevant written evidence, in order to fill out the picture derived from archaeology. The word 'relevant' must be stressed, because the choice of documents is deliberately eclectic rather than comprehensive. Scholars with other interests might well quote other texts, and place other emphases upon them. The hope is that the ones cited here will lead to a convincing synthesis of the two forms of evidence: documents and archaeology.

We may begin with the interlinked topics of forts, kings and battles. Gildas, writing in the sixth century about a period three or more generations earlier, tells of Britons holding out on 'lofty entrenched hills', *montanis collibus vallatis* (ed. Winterbottom 25.1; commentary in Sims-Williams 1983). If this reflects a genuine tradition, then what we see here is a place of refuge: the *Fliehburg* or *Fluchtort* of continental scholars. This is indeed one of the models which has been proposed for Cadbury 11 (Burrow 1981, 156–8), though as we shall see it is an inadequate one. In any case, a *Fliehburg* may have been no more than a derelict pre-Roman hillfort, with no implications for either post-Roman fort-building or the activities of kings.

More to the present point is that Gildas attributes to his contemporary, King Cuneglasus, a place described as *receptaculum ursi*, literally the 'bear's den'. *Receptaculum* has been seen as a translation of British *din*, fort, so that a better translation might be 'Fort of the Bear'. Given that 'bear' was *arth* in British, this may then be identified with Dineirth or Dinarth, near the coast of north-east Wales, where a stone-walled citadel and outer enclosure crown a craggy hill.

Other associations between kings and forts were embedded in the traditions of the Iona monastery, which formed the basis for Adomnan's *Life* of Columba, written about a century after the saint's death. Thus, Columba was consulted by Roderc son of Tothal, *qui in petra Cloithe regnavit*, 'who ruled on Clyde Rock'. From Bede we can identify this with Castle Rock, Dumbarton, and a minimal inference would be that, at least by Adomnan's day, the late seventh century, this was a seat of a British dynasty. Adomnan likewise thought that the Pictish King Brude son of Maelchon should possess a *munitio*, 'fortress', with a 'royal hall', *aula regia*.

These references show that forts might be seats of kings, and centres of royal power. For a more active relationship between forts and kings we may turn to the *Iona Annals*. These are held to have been compiled originally at the time of the events which they record, but subsequently they were incorporated in other Irish Annals such as those of Ulster and Tigernach, and the manuscripts in which they are preserved are very late indeed (Smyth 1971; Bannerman 1974; Ó Corráin 1980). They are not totally free from garbled entries and possible duplications, but substantially they are reliable: at least as reliable, it may be said in the present context, as most excavators' published reports. Over the century from 638, there are 24 references to forts or strongholds which, so far as they can be located, are all in Scotland. In detail, there are records of ten sieges, five burnings, three destructions and one capture. The annals themselves are notoriously laconic: 638 obsesio (sic) Etin: 'siege of Edinburgh'. 694 obsesio (sic) Duin Fother: 'siege of Dunnottar'.

Rather more can be learned by looking at the cases of Dun Ollaigh (Dun-ollie) and Dun Att (Dunadd). Excavation has shown that the former occupies a naturally strong headland overlooking Oban Bay which was probably the most convenient harbour for travellers to and from Iona itself. The site has a long history, but the first two phases may be dated by artefactual and radiometric evidence to the late seventh and early eighth centuries. The *Annals* record that Dun Ollaigh was burned in 698 (and possibly in 686), that it was destroyed by Selbach in 701, and built (presumably to be understood as rebuilt) by Selbach in 714. Selbach was king of Dalriada, or at least of the kindred of Lorn (Cenél Loairn). His activities at Dun Ollaigh, as well as his siege of Aberte in 712, may be incidents in the internal struggles of the three kindreds of Scottish Dalriada.

Dunadd is the subject of an unusually long entry, which opens up wider horizons for us:

> 736 Oengus, son of Fergus, king of the Picts, laid waste the provinces (*regiones*) of Dal Riata, and captured Dunadd, and burned Creic (unidentified), and bound with fetters the two sons of Selbach, namely Dungal and Feradach.

The abduction of the two sons (whether for political reasons or for ransom), was obviously a blow to the kindred of Lorn. Yet more serious was the devastation of Dalriada, and the capture of a major fortification and inauguration centre.[11] The fuller details of the annal for 736 may help us to understand the brief record in 683 of 'siege of Dunadd and siege of Dundurn'. May we see here reciprocal attempts by Picts and Scots to capture and destroy a rival stronghold? Whatever the truth of that, the later annal demonstrates a serious attempt by the Picts, under a notably vigorous king, to establish control over mainland Dalriada. Here we can discern, in a contemporary record, the part played by kings and fortifications in the seizure and defence of territory. In this connection we must recall Bede's statement that, after the slaughter of Ecgfrith at Nectansmere, the Picts recovered territory from Northumbria while the Scots of Dalriada and some of the northern Britons regained their political independence.[12]

Not all the burnings, sieges and destructions recorded in the *Iona Annals* were necessarily of territorial significance. Some may have been carried out in the course of blood feuds or in pursuit of dynastic ambitions. Among the Celts, as among other barbarian peoples, the road to the throne was frequently violent. This does not necessarily mean that attacks on fortifications were always involved in the seizure or defence of kingship, simply that violence was endemic among rulers who might also be associated with fortified places.

So far, a selection of written evidence has been deployed for the threefold association of kings, forts and military actions; but to stop at this point would be to leave the enquiry in the mythical world of Celtic war-lords and their defended homesteads. We must now consider some of the Latin words which contemporary writers used for fortifications. Bede, for instance, calls Castle Rock, Dumbarton, *urbs*, and also *civitas Brettonum munitissima*. He uses *urbs* again for another British place, *Giudi*, which is questionably identified with Castle Rock, Stirling. These are the only forts in Celtic hands to which Bede refers, but the list may be extended by the recognition that Anglian Bamburgh was founded on the British fortified headland of Din Guaroy, and that Anglian Dunbar likewise has a British name: Dynbaer. Bamburgh, like

Dumbarton, is occasionally called *civitas* by Bede, but it is more frequently *urbs*, and *urbs* is likewise the term which Eddius uses for Dunbar. Another Latin term used in a Celtic context is *caput regionis*, 'chief place of the province'. It was at such a place that Columba, according to Adomnan, was able to meet and question the skipper and sailors of a vessel newly arrived from Gaul (*VC* 31a) The *caput regionis* is sometimes identified with Dunadd; but Dunollie, with its better harbour and closer link with Iona has a stronger claim.

It is one thing to show that Latin terms may be used about Celtic fortifications, but quite another to understand what they might mean in political, social and economic terms. That a *caput regionis* should be visited by Gallic merchants reminds us of the emergence of *emporia*, market places for overseas trade under royal control, in southern and south-east England: Ipswich, perhaps under the influence of the Wuffingas dynasty, in the early seventh century, and Hamwih under the Wessex monarchy, from *c*.700 (Hodges and Whitehouse 1983, 93–8). As for *urbs* and *civitas*, it has been suggested that the main characteristic of an *urbs* was that it was fortified, while a *civitas* was normally a place with a significant Roman past. This can hardly apply in the cases of Dumbarton and Bamburgh, so there, it is suggested, Bede 'is using *civitas* for a particularly important kind of *urbs*, the main royal fortress' (Campbell 1979, 36–7). It should also be recalled that he attaches a national name, *Brettonum*, to Dumbarton.

Dunbar, the royal town (*urbem suam*) of Ecgfrith of Northumbria, deserves further consideration. Although no early work can now be seen beneath the later castle, the site itself – a rock stack beside a good harbour – is comparable with Dunollie or even Dumbarton. As a royal *urbs* it should be added to the list of pre-Conquest royal *tuns*, with all that is implied thereby (Sawyer 1983a). In particular, although it was *urbem suam* in relation to King Ecgfrith, it was actually in the charge of a *praefectus* (VW 38). This term, perhaps translatable as earl or thane, introduces us to a level of potentate below that of the king: a royal official, member of a nobility of service. It has been suggested that this particular *praefectus* had administrative responsibility for a wide area of north-eastern Northumbria, in fact the kind of area, centred on an *urbs*, which was the forerunner of the shires and thanages of medieval Scotland (Barrow 1973, 66–7). We are beginning here to see concepts that are considerably more sophisticated than those of the defended homesteads of war-lords.

The direct evidence for them, however, is restricted to northern Britain, within and adjacent to the Northumbrian area of early literacy. Can we legitimately extend them to the British forts in Wales and south-west Britain? Some justification for doing this may be found in the long-standing belief that Celtic legal, social and economic institutions were especially well preserved in Anglian Bernicia.[13] One factor in such preservation may have been the Anglian take-over of British centres of power at Bamburgh, Doon Hill, Dunbar and Yeavering as going concerns. Without suggesting that British society was uniform regardless of region, we may nonetheless find a useful conceptual tool in the idea that the fortifications of Northumbria are relevant to those of Wales and Dumnonia. The relevance of Dumbarton, *urbs* and *civitas Brettonum munitissima*, is quite beyond question.

If we might also assume that the size of a fortification is a matter of deliberate choice, dependent more on function and status than on topography, it is relevant to observe that Bamburgh is rather smaller than Congresbury, and markedly smaller than Cadbury-Camelot or the habitable area at Tintagel. It may further be suggested that Cadbury 11 took over the administrative role of the Roman *civitas Durotrigum Lindiniensis*, Ilchester, in the troubled years of the fifth century, just as it certainly took over its role as a mint town in the no less troubled eleventh century. As for the term *urbs*: in so far as the area of the royal *urbs* of Dunbar can be estimated, it is about the same as that of Chûn and Dinas Powys (Burrow 1981, 159; Alcock 1982a, 380–4).

Another unit in the hierarchy of Northumbrian royal centres was the king's township: *villa* (or *vicus*) *regis*, *regia* or *regalis*. The relevance of these to the pre-Anglian, British organisation is seen at Yeavering, *villa regia quae vocatur Adgefrin*. Yeavering was celebrated by Bede as the place where Paulinus spent 36 days baptising converts in the river Glen. More recently, Dr Hope-Taylor's research has made it a classic of archaeological excavation. In Paulinus' day, under the rule of Edwin, the extensive township included a great timber enclosure, an assembly stand, a pagan temple and a royal hall. This had grown, over many decades, out of an architecturally modest British township, which had consisted simply of a palisaded fort, no doubt enclosing circular wooden houses, and a cemetery which occupied the site of a dismantled stone circle.[14] The latter was only one element in Yeavering's long ancestry of ritual, ceremonial and power, which stretched back through the hill-top town on Yeavering Bell to a Late Neolithic henge monument. It is reasonable to believe that pre-Anglian Gefrin – the name itself is British – was just as much a royal township as was its successor under Aethelfrith, Edwin and Oswald.

If this is accepted, then the concept of the royal *villa* or *vicus* can usefully be transferred to Celtic areas. In Northumbria its place in the hierarchy of power may be expressed by Eddius (*VW* 39) when he writes of Ecgfrith and his queen journeying through *civitates et castella vicosque*, 'chief towns, forts and townships', in that order. The townships were probably more common than *civitates* and *urbes*. One of them was at no great distance from Bamburgh itself. Bishop Aidan had a church and cell in each of several *villae regiae*, where he would stay when travelling on a preaching mission. Historians have seen the *villa regia* as a centre for the administration and economic exploitation of an estate with varied resources (Campbell 1979, 43–51). In archaeological terms, this is just what appears at Dinas Powys 4: a relatively small and weakly-embanked enclosure, which none the less commanded a rich variety of resources at both subsistence and luxury levels. Had others of our forts been excavated and published to the same level, there is no doubt that this picture would have been widely repeated.

Eddius also enables us to see something of the mechanics of royal administration and exploitation:

The king with his queen was making a progress through chief towns, forts and townships, with worldly display, and daily rejoicing and feasting (*VW* 39).

This progress or circuit was a periodic visitation of royal centres, which were themselves at various levels of importance. The banqueting represents the consumption or redistribution of food renders and other surpluses which had been accumulated as tribute at the centre, again on a periodic basis in anticipation of the circuit. In the worldly display, *pompa saeculari*, and in the rejoicing we see the non-material, symbolic aspects of kingship. These, then, are the major non-military royal activities at enclosed places. The immediate evidence is from the Northumbria of Eddius and Bede; but it would be unreasonable to believe that the organisation which it reveals was a creation of the late seventh century, or an Anglian innovation at all.

A further topic on which we might particularly wish to interrogate the documents is how the building and manning of royal forts were financed. It is not difficult to demonstrate the widespread existence, in both Britain and Ireland, of a system of land assessment. Bede's well-known comment about the number of 'hides according to the English reckoning' on Man and Anglesey implies the existence of a common unit, the *terra unius familiae*, in the two Celtic islands as well as in England. Parallels have been drawn between the hide and the *treb* and *tech* in Ireland as well as in Dalriada. The latter is of immediate military significance, because *tech* appears in the *Senchus Fer n'Alban*, in origin a seventh-century document, as the unit of assessment for the sea muster in units of seven-benched vessels which was obviously of high importance among the islands and coastlands of Dalriada (Bede *HE* 2.9; Charles-Edwards 1972; Bannerman 1974; Ó Corráin 1980).

Among the Britons, the best evidence for the tribute and services due to the king is to be found in the Laws of Hywel Dda (Richards 1954 for an accessible translation). These are not easy to use for our period, because the available manuscripts are no earlier than the late twelfth century, and the laws themselves purport to have been promulgated in the mid-tenth century. It is, nevertheless, recognised that they are highly stratified, and that one stratum is certainly primitive customary law. In particular, some historians have pointed to parallels between the Welsh Laws and a twelfth-century custumal of the lands of the bishop of Durham, and have argued that these parallels indicate a stratum which predates the Anglian settlement of Bernicia (Jolliffe 1926; Kapelle 1979). The dues in question refer to the buildings erected on the king's (or bishop's) behalf by the bondmen, *villani regis*. Other clauses show that these bondmen were settled in nucleated villages under the supervision of a royal official known as a *maer*. The distribution pattern of *maerdref* place-names in Wales argues that this institution goes back before the intrusion of Normanising influences (Ordnance Survey 1973).

The buildings common to the Laws of Hywel Dda and the Durham custumal are a hall and satellite buildings. The Latin version of the Laws then continues:

The king ought to have packhorses from the bondmen on his hostings; and from each bond township (*villa rusticana*) a man with a felling-axe and a horse to build the king's forts (*castra*); but they are at the king's expense (Emanuel 1967, 137, 204–5, 377). This appears to refer to the erection of stockaded encampments during the course of a hosting (*expedicio*), and it is therefore of doubtful relevance to the construction of substantial permanent fortifications. Nor is the phrase 'at the king's expense' revealing in the present context. Finally, despite the value of the *Senchus Fer n'Alban* as a record of the sea-muster of Dalriada, it says nothing about either the building or the manning of fortifications.[15]

From essentially military affairs, I turn now to the potential relevance of the written evidence for our understanding of economic activities, beginning with the work of craftsmen. The place of the craftsman in Celtic society has recently been reviewed through the medium of literature, especially that of Ireland. It is admitted that the written accounts are not easy to use, and that a real collaboration is called for between archaeologists and literary scholars. Among other points of special relevance here are the high status accorded to the builders of forts and houses, and the respect, not unmixed with superstitious awe, with which the metalsmith's works of power were regarded (Gillies 1981).

When, however, we look at the archaeological actuality of jewellery and other works of craftsmanship, we find that the literary sources are a doubtful guide. In the *Gododdin*, for instance, two phenomena may be noticed: anachronism, and poetic enhancement. Thus, the warriors of the *Gododdin* frequently wear gold torques, despite the fact that these had gone out of fashion several centuries earlier. Moreover, objects which the archaeologist finds in wood, bronze or silver are, for the poet, regularly made of gold (Alcock 1983). We must sometimes remind ourselves that sources such as the *Gododdin* or the Irish epics are works not of reportage, but of the imagination; and that the picture of the past which they hold up to us is perceived not through a window but through a distorting mirror.

Another field of economic activity where documents can fill out some of the gaps in the archaeological record is that of raiding, whether for men or animals; but this is too large a field to be surveyed here.[16] There is little unambiguous evidence that pre-Viking Celtic Britain was involved in organised slave-trading within a wider system embracing the Mediterranean, Gaul or even Anglo-Saxon England. In consequence, we should not see the export of Pictish, Scottish or British captives as a large element in paying for imports of Gaulish or Mediterranean wine, or of scrap metal and glass. We should rather consider the possible export of light and transportable luxury items, whether natural products such as white furs, river pearls, rock-crystal, tin and even gold, or manufactured goods including leather work and fine woollens.

To illuminate and amplify the archaeological evidence for the basic farming economy, and other aspects of material culture, we can best turn to the Welsh Laws (Jones 1972). The periodic renders of food to the king demonstrate how kingship itself was maintained. They also reveal elements of agricultural surplus which cannot readily be attested archaeologically. Whatever the date of the manuscripts, we cannot believe that beer was first brewed, or honey first gathered, in the late twelfth century. As it happens, both are mentioned as part of a food rent in a Llandaff charter which has been dated *c.*780 (Davies 1978, 47; 1979, 118). Attention has also been drawn to the list of domestic equipment which appears in the Laws, and which far exceeds the artefact catalogues of even the richest excavations (Alcock 1971; 1973, 145, 229–31). It is at least unlikely that these are all innovations contemporaneous with the manuscripts. Finally, we may notice the suggestion that in *Culhwch ac Olwen* we can discover a list of 'the ceremonial possessions of a traditional ruler – sword, knife, whetstone, drinking-horn, cauldron, draughtsboard, mantle and the like' (Edel 1983, 264–5).

The most valuable caution which the documents have to offer lies in their references to social ranks below those of kings and nobles, and to grades in the settlement hierarchy lower than the enclosed places which are our main source of archaeological evidence. When Eddius mentions *civitates et castellas vicosque*, in that order, this may be no more than a euphonious literary effect. But if it represents an actual hierarchy, then it is evidence for townships at a lower level than the greater and lesser fortified sites; and townships, moreover, which the king might visit on circuit. These are echoed by the *villae rusticanae*, inhabited by *villani regis* of the Welsh Laws. These have been seen as nucleated townships of bondmen, which were often sited on the best agricultural land. It is not germane to the present discussion to explore the documentary evidence for these arrangements any further.

It is clear, nevertheless, that the archaeological evidence itself demands the existence of peasant townships to produce the surplus on which kingship, fort-building, and high quality craftsmanship were founded. At present, our knowledge of the monuments does not allow us to recognise settlements of this order, or to generalise about them with anything like the confidence which we feel when writing about royal or noble fortifications. Indeed, over much of Celtic Britain these lower ranks of settlement, and their inhabitants, cannot be perceived at all in the archaeological record. This in itself is a major rebuttal of the belief that we should treat the archaeology in isolation from the documents.

NOTES

1   Versions of this paper have been delivered at State University of New York, Binghampton and University College, Cardiff; and the whole has been refined through discussions with colleagues and, more especially, several generations of graduate students. I am grateful to all these persons and institutions, and also to the colleagues who have readily answered queries and provided information in advance of publication.

In explanation of the title, I had deliberately sought a neutral and imprecise term before I discovered the late E. M. Wightman's major discussion of potentates and peasants (Wightman 1978). Note Thomas' use of 'Cornish grandee' and also *princeps* and *tigernos*, in relation to Tintagel (1982, 19-21).

2 For an extreme statement of this view see Arnold (1982c, 458).

3 On the assumption that some duns were completely roofed over, the floor area would be equal to that of some major halls, such as Doon Hill A or Buiston. It is worth noting that the Norman *Consuetudines et iusticie* of William the Conqueror prohibited the building of strongholds on rocks or islands (Haskins 1918, 277-84).

4 Bateson (1981, 59-65, 102-7). An exceptional open site is Bac Mhic Connain, N. Uist (Callander 1932). Brough of Birsay is an enclosed place within my terms, which has abundant metalworking evidence (Curle 1982). It is often regarded as a monastic site in its pre-Viking phase, but the evidence for this, rather than for secular use, is hardly conclusive.

5 Note, however, that in proto-urban and urban environments of slightly later date in north-western Europe, it is a commonplace that tanning and comb-making were specialist occupations; and this may perhaps be inferred for weaving both among the pagan Saxons and in a peripheral Pictish context at Broch of Burrian.

6 We may recall the Laws of the West Saxon king, Ine (688-94), *cap.* 13.1: 'We call up to seven men "thieves"; from seven to thirty-five a "band"; above that it is an "army"' (Whitelock 1979, 400).

7 Applied with due caution, analogies with the medieval castle are suggestive here. Thus King (forthcoming) has stressed that the most military of all structures, the Norman keep, might none the less be a commodious residence. Elsewhere he has discussed the function of castles under the headings of aesthetic and symbolic; practical uses in time of peace as a dwelling and as an administrative centre; and warlike employment in defence, in attack, and for criminal purposes (1983, xvi-xx). Coulson (1976; 1979) has further explored the non-military, and especially the symbolic, functions of fortresses and castles.

8 For inauguration footprints (Thomas 1879; Hamilton 1968, 151-6); for inauguration on a prominent stone, or a stone chair, on a hill (Hayes-McCoy 1970; Donaldson 1977, 9-11). At Dundurn, the possible significance of a circular churchyard below the hill should be noticed.

9 Contrast Bede's reference (*HE* 3, 24) to monks waging heavenly warfare.

10 There are two reasons for suggesting that the helmeted figure represents a king: (1) the rarity of helmets in the archaeological record of the period argues that they were a prerogative of the very highest rank of potentates; (2) Nelson (1980, 44-6) has drawn attention to the use of helmets, not crowns, as the principal symbol of kingship. For a very different interpretation of the scene, cf. Stevenson (1955b; 1980, 113-14).

11 It is difficult to assess the significance of devastation in this period because of the laconic nature of the Annals. For a detailed study of the political purposes and the effects of military devastation in the later Middle Ages, cf. Hewitt (1966).

12 *HE* 4, 26; this is far removed from the concept of Celtic warfare as a purely ritual act, in which territory did not change hands. Nectansmere reminds us that not all battles were at forts; especially in southern Britain, they appear to have occurred principally in the open, especially at river crossings (Alcock 1978).

13 The basic exposition was by Jolliffe (1926). For a recent critique which does not demolish the central proposition, see Kapelle (1979, 50-85). Recent papers by I. M. Smith and N. Gregson in Clack and Ivy (1983) appeared too late for me to use in this paper.

14 This interpretation of pre-Anglian, British, Yeavering leans heavily on the work of Miket (especially 1980, 301-4). Beyond this it is unreasonable to believe, on the basis of very limited excavation, that the Great Enclosure was devoid of buildings.

15 For apparent fort-building services in the Irish Laws, Gerriets (1983, 54).

16 The supposed archaeological evidence for slavery has been diminished by Scott's suggestion (1978, 229) that the alleged 'slave collars' from Lagore were intended for restraining fierce pet dogs, perhaps specifically Irish wolfhounds. For historical evidence in Wales, see Davies (1978, 43-7); for England, Pelteret (1981).

Appendix:
Enclosed Places, AD 500–800
by Elizabeth A. Alcock

This appendix provides a summary catalogue of those sites which furnish evidence for the generalisations of the preceding pages. Formally, it comprises a map and numerical index; and an alphabetical gazetteer of enclosed places. The normal form for each entry is: map index number, modern name (and ancient name where appropriate), and national grid reference; a digest of the evidence supporting a date in the sixth to eighth centuries; and a (non-comprehensive) list of key references. Exceptional references are those for the fort of the Pictish king Brude son of Maelchon, *Brudei munitio*, and for Giudi or Iudeu; both of them sites well attested in written documents, but of disputed, or at least uncertain, location.

KEY TO MAP AND GAZETTEER (p.43)

1 Broch of Burrian, North Ronaldsay, Orkney.
2 Broch of Burwick, Mainland, Orkney.
3 Broch of Oxtro, Mainland, Orkney.
4 Brough of Birsay, Mainland, Orkney.
5 Broch of Midhowe, Rousay, Orkney.
6 Broch of Gurness, Mainland, Orkney.
7 Broch of Ayre, Mainland, Orkney.
8 Broch of Burray, Burray, Orkney.
9 Freswick Sands Broch, Caithness.
10 Keiss Broch, Caithness.
11 The Udal, North Uist.
12 Dun Cuier, Barra.
13 Dun Ardtreck, Skye.
14 Urquhart Castle, Inverness-shire.
15 Craig Phadrig, Inverness-shire.
16 Castle Hill, Inverness, Inverness-shire.
17 Burghead, Moray.
18 Green Castle, Portknockie, Banffshire.
19 Cullykhan, Castle Point, Troup, Banffshire.
20 Dundarg Castle, Aberdeenshire.
21 Dunottar Castle, Kincardineshire.
22 Aldclune, Perthshire.
23 King's Seat, Dunkeld, Perthshire.
24 Inchtuthill, Perthshire.
25 Dundurn, Perthshire.
26 Clatchard Craig, Fife.
27 Stirling, Stirlingshire.
28 Dunollie, Argyll.
29 Dùn an Fheurain, Argyll.
30 Loch Glashan Crannog, Argyll.
31 Ardifuar, Argyll.
32 Dunadd, Argyll.
33 Tarbert, Argyll.
34 Little Dunagoil, Bute.
35 Dun Fhinn, Argyll.
36 Ugadale, Argyll.
37 Kildonan Bay, Argyll.
38 Kildalloig, Argyll.
39 Dunaverty, Argyll.
40 Dumbarton Rock, Dunbartonshire.
41 Dalmahoy, Midlothian.
42 Castle Rock, Edinburgh, Midlothian.
43 Harehope, Peeblesshire.
44 Traprain Law, East Lothian.
45 Dunbar, East Lothian.
46 Doon Hill, East Lothian.
47 Kirk Hill, St Abbs, Berwickshire.
48 Ruberslaw, Roxburghshire.
49 Yeavering, Northumberland.
50 Bamburgh, Northumberland.
51 Castlehill, Dalry, Ayrshire.
52 Lochlee Crannog, Ayrshire.
53 Buiston Crannog, Ayrshire.
54 Black Loch Crannog, Wigtownshire.
55 Tynron Doon, Dumfriesshire.
56 Mote of Mark, Stewartry of Kirkcudbright.
57 New Pieces, Breiddin, Montgomeryshire.
58 Bryneuryn, Dinarth, Denbighshire.
59 Degannwy Castle, Caernarvonshire.
60 Aberffraw, Anglesey.
61 Carreg y Llam, Caernarvonshire.
62 Dinas Emrys, Caernarvonshire.
63 Coygan Camp, Carmarthenshire.
64 Dinas Powys, Glamorgan.
65 Cadbury-Congresbury, Somerset.
66 Cadbury-Camelot, Somerset.
67 Tintagel, Cornwall.
68 Killibury, Cornwall.
69 Trevelgue, Cornwall.
70 Chûn Castle, Cornwall.
71 Goldherring, Cornwall.
72 Maen Castle, Cornwall.
73 Grambla, Cornwall.
74 Trethurgy, Cornwall.
75 Castle Dore, Cornwall.

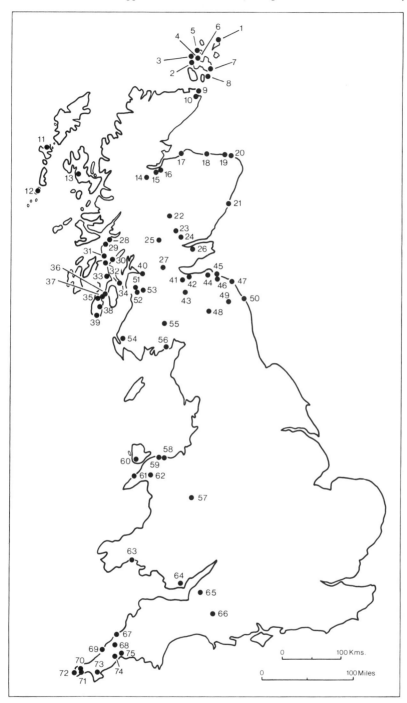

Figure 1. Enclosed places, AD 500–800.

The digest of chronological evidence includes documentary references from contemporary sources, radiocarbon age estimates, stratification and typology of ramparts and buildings, and artefactual evidence. The latter includes jewellery and lesser trinkets typologically assigned to the period, and also metalworking debris, especially the moulds and raw materials (scrap metal and glass) for making such jewellery. Certain forms of comb and bone pin are also regarded as chronologically diagnostic. Another major class of evidence is that of imported pottery of Classes A, B, D and E; here the list is derived almost entirely from Thomas (1981). It scarcely needs saying that the occurrence of artefacts of our period on a particular site – for instance, bone pins on a broch – is no guarantee that there are structures of that period, or even a substantive reoccupation; but it is none the less a suggestive pointer.

Previous versions of this register of sites have been discussed at several conferences, and have been published, for Wales, in *Welsh History Review 2*, 1965, 1-7; for Wales and the Marches and Dumnonia in Hinton (1983, 58-60); and for Britain (and Ireland) in Alcock (1971; 1973, 209-29) with map 6. These earlier lists differ in detail from the present one, and they are mentioned here in order to emphasise the point that there is nothing definitive or permanent about any of them. While the digest of chronological evidence is normally both objective and irrefutable, the inferences drawn from it, even the inclusion of a site in the present gazetteer, is a matter for conjecture and debate in varying degree. Indeed, a major intention of this appendix is to provide ammunition for dialectic, not fossilised doctrine.

In this connection, attention should be drawn to certain biases and omissions. In Wales and Dumnonia our knowledge has undoubtedly been skewed by the attention paid to forts with mythical associations, especially those connected with the Arthurian cycle. In northern Britain the bias has been in favour of excavating vitrified forts on the mainland, and brochs in the far north and west. Even so, brochs are probably under-represented in the gazetteer. More recently, there has been some concentration on historically documented fortifications. In all areas, research has focused on fortified hill-tops, to the neglect of unfortified places known to have been used by potentates (cf. Alcock (1981a, 180) on the Pictish and Scottish royal centre at Forteviot). All this means that our data base is a far from random sample.

Moreover, certain sites that might have been thought relevant have been excluded, either because their attribution to the period is questionable, or on the more subjective ground that their relatively feeble enclosing work is regarded as more appropriate to a rural homestead than to the seat of a potentate. In Wales these would include Pant y Saer and Garn Boduan, which have both featured in earlier lists; in northern Britain, Crock Cleuch and Phase IV at Hownam Rings are examples. Moreover, sites of an essentially 'Roman' rather than 'native' character have been excluded even when, as at Carlisle, they were important political centres in our period. (For these see R.Cramp in Chapman and Mytum (1983,263-97, especially 265-6 and 274).) Finally it must be stressed that any wider treatment of the evolution of the

Northumbrian *civitas, vicus* or *villa regalis* out of the administrative arrangements of Roman Britain must take account of places such as *Campodunum,* Carlisle, Catterick and *Deruentio,* in addition to those discussed above and listed in this appendix.

Alphabetical Gazetteer

60 Aberffraw, Anglesey (SH 3568)
character and stratification of rampart
White (1980)

22 Aldclune, Perthshire (NN 8964)
jewellery
Triscott (1980; 1981)
Alcock (1984)

31 Ardifuar, Argyll (NR 7896)
metalworking
Christison (1905, 259-70)

50 Bamburgh (*Din Guoaroy, Bebbanburh*),
    Northumberland (NU 1834)
documentary references
HE 3, 6; 3, 12; 3, 16
Hope-Taylor (1966)
Alcock (1983)

54 Black Loch (Loch Inch-Cryndi) Crannog,
    Wigtownshire (NX 1161)
bonework
Munro (1882, 57-60)

7 Broch of Ayre, Mainland, Orkney
    (HY 5804)
bonework
Graeme (1914)
Stevenson (1955a)

8 Broch of Burray, Burray, Orkney
    (HY 4998)
bonework
Anderson (1883)
Stevenson (1955a)

1 Broch of Burrian, N. Ronaldsay, Orkney
    (HY 7651)
Pictish symbols, bonework, iron bell
Anderson (1883)
MacGregor (1974)

2 Broch of Burwick, Mainland, Orkney
    (HY 2216)
bonework
Watt (1882)
Anderson (1883)
Stevenson (1955a)

6 Broch of Gurness, Mainland, Orkney
    (HY 3826)
bonework
Richardson (1948)
Hedges and Bell (1980)

5 Broch of Midhowe, Rousay, Orkney
    (HY 3730)
bonework, trinkets
Callander and Grant (1934)
Stevenson (1955a)

3 Broch of Oxtro, Mainland, Orkney
    (HY 2526)
bonework, trinkets
Petrie (1890)
Anderson (1883)
Stevenson (1955a)

4 Brough of Birsay, Mainland, Orkney
    (HY 2328)
bonework, jewellery, metalworking, glass
Radford (1959; 1978)
Curle (1982)

   Brudei Munitio, see Castle Hill, Inverness
    and Urquhart Castle
documentary references
VC 40a, 80a
Alcock (1981a, 159-61)

58 Bryneuryn, Dinarth (Din Eirth),
    (*Receptaculum ursi*), Denbighshire
    (SH 8379)
documentary reference
DEB 32.1
Sims-Williams (1983, 8)

53 Buiston Crannog, Ayrshire (NS 4143)
imported pottery (E), bonework, jewellery,
metalworking
Munro (1882, 190-239)
Alcock (1983)

17 Burghead, Moray (NJ 1069)
C-14 age estimates, Pictish stones
Small (1969)
Edwards and Ralston (1978)
Shepherd (1983)

66 Cadbury-Camelot, Somerset (ST 6325)
imported pottery (A, B, D), jewellery, glass
Alcock (1972; 1982a)

65 Cadbury-Congresbury, Somerset (ST 4465)
imported pottery (A, B, D), trinkets, metalworking, glass
Fowler, Gardner and Rahtz (1970)
Burrow (1981)

61 Carreg y Llam, Caernarvonshire (SH 3343)
wheel-thrown pottery
Hogg (1957)

75 Castle Dore, Cornwall (SX 1054)
post-Iron Age structures, ?imported pottery
Radford (1951)
Rahtz (1971)

51 Castlehill, Dalry, Ayrshire (NS 2849)
trinkets, glass
Smith (1919)

16 Castle Hill, Inverness (?*Brudei Munitio*),
Inverness-shire (NH 6645)
Henderson (1975, 91-108)

70 Chûn Castle, Cornwall (SW 4033)
imported pottery (B)
Leeds (1927; 1931)
Thomas (1956)

26 Clatchard Craig, Fife (NO 2417)
imported pottery (E), C-14 age estimates,
metalworking
Close-Brooks (1986)

63 Coygan Camp, Carmarthenshire (SN 2809)
imported pottery (A, B)
Wainwright (1967)

15 Craig Phadrig, Inverness-shire (NH 6445)
C-14 age estimates, imported pottery (E),
metalworking
Small (1972)
Small and Cottam (1972)
Alcock (1984)

19 Cullykhan, Castle Point, Troup, Banffshire
(NJ 8267)
C-14 age estimate
Greig (1971; 1972)
Shepherd (1983)

41 Dalmahoy, Midlothian (NT 1366)
jewellery, metalworking
Stevenson (1949)
Alcock (1983)

59 Degannwy Castle, Caernarvonshire
(SH 7879)
documentary references, imported pottery (B)
Annales Cambriae s.a. 812, 822
Alcock (1967)

62 Dinas Emrys, Caernarvonshire (SH 6049)
imported pottery (B, E), metalworking, glass
Savory (1960)

64 Dinas Powys, Glamorgan (ST 1671)
imported pottery (A, B, D, E), bonework,
jewellery/trinkets, metalworking, glass
Alcock (1963)

46 Doon Hill, East Lothian (NT 6875)
building plans and stratification
Hope-Taylor (1980)
Reynolds (1980b)
Alcock (1983)

40 Dumbarton Rock (*Alcluith*), Dunbartonshire (NS 4074)
documentary references, C-14 age estimates,
imported pottery (B, E), glass, metalworking
HE I, I; I, 12
Alcock (1976)

32 Dunadd (*Dun Att*), Argyll (NR 8393)
documentary references, imported pottery (D,
E), metalwork, metalworking, inscriptions
AI s.a. 683, 736
Christison (1905, 292-322)
Craw (1930, 111-27)
Lane (1980, 31; 1981, 30-1)
Alcock (1981a, 166-8)

29 Dùn an Fheuran, Argyll (NM 8226)
bonework
Ritchie (1971)

13 Dun Ardtreck, Skye (NG 3335)
imported pottery (E)
MacKie (1965a; 1965b)

39 Dunaverty (?*Aberte*), Argyll (NR 6807)
documentary reference (note Watson's
reservation about the identification, Watson
(1926, 237, n.1))
AI s.a. 712
Alcock (1981a, 157)

45 Dunbar (*Dynbaer*), East Lothian (NT 6779)
documentary references
VW chap. 38
Alcock (1981a, 174-5)

12 Dun Cuier, Barra (NF 6603)
bonework
Young (1956)

20 Dundarg Castle, Aberdeenshire (NJ 8964)
suggested in Shepherd (1983, 330), Simpson
(1954)

25 Dundurn (*Dun Duirn*), Perthshire
(NN 7023)
documentary reference, C-14 age estimates,
imported pottery (E), jewellery, metalworking,
glass
AI s.a. 683
Alcock (1981a, 168-71)

35 Dun Fhinn, Argyll (NR 6530)
glass
RCAHMS (1971, 83-4)

28 Dunollie (*Dun Ollaigh*), Argyll (NM 8531)
documentary references, imported pottery (E),
bonework, metalworking
AI s.a. 686, 698, 701, 714, 734
Alcock (1981a, 172-3; 1981b)

21 Dunottar Castle (*Dun Fother*), Kincardineshire (NO 8883)
documentary references
AI s.a. 681, 694
Alcock (1981a, 171-2)

42 Edinburgh (*Din Eidyn*), Midlothian (NT 2573)
documentary reference
AI s.a. 638
Alcock (1981a, 165-6; 1983)

9 Freswick Sands Broch, Caithness (ND 3866)
bonework
Anderson (1901, 143-4)
Stevenson (1955a)

Giudi, Iudeu – ?Stirling
documentary references
HB chap. 64
HE 1, 12
Alcock (1981a, 175-6)
Jackson (1981)

71 Goldherring, Cornwall (SW 4128)
platters compare Gwithian
Guthrie (1969)

73 Grambla, Cornwall (SW 6928)
imported pottery (?A, B)
Saunders (1972)

18 Green Castle, Portknockie, Banffshire (NJ 4868)
C-14 age estimates
Ralston (1978)
Shepherd (1983)

43 Harehope, Peeblesshire (NT 2044)
palisade-typology
Feachem (1960)
Alcock (1983)

24 Inchtuthill, Perthshire (NO 1139)
?re-used Roman masonry
Abercromby, Ross and Anderson (1902, 230-4, fig.206)

10 Keiss Broch, Caithness (ND 3561)
bonework
Anderson (1901, 122-7)
Stevenson (1955a)

38 Kildalloig, Argyll (NR 7518)
imported pottery (E)
RCAHMS (1971, 87-8)

37 Kildonan Bay, Argyll (NR 7827)
C-14 age estimate, trinkets
Fairhurst (1939)
Peltenburg *et al.* (1982)

68 Killibury, Cornwall (SX 0173)
imported pottery (B)
Miles *et al.* (1977)

23 King's Seat, Dunkeld, Perthshire (NO 0142)
place-name, fortification-typology
Watson (1926, 21-2)
Feachem (1966, 73-5)

47 Kirk Hill, St Abbs (*Colodaesburg, Urbs Coludi*), Berwickshire (NT 9187)
documentary references, C-14 age estimates
HE 4, 19; 4, 25
Alcock (1981b; 1983)

34 Little Dunagoil, Bute (NS 0823)
imported pottery (E), bonework, glass
Marshall (1964)

30 Loch Glashan Crannog, Argyll (NR 9193)
imported pottery (E), jewellery
Scott and Scott (1960)

52 Lochlee Crannog, Ayrshire (NS 3045)
trinket, glass
Munro (1882, 68-151)

72 Maen Castle, Cornwall (SW 3425)
grass-marked base
Crofts (1955)

56 Mote of Mark, Stewartry of Kirkcudbright (NX 8454)
imported pottery (D, E), C-14 age estimates, bonework, metalworking, jewellery/trinkets
Curle (1914)
Longley (1982, 132-4)
Alcock (1983)

57 New Pieces, Breiddin, Montgomeryshire (SJ 2913)
glass (identified by J. R. Hunter, ex info. C. R. Musson)
O'Neil (1937, 107-12)
Mytum (1982)

48 Ruberslaw, Roxburghshire (NT 5815)
re-used Roman masonry
Curle (1905, 219-32)
Alcock (1979)

27 Stirling (?*Giudi*), Stirlingshire (NS 7993)
for references and discussion of identification see *Giudi*

33 Tarbert (*Tairpert Boitter*), Argyll (NR 8668)
documentary references
AI s.a. 712, 731
Alcock (1981a, 177)

67 Tintagel, Cornwall (SX 0489)
imported pottery (A, B, D), glass
Radford (1935)
Burrow (1973, 99-103)
Thomas (1982, 17-34)

44 Traprain Law, East Lothian (NT 5874)
jewellery/trinkets
Burley (1956)
Jobey (1976)
Alcock (1979)
Close-Brooks (1983)

74 Trethurgy, Cornwall (SX 0355)
imported pottery (A, B, E)
Miles and Miles (1973)

69 Trevelgue, Cornwall (SW 8263)
?imported pottery (?B)
Andrew (1949)

55 Tynron Doon, Dumfriesshire (NX 8293)
bonework, jewellery
Williams (1971)
Alcock (1983)

11 Udal (Coileagan an Udail), North Uist
(NF 8277)
C-14 age estimates, jewellery, bonework,
metalworking, native pottery
Crawford and Switsur (1977)

36 Ugadale, Argyll (NR 7828)
metalworking, glass
Fairhurst (1956)

14 Urquhart Castle (?*Brudei Munitio*),
Inverness-shire (NH 5328)
Alcock (1981a, 159-61)

49 Yeavering (*Ad Gefrin*), Northumberland
(NT 9331)
documentary reference, architectural
comparisons
HE 2, 14
Hope-Taylor (1977)
Alcock (1979, 136)

The archaeology of Early
Historic Irish kingship

Any discussion of matters pertaining to the Early Historic period[1] in Ireland must take cognizance of both the fine survival of textual evidence and the rich artefactual and monumental assemblages. Despite the fact that the information sets available to each discipline derive from the same society, it is surprising how seldom correlation of the information sets, with equal weight being given to each, is attempted.[2] Clearly there are problems of unfamiliarity with the sources and methodology of each discipline by the practitioners of the other, the consequences of which are either distrust or misuse of the unfamiliar evidence. Renfrew (1979) has aptly described the often antagonistic or patronising relationship between the two disciplines as 'dialogues of the deaf'. As an archaeologist with no basic historical training, but working in a historical period, I am acutely aware of the criticisms which my own reading of the historical evidence will bring. I can only plead the best intentions.

I will, in this chapter, make very few allusions to non-Irish matters, or to the very extensive evidence for Irish late-medieval kingship (heavily relied on by Byrne 1973), for the following reasons. A fair proportion of the evidence of the past illuminates a well-defined and narrow part of the chronological, cultural or geographical spectrum. Because the survival and recovery of these evidential segments are both limited and adventitious they are, even within the same discipline, most unlikely to illuminate the same event. The rest of the evidence, on the other hand, has the contrary property that its chronological, cultural or geographical status cannot be defined closely. The necessity to accommodate these limitations often encourages an assumption of homogeneity and the casting of a wide net. Thus, by using such generalised labels as 'early Christian' (chronological), 'Celtic' (cultural) and 'Irish sea province' (geographical) the combination of otherwise unconnected evidence can be undertaken without too much justification. This practice of eclectic data collection may often be unavoidable, but it must be expected to set up severe contradictions, especially as the details become better understood.

It will also be noted that I eschew the use of generalised 'models'. The generalising practice mentioned above is particularly encouraged by the present fashion of model-building, the models being drawn, in an ever more eclectic fashion, from history, social theory, anthropology, biology, geography, and empathetic hypothesising.[3] There is nothing inherently wrong with models, or with empathy and 'logic', as long as the appropriateness of the particular model or hypothesis is always demonstrated. I doubt very much whether archaeological interpretation is even possible without some use of

models, even when they are not overtly described; but as Leach has put it
'. . . the guessing ought to be on the basis of what you definitely know, not just
wild free-ranging speculation' (1979, 123). There even seems to be a current
view that the archaeologist working in a historical field should, in order to keep
some sort of methodological purity of interpretation, be blind to the historical
background of his period while interpreting his archaeological data, using this
impartial model-based methodology. The practice of ignoring one set of
evidence of the past, for whatever reason, has been called 'counterfactual
history' and rightly criticised (Hobsbawm 1979, 248). Indeed the models used
consciously or unconsciously by archaeologists are, at least partly, historically
based, so the use of the historical model appropriate to the particular archaeological problem can hardly be bad archaeology.

I have dwelt on this issue because the topic of Early Historic Irish kingship
is very dependent on the combination of both historical and archaeological
evidence. A high-status site may certainly be recognisable from archaeological
evidence alone by using various 'ranking' models. It may even be claimed to
be 'royal compatible'. But the conclusion that it was actually the residence of
a king can only be proved from historical sources.

Historical source material

The levels of reliability in the ancient Irish laws, genealogies, tales and annals
are variable, and well studied by the historians. The laws and tales are the most
useful sources for details of kingship but suffer from the problem that the
details may be virtually undatable within the Early Historic period. At one
extreme it is usually clear to what date a manuscript copy of a text belongs.
Even the date of the original, or of a lost intermediate recension, can often be
judged from internal evidence. At the other extreme the text (particularly if it
is from the laws or heroic sagas) may well contain archaisms and even an
ancient or mythical core. It has recently been shown that even the most archaic
sagas consist of a palimpsest of details added and changed over the course of
the telling or during the writing or copying of the document (Mallory 1981).[4]

The historical picture of society[5]

Early Irish society was 'tribal, rural, hierarchical and familiar' (Binchy 1954,
54). The 'tribe', a not wholly satisfactory rendering of Irish *tuath*, was a
population unit with a king (*rí*) at its head. There were some 150 tribes in
Ireland at any one time during the Early Historic period, giving for each a
mean size of about 500 square kilometres, aptly described by Byrne as 'Lilli-
putian' (1971, 140), and a *mean* population of perhaps around 5,000. Such
averages are an academic convenience rather than a reflection of reality for
neither the individual power, allegiances, size, boundaries, nor location of the
tribes remained unchanged (Byrne 1971), nor were they in any sense equal.
The archaeological evidence we find for one royal site at any one time cannot
safely be assumed for other sites or other times. The early Irish lawyers
however, as is the wont of all lawyers, attempted to generalise society. Their

descriptions of the privileges, responsibilities and possessions of the social grades can perhaps be taken as a sort of average level of wealth and status of each grade, including that of the king.[6]

The cement of early Irish society was clientship, a contractual and strictly defined relationship between people of different rank which conferred benefits and obligations on both parties.[7] Two forms of clientship are described by the contemporary lawyers: 'base' and 'free'. The base client, though he may have had some land and stock of his own, obtained from a noble a grant of land or cattle and legal and physical protection. In return the client paid an annual render of cattle and food, contributed military service and provided hospitality for his lord's entourage. The free client, who would usually have been of noble status himself, had slightly different duties, including companionship, and his render might include non-agricultural items such as horse-bridles. Clientship partly freed the noble from personal agricultural involvement to pursue drinking, hunting and fighting, and freed the client from concerns of law and security in order to concentrate on his farming.

Within the non-ecclesiastical, non-skilled social hierarchy it is convenient if we make four divisions, albeit a gross simplification of the complex divisions of the contemporary lawyers. At the bottom were the landless, and to all intents and purposes archaeologically invisible, peasants and slaves. Above these were the non-noble farmers of various levels of wealth, who would all have been clients, mostly of the base form, of a noble. Above the farmers were the various grades of nobility. The nobles would have had at least the requisite numbers of inferiors as free and base clients and the lower nobility may well have been free clients themselves of higher nobles. At the top of the nobility were the kings, whom we may conveniently divide into the king of a tribe and the overking of a number of tribes. The so-called high-king of Ireland, when it came to mean anything at all, meant the overking of other overkings. This was, as it were, the secular hierarchy. Parallel to it was a hierarchy consisting of the ecclesiastics, craftsmen and men of learning. Each level of skill had a defined equivalence to a level on the secular scale with, at the top, the senior bishop of the tribe having the status of the king. As with the secular nobility the upper ranks of the 'men of skills' would almost certainly have been, and have had, clients.

The aristocratic section of the upper grade of society, the grade of nobility, held that position through a carefully defined combination of wealth and family. In other words, if a man belonged to a noble kin-group his legal status (for instance his honour price) was then dependent on his wealth, which would be measured by the number of cattle and clients he possessed. If a man of noble background lacked the defined wealth for a particular level of nobility then his position at that level was forfeited, and he could even fall out of the nobility, a real threat as his clients could buy themselves out and decrease his client base. Alternatively, he could climb the noble ranks by increasing his wealth, as far as the level below that of kingship. The same wealth-connected qualifying rules applied to the rank of kingship, with the added necessity of being within the *derbfhine* of a king.[8] It was, therefore, possible to fall out of kingship by falling below the required level of wealth.

The field archaeology

The commonest field monument in Ireland is the ringfort. Despite wide variation it is possible to include most members of the class in a generalised description (Proudfoot 1961). The typical ringfort was a roughly circular enclosure of between 20 and 60 metres internal diameter, surrounded by one or more, usually close-set, earthen banks and ditches or one or more substantial stone walls. Its siting was not usually defensive or strategic but rather the sort of position that would be expected for a working farm, on well-drained level or moderately sloping land below 200 metres altitude. It typically belonged between the sixth and twelfth centuries AD, and was probably the homestead of a single family.[9] It was likely to contain a single main house and perhaps some outbuildings, and possibly a 'souterrain' (defensive artificial cave). Its economic base was mixed farming with a very strong bias towards cattle. The artefacts recovered by excavation suggest in most cases only a moderate level of wealth, the items being those expected in a working farm, but a few have produced artefacts indicative of a higher status. The distributional evidence points to an area of immediate exploitation of between 20 and 100 hectares, which matches very well the expected size of holding of a farmer as defined by the contemporary lawyers.

It seems, then, a reasonable inference that the ringfort was the defended homestead of someone belonging to the land-owning classes of early historic society, let us say from the wealthy non-noble farmer (*bóaire*) upward. The commonest form of ringfort found today is univallate and unspectacular. Rather rarer are bivallate ringforts and the rarest the trivallate. An easy explanation of this pattern would be to suggest that the progression from univallate to trivallate correlates to the social hierarchy, the trivallate ringforts being those of the kings, but we will see later that such a simplistic 'size-ranking' approach is not completely satisfactory.

There are a number of sites with the features or size of a ringfort, but sited strategically or defensively or in an inconvenient situation for normal intercourse of farming. These include promontory forts, outcrop forts and crannogs. The last are artificial or modified lake islands strengthened by a palisade or stone wall (Wood-Martin 1886). The chronological spread of these primarily defensive types of sites, wider than that of ringforts, runs from the seventh to about the sixteenth century AD. It is difficult to believe that the economic base of these inconvenient sites was immediately agricultural in the sense that the occupant was himself a farmer, although their internal size is very comparable to that of the ordinary ringforts. Unfortunately their excavation has not been extensive, but the crannogs belonging to our period have tended to be significantly richer in high quality artefacts than the contemporary ringforts, even allowing for the better preservation in waterlogged conditions, and contemporary descriptions note the high status of the occupants.

Although the major part of the cattle holding of a noble would have been distributed among his clients it was still necessary for him to have a certain number of his own animals. We can assume that if the occupants of these strategic or inconvenient sites belonged to the noble classes, as seems likely, they had some means of maintaining their own stock somewhere else.

Large enclosures with internal areas of several hectares are relatively common (Swan 1983). They are usually roughly circular, surrounded by earthen banks and ditches or stone walls, and in the same sort of topographcal situation in which we find the ringforts. Where they are multivallate the banks (or walls) are invariably wide-set. They are defensive in the same secondary sense as the ringfort, and are not to be thought of as 'hillforts' in the English sense. In a fairly large proportion of cases the presence of ecclesiastical elements indicates that they were monastic. We know from the contemporary literature, confirmed by the archaeology, that the monastic settlements were population aggregations, in fact small towns in the loosest sense. They had a complex and increasingly wealthy economic base drawing both on the surrounding countryside and on commerce and manufacture (Doherty 1980).

Defence

The defensive nature of these settlements is not to be wondered at. The cattle-based economy, the confinement of law and protection to the tribe (see below), the small size of the tribes and the often bad relations between them described in the contemporary annals, all conspired towards a rather insecure situation for the farmers. At the lowest level the cattle-raid (*crech*) was a favoured pastime of the younger nobility (combined with the taking of noble heads) and a convenient way of obtaining cattle. At the highest level the king could, after a formal announcement at the tribal assembly, undertake a hosting into another territory or muster his people to repel an invader. There is no indication that, apart from calling such a defensive muster, the king provided a means of tribal defence. Binchy (1954, 64) has suggested that the status of sanctuary held by the large, semi-defensive monastic *enceintes* would have served to protect the common people in their vicinity. But the defensive structure of the ringfort, with the added security of clustering and avoidance of the tribal boundary, was a convenient form of personal defence against raids by small bands.

Prehistoric royal/ritual sites

Wailes (1982) has discussed the 'royal' and 'ritual' sites of the pagan era described in the archaic sagas. He argued that the places named therein as pre-Christian centres of kingship and ritual (and described as 'grass grown' and deserted in the Early Historic period) belonged to the core level of the tales and could be interpreted as prehistoric reality rather than mythical fiction. At the same time he wisely ignored the descriptive details and explanations. Wailes listed some empathetically based archaeological expectations for places of major ritual and kingship as follows:

1. Unusual importance should imply unusual size or form, or both.

2. Sites with similar status might be expected to be archaeologically similar.

3. Evidence should be forthcoming (as far as it might survive archaeologically) of both residence and ritual.

4. The residential evidence should indicate a high status.

5. The culture implied by the archaeology should coincide with that implied by the texts.

Only two of the sites with which Wailes dealt have been excavated carefully, if on a necessarily restricted scale, but all have been studied in the field. We may summarise the elements more or less common to these sites thus, though being careful not to give them the status of rules:

1. The presence of a complex of monuments, including

2. a large circular enclosure defined by a massive bank with an inner ditch,

3. one or more smaller inner-ditched earthen circles ('ring-barrows'),

4. a prominent mound in or near the large enclosure,

5. a banked roadway.

In addition, all these sites retain a local tradition of early importance which is unlikely to be mere antiquarianism. Wailes concluded that the hypothetical expectations were demonstrated. It would seem reasonable to suppose that these general expectations, and some of the descriptive elements of the prehistoric royal/ritual sites, will be relevant to the study of Early Historic kingship.

Identification of historic places

Clearly one of the most important concerns in an attempted archaeological description of textually attested places must be their correct identification. The survival of ancient Irish place-names is not, despite the continuity of the Irish language, quite as good as might be hoped. In fact only a small minority of the huge number of Early Historic places listed by Hogan (1910) have been located more precisely than to a general district, and fewer still to an actual surviving site.

Within an area in which it is thought a historically named place ought to lie, or which contains a place-name which may be the descendant of that early name, there may be a number of claimants for identification as the archaeological remains of that historical place. Whether a particular class of field monument appears in the list of claimants will depend on the prevailing archaeological expectation of typology. Clearly if this expectation is wrong or too narrow, the identification may also be wrong but there is the added problem that, within the constrained list of claimants, the most physically outstanding site would almost certainly be identified with the historical place. I call this the 'outstanding-site tendency' and I believe it has caused a great deal of misidentification, or at least unproven identification, of Early Historic places.

Royal places

Many royal places are attested in the Early Historic sources, some with reference to detailed events, some with descriptions and most simply in passing. The main forms of reference are as follows:

1. Tales, poems or other texts in which it is specifically stated that a king lived at a certain place – for instance '*Fiachna Lurgan* . . . left his wife . . . in his *dún* (stronghold) in *Ráith Mór* of *Mag Line* (Great Fort of the plain of *Line*)'.

2. The use of the form 'king of place', for instance *Cathal rex Ratho Airthir* (Cathal king of the Eastern Fort).

3. The use of a place-name as an epithet attached to a king's name (*Congalach Cnogba*, Congalach of Knowth).

There are problems in the interpretation of the nature of the ostensibly named royal place. In some cases it is clear from the textual description, as for example in the one above, that the place was the habitation of the king in a perfectly normal sense. But as we shall see, a king might well have constructed or used a number of places and we may not be sure which named place was his main residence. Also, as the kingship moved between rival dynasties within the tribe it was not unusual for the place of royal habitation to move also. For instance, when the kings of *Clochar* in Co. Tyrone lost the kingship of the tribe of *Uí Crimthainn* to their kinsfolk at *Loch Uaithne* (Lough Ooney, Co. Monaghan) the centre of kingship passed to the latter place. Nor need the naming of a place of kingship imply that it was a settlement at all. Assembly places, feast places, inauguration places, places of ancient or historic significance, places of major topographical importance may all appear as royal epithets. For instance, the overking of the federation of the *Ulaid* (north-east Ulster) was occasionally known in the Early Historic period as the king of *Emain* (now Navan, Co. Armagh). This was a purely symbolic title, for this prehistoric royal/ritual capital of prehistoric 'Ulster' was by that time outside the *Ulaid* king's area of influence. There is also the danger that if the date of the text is later than the supposed date of the event the writer may have made an unwarranted assumption that the place known to him as the contemporary capital of that tribe or dynasty, or habitation of that king's descendants, had the same status at the time of the event. It is partly for these reasons that I have avoided the phrases 'capital of the tribe' or 'tribal centre'.

The identified royal sites

When we come to discuss the archaeological results obtained from a study of Irish royal sites, and assuming we are happy about the identification, we come up against a dearth of information, either because of the lack of detailed site study or because of intensive later use and change. As an example, one of the most important Early Historic centres of kingship was *Caisel*. The king of *Caisel* was a tribal king, usually overking of most of the province of Munster and occasionally high-king of Ireland. It is one royal place whose identity can

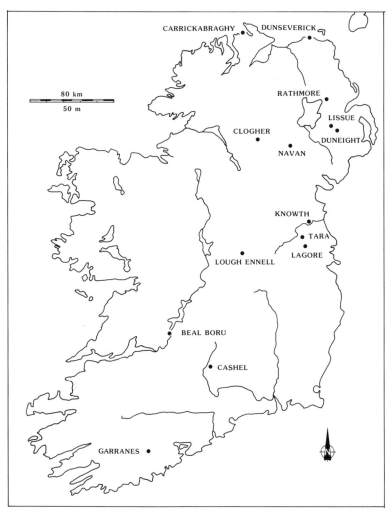

Figure 1. Map showing the main sites mentioned in the text.

be regarded as certain – (the rock of) Cashel, Co. Tipperary. Here a prominent and extensive rock outcrop is now crowned by a range of ecclesiastical buildings and no obvious early secular features can be made out. Therefore, despite the fact that it is precisely located and was a place of major kingship for the whole of our period nothing archaeological is known about it as an early royal site. This is typical of the majority of the identifiable royal sites in Ireland, whose surviving condition prevents more than the most general and uncertain observations. But there is a small number of excavated sites for which there is far more information.

In Munster the habitation of the Kings of *Raithliu*, *Ráith Raithleann* ('Fort of *Raithliu*'), was identified many years ago as the trivallate ringfort of

Garranes, Co. Cork and excavated by Ó Ríordáin (1942). The excavation provided some important finds dating the occupation as starting in the sixth century AD. Other earthworks in the near vicinity of Garranes may well have been associated with it (they included a pond and some small ring ditches), but little is known about them. Unfortunately the identification of this site cannot be regarded as certain.

The crannog of Lagore, Co. Meath, excavated by Hencken (1951) after very severe disturbance, is believed to be the island of *Loch Gabor,* capital and home of the kings of Southern *Brega,* attested in the historic sources from the mid-eighth to the late tenth century AD. The rich and reasonably well stratified assemblage of excavated material spanned the same period. As no other crannog has been identified in the lake it seems reasonable to accept the identification. No other sites are reported as being closely associated with Lagore, although the early (pre-Patrician?) church of *Domnach Sechnaill* (Dunshaughlin) was very near.

An allied tribe had their royal capital, from the early ninth to the tenth century, at *Cnogba,* which is identified without much doubt as the Neolithic passage grave at Knowth, Co. Meath. Extensive excavations at this site by Eogan showed that the huge mound of the passage grave had been fortified with a double ditch in, perhaps, the seventh century and occupied from then on (Eogan 1974). Unfortunately the interior of the fort had later been damaged by the erection of a castle and by quarrying, but the houses of a settlement of about the tenth or eleventh century were found around the base of the mound. Its location, within the extensive prehistoric necropolis of *Brug na Bóinne* and adjacent to an iron age inhumation cemetery, is worthy of mention.

The last site, *Clochar,* was capital of a relatively powerful tribe in central Ulster, the *Uí Crimthainn,* from at least the sixth to the ninth century. Its kings were frequently overkings of a substantial federation of tribes. The identification of this royal place with a complex of earthworks at Clogher, Co. Tyrone, based mainly on descriptions in the early texts, can be regarded as certain (Warner 1982). Excavations at this site, not yet published (Warner 1973), and analysis of the field evidence, have revealed a mass of information confirming the historical date span. The central feature, a strong univallate ringfort, was surrounded by a large internally ditched enclosure (a re-used hillfort) containing a ringbarrow and a substantial mound. Very close to this site was an important early monastery (see figure 2 and plate 1).

Early changes

Until at least the seventh century Irish society was in a state of severe flux, with rapid but obscure changes taking place. By that time the great prehistoric royal/ritual sites had lost their residential status as royal centres, retaining only their symbolic and perhaps ritual status. By mechanisms not yet fully understood Irish material and social culture was heavily influenced by late Roman Britain, aided by the spread of new dynastic groups through the country. We would expect royal sites to show these changes and, despite the

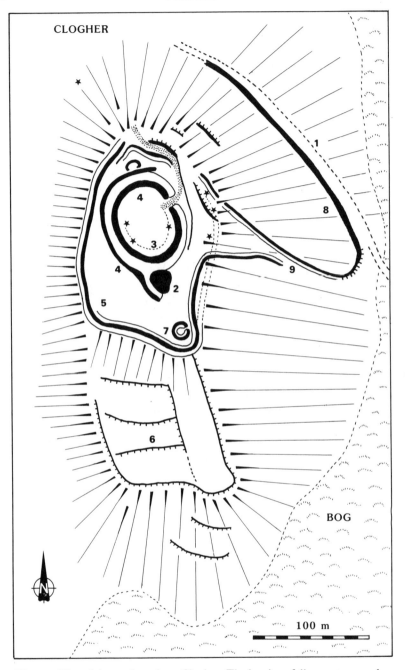

Figure 2. Plan of the earthworks at Clogher. The key is as follows: stars mark evidence for metalworking; 1 'droveway'; 2 mound; 3 ringditch; 4 ringfort; 5 outer enclosure/hillfort; 6 fields; 7 ringbarrow; 8 bank of unknown date; 9 embanked 'funnel'.

small size of our sample, they do. Intrusive Roman material has been found at two of the prehistoric royal/ritual sites and at the Early Historic royal sites of Cashel (a stray find) and, with examples of the new Irish derivative forms, Knowth and Clogher.

Royal and ritual

It seems to be generally agreed, if I interpret the historians correctly, that there was a change in the practice, if not in the theoretical concept, of Irish kingship at this early stage in our period. The proto-historic kingly status of being the personal embodiment of the ethos of the tribe, a combination of royal and sacred, became secularised. Byrne has described it as changing from quasi-divine warrior-kingship to farmer-kingship. There seems to be little doubt that Christianity encouraged this separation of royal and sacred, and it is no surprise that we find a close physical association of royal habitations and major early church sites, an association apparently illustrated by the legend of the foundation of Armagh by Patrick. The prehistoric royal/ritual sites were associated each with its own major fertility rite (*feis*), at which the king was inaugurated, or symbolically mated with the tribal deity. *Caisel* was one of the most important, newly created, Early Historic sites of kingship, and had no place in the earliest myths. Significantly, as Binchy has pointed out (1970, 40), it had no *feis*. This is not to say that the ritual side of kingship did not survive, for it patently did, as late as the end of Irish kingship in the early seventeenth century. It does suggest, however, that the archaeological evidence from royal sites might be expected to be proportionally heavier on the 'royal' than the 'ritual'.

The sacred aspect of the prehistoric royal/ritual sites seems to be evidenced by the field monuments. Burial is usually represented, or rather implied, by ringbarrows (Raftery 1982). Some sort of assembly, or sanctuary, is indicated by the large inner-ditched enclosures and prominent mounds. Tara is perhaps the most important of the prehistoric royal/ritual sites, whose use as a place of inauguration, and great symbolic importance, continued through the Early Historic period. The site contains three mounds relevant to this discussion (Ó Ríordáin 1953). The Early Historic writers called the main mound at Tara *duma na ngiall* ('mound of the hostages'), with the clear indication that they regarded it as part of kingly ritual. Another, ditched, mound was called *forrad*, which might mean 'high seat' (cf. Welsh *Gorsedh*). The third mound lies between the two outer banks of the trivallate ringfort in Tara called *Ráith na senad* ('Fort of the assembly'). I would interpret this ringfort as the king's residence at times of inauguration or other ritual in the Early Historic period. Its adjoining mound is paralleled by the mound integrally associated with the royal ringfort at Clogher (which also has a ringbarrow and a large internally ditched enclosure). In one Early Historic story two kings meet to discuss a joint military project on the mound next to the unnamed fort of one of them, and it may well transpire that a royal convention (*rígdál*) was wont to take place on just such a mound. The word *síd*, applied to mounds and barrows in

Irish tales, has etymological connotations of 'peace', 'other world' and 'seat'. The royal/ritual status of mounds is finally confirmed by their frequent textual appearance as places of inauguration in late medieval Irish kingship.

These examples appear to suggest that the monumental evidence of the rituals of Early Historic kingship (assembly and inauguration, for instance), of a form familiar in the prehistoric sites, might be expected at these later royal sites. Unfortunately few have yet been shown to possess these features, either in the field or in the early texts. Similarly, where an occasional Early Historic assembly site (óenach) can be identified it is found to be remote from any royal site (MacNeill 1962). As a clear example of this the royal residences of three dynastically connected east-midland tribes, at *Ráith Airthir* (an unidentified ringfort near Oristown), *Cnogba* (Knowth) and *Loch Gabor* (Lagore) were a considerable distance from their joint main places of assembly at *Tailtiu* (Teltown) and of inauguration at *Temair* (Tara, the prehistoric royal/ritual site) (Binchy 1958). The locational separation of the sacred, represented by the removal to the church of burial and religious ritual is, then, echoed for the profane by the separation of habitation from inauguration and assembly. It is clear from the example given, and may prove to be the pattern, that it was the royal habitation that was relocated rather than the ritual site.

Site typology

The Irish prehistoric royal/ritual sites have in common a completely non-defensive nature. Though it is evident from the early tales that the mytho-logical kings were perceived as warrior-kings there is no evidence of this aspect from the archaeological study of their places of kingship. The earliest archaeo-logical evidence for the structure of an Early Historic royal habitation comes from Clogher. Here there was a sixth-century AD oval enclosure of about 50 metres mean diameter bounded by a massive wooden palisade, outside which was a flat-bottomed ditch and beyond that a low bank and further palisade. The internally ditched enclosure seems to echo on a small scale the great 'ritual' enclosures of the prehistoric royal sites; that at Tara also had a palisade on its inner lip. It may be in reference to this sort of palisaded site that an occasional name for royal places in the Early Historic texts was *Durlas*, which has been taken to be from *Dar-les*, 'oak-enclosure', the linguistic construction implying a very early date for the name. The name *Clochar* does not include any defensive element but refers to stone ruins visible, but ancient, when this first royal site was built.

In about AD 600 the palisaded ringditch enclosure at Clogher was replaced by a strong univallate ringfort of 60 metres internal diameter. The defensive nature of this new site is not in doubt and the texts use the name *Ráith mór* ('great fort') for it. Both Clogher and the Garranes trivallate ringfort which might be slightly earlier were found to have unusually strong and complex gateways. From the contemporary texts it is clear that the settlements of the kings were expected to be fortified or defensively constructed. The generic word usually used of a royal habitation was *dún* ('fort' or 'stronghold'), often when the specific element in the name was *ráith* ('earthwork'), *les* (enclosure) or *inis* (island) (Flanagan 1981). The contemporary lawyers suggested that 'seven score feet . . . are the measure of his [the king's] fort (*dún*) on every side. Seven feet are the thickness of its (?)earthwork, and 12 feet its depth'. The clear implication of this is that it should be circular and about 40 metres in (?)internal diameter, just the shape and size of the average ringfort. Some early texts describe high-status forts as being 'three-banked', or 'three-mounded'. Indeed, this is one explanation of the name, *Dún Trédúi*, of an Irish colonial fort in Britain mentioned by the ninth-century king-bishop *Cormac* in his glossary. A contemporary legal reference, not easily translated, seems to indicate that the fort of a king was expected to have an extra bank, the 'rampart(?) of clientship', with the information that only a reigning king could expect to have his fort built by his clients. I have already mentioned the ubiquity of the ringfort and the suggestion that the top-of-the-range trivallate ringfort may represent the dwelling of a king, and this certainly fits the historical evidence that I have outlined. Unfortunately the full archaeological evidence as we have it at present does not confirm this as a safe generalisation. Garranes was certainly trivallate, perhaps from as early as the mid-sixth century, but it was not certainly a royal site. Clogher, from the seventh century on, was univallate, though with an outer banked enclosure. The capital of the *Dál nAraide* of Ulster, *Ráith Mór*, was described in one heroic text as 'triple-banked'. The best candidate for this site, a very strongly ditched ringfort in Rathmore townland, is and almost certainly always was, univallate. The trivallate description may well have been a literary convention.

Neither Clogher nor Garranes were sited strategically or defensively, their defensive function being, as was that of the ringforts of lesser status, secondary to considerations of accessibility and convenience. This may well explain the comparative annalistic rarity of sieges and stormings and the comparative frequency of demolitions of royal sites, and submissions and intra-mural burnings of kings. When opposed by an army the first is unnecessary and the others easy. Furthermore, any idea that these royal sites provided a defensive centre for the local people or for the tribe cannot be entertained.

The contemporary historical sources tell us that from the seventh century there was a fashion among Irish kings to live in island dwellings, which continued until the sixteenth century. Some crannogs and natural islands can be identified with reasonable certainty as named historic royal sites. The only excavated example is Lagore, and the habitable area of this site, as of several other royal sites, was about that of an average ringfort. Unlike the ringfort the defensive nature of the crannog must be considered to be primary, although the general situation may still have been convenient to traffic and agricultural needs.

The Early Historic royal place *Caisel*, though providing us with little specifically useful archaeological information, does have one value. The name is a borrowing of the Latin *castellum*, at a time not likely to have been later than the fifth century. The strong implication that this name gives of fortification can hardly be overlooked, indeed the word *caisel* became a common place-name element meaning 'stone fort'. There are no remains now of fortification, but the situation, a prominent naturally scarped outcrop, must be considered to be at least a defensive position. It would be useful to explore the primary-defensive or strategic aspect of some royal sites further but we are seriously limited by the reliability of our evidence. I will give two examples, but I must stress that their identification is in both cases unproven. The kings of a small tribe in the Inishowen peninsula of Co. Donegal had their residence at *Carraic brachaidhe*. The name implies a rock outcrop and can be identified with just such a feature, now Carrickabraghy, crowned by a medieval castle (Dobbs 1947). The royal residence of the Irish *Dál Riada* seems to have been *Dún Sobairche*, a place of such strength that its sacking in AD 872 was described as 'never achieved before'. The best candidate for this stronghold is a shoreline stack fort of great natural strength at Dunseverick in north Co. Antrim, now crowned, like many other examples, by a medieval castle (McNeill 1983, 107). Close by is a possibly artificial mound.

There is, then, a case for believing that some of the Irish Early Historic royal sites were primarily defensive, particularly the island and outcrop sites. One is struck by the similarity between this last type and the Scottish royal sites studied by Alcock (1981a), as also by the repetitive siting of medieval castles on these outcrop sites, again a situation paralleled in Scotland.

Around the turn of the millennium some of the kings became increasingly powerful, almost 'feudal' in the European sense, controlling extra-tribal areas by force and ignoring the rules of title to kingship. In Byrne's view this was a sort of return to 'warrior-kingship' without its quasi-divine property. Strategic forts were now being built, particularly along borders and at vulnerable river crossings (Ó Corráin 1972, 256). The only such site to have been excavated is Beal Boru, Co. Clare, supposedly a fortress marking the boundary of *Dál Cais* in the twelfth century. It proved to be a quite normal, artefactually dull, eleventh-century ringfort, rebuilt as a massive ringwork or unfinished motte some time later (O'Kelly 1962a). It was not clear which phase represented the named place, nor whether the second phase was pre-Norman or Norman. It was not a royal site in the strict sense despite its royal literary connections, and it is important that we distinguish these 'garrison' sites from royal places in the sense in which we are discussing this concept. Some of the many forts listed as having been built by the great king *Brian Bóruma* (or by his successors) actually had stewards and nobles in residence. They were, in other words, high-status places belonging to the nobility but incorporated into an area-defensive plan as garrisons. These late fortifications, and others that were certainly royal residences, were frequently described by the newly coined, or borrowed, terms *caislén* and *caistél*, which, with the contemporary descriptions, make them seem rather like semi-military castles (Ó Corráin 1974).

Much as it might appear that the militarisation of royal, or royal associated, places was a chronological process throughout the early historic period we may

well find that we are being misled by these strategic sites, and that the places
of normal kingship did not change substantially.

Multiple sites

In the laws a king was expected to have three forts, between which his property
was divided. It seems probable that they would have been spread around the
tuath, to be visited at some time during the year. It seems to me, however, that
only one of these would be the royal fort in the true sense, the place with which
the king was identified, his residence and the place of his hospitality. The
others would have had a steward or client in residence.

There is, however, some evidence that even the main place of residence may
have consisted of more than one substantive and monumentally recognisable
site. By this I mean more than just the existence of an extra-mural settlement,
as at Knowth, or of accompanying 'ritual' earthworks, as at Clogher. In a
punitive eleventh-century hosting into Ulster the high-king 'burned the *dún*'
of the king of the *Dál Fiatach* and 'broke down its *baile*'. The implication of
this reference is that there was a separation of fortification and settlement or
farm. The place, *Dún Echdach* is plausibly identified as Duneight in Co. Down
where there are two imposing sites. One is a bivallate ringfort of normal
proportions and form and the other an Anglo-Norman motte-and-bailey,
again of normal form. Excavation in the bailey of the latter showed it to have
been originally, in the tenth or eleventh century, a bivallate earthwork enclosure (Waterman 1963). It was therefore equated with the *dún* of *Dún
Echdach* burnt in 1011. It seems quite possible that both sites were part of the
royal settlement, and we do not know which was the royal habitation proper.
The high-status ringfort of Garryduff in Co. Cork had an artefactually sterile
close neighbour which the excavator suggested might have been its cattle
compound (O'Kelly 1962b) and the Clogher royal site is connected by an
ancient roadway to a substantial stone ringfort two kilometres away. The
eleventh-century high-king *Máelsechnaill* had two textually attested adjacent
residences – the crannog of *Cró-inis* in Lough Ennel, Co. Westmeath, and the
fort of *Dún na Sciath* on the shore of the same lough.

Status and wealth

We have seen that no matter how wealthy a noble was he could not legitimately
claim kingship without the necessary family history, although nothing prevented a noble from equalling a king in terms of wealth. Even a commoner
could get noble status by acquiring double the qualifying wealth. I have
already mentioned the potentially high status of ecclesiastics and men of skill,
and we might suppose that the 'royal' status of the senior bishop meant a royal
level of wealth. The hosteller (*briugu*), an important member of Irish society,
could also have an honour price equal to that of a tribal king. In order to fulfil
his role, however, he was expected to possess in *double* measure the agricultural
property of a king. The normal fruits of trade, no matter how exotic, were
obviously available to any members of society who could afford them, and as

we have seen the potential customer base was far larger than the royal family. As Byrne (1971, 144) has written, 'Not what the king owns or wears but what he does reveals his kingship'.

It is clear then that although wealth was necessary for kingship, kingship was not necessary for wealth. It can be regarded as a rule, in an Irish context, that the status of kingship implies archaeological evidence of wealth. But we can be equally dogmatic in the assertion that the archaeological evidence of wealth does not of itself unequivocally imply royalty.

The tribal king was the ultimate power within his *tuath* on matters of tribal importance, though not concerned with minor legal matters relating to individuals, for which the client system and the ties of the kin-group would have sufficed. He could promulgate laws in tribal assemblies and call for hostings both inside and outside his tribal area. His duties do not seem to have been particularly onerous, and were discharged with the aid of a few functionaries such as the steward (*rechtaire*). The lawyers proposed that the king should spend two days a week on legal and tribal matters, compared, for instance, with one for horse-racing and one for hunting. No time was apparently put aside for farming, clearly for the reason that his minimum of thirty-seven clients freed him from such necessity with their render of food and service. MacNiocaill has suggested (1981) that the client base of nobility should be recognisable in the archaeological record, through the bone material. The render particularly included young animals, which should therefore be proportionately over-represented. Unfortunately, the bone records from excavated high status sites are not yet adequate for this sort of study (McCormick 1983), but the prospect is interesting.[10]

The king, of course, possessed much stock of his own, sixty cows according to the lawyers. Around the Clogher ringfort is a two-hectare enclosure which is joined by a banked funnel to a banked road. This 'droveway', as it must be, runs for two kilometres across neighbouring hills on to low mountains, where it ends in another funnel and is connected to a large stone ringfort. We can hardly doubt the explanation in terms of transhumance of cattle to summer pastures, nor can we doubt that the large Clogher enclosure had at least partly the function of cattle corral (see figure 3).

The relationship of the tribal king to his overking was almost one of clientship itself, in which he received gifts and protection in return for tribute, companionship, military support and, if necessary, hostages. The sort of stipends and tributes that passed between the kings are listed in the twelfth-century 'Book of Rights' (Dillon 1962), and included weapons, slaves, animals (including dogs),[11] ships, chariots, clothes, ornaments and foodstuffs. The tribe was the main social unit for the protection and control of its people, who neither owed allegiance nor (unless they were men of skills or learning) received any automatic protection outside their own tribal area. Non-tribal visitors had to gain the protection of a noble or the king to ensure their own safety, which was strictly upheld, and a merchant or traveller would obtain such protection in return for service or a gift. The giving of royal stipends and

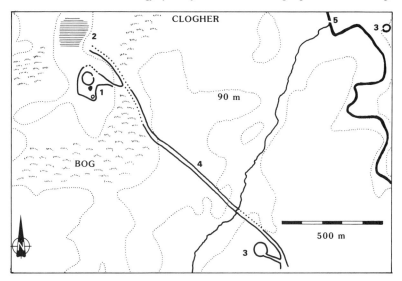

Figure 3. The Clogher 'droveway' and adjacent sites. Key: 1 royal site; 2 monastic site; 3 ringforts; 4 'droveway'; 5 ford.

the need of outsiders to buy protection might well indicate that the royal site would have an exotic element in its material assemblage. The problem is to identify such exotica (which may well have been perishable) within the assemblage of high-status material more widely available.

Feasting was a major responsibility of the king. The lawyers set aside one day of the week for his drinking, towards which the clients were expected to include malt in their render. A poem mentions the wine-ship (*finbarc*) of the capital of Leinster. The king's house (*rígthech*) is, in some early sources, called *tech midchuarta*, which Wagner (1974) would translate as 'the house of the mead circle'. Both excavated royal sites whose date goes back to the sixth century have produced sherds belonging to amphorae imported from the Mediterranean area ('B' ware), and wine would have been the content of at least some of these. Fine red bowls ('A' ware) of the same general date, and from the same general area have also been found on these sites. The indication these give of high status is undeniable, and no small, non-royal residential sites have produced them; but they have occurred at monastic sites and at two large coastal promontory forts (Thomas 1981). The imported 'Gaulish'(?) pottery ('E' ware) stands in the same position, for although the wine itself was likely to have been in barrels the best explanation of the 'E' ware vessels is as drinking accoutrements. These vessels have been found in all the excavated royal contexts of the seventh and eighth centuries, but also in small secular sites of unproven, or unlikely, royal status.

The lawyers called the king of a tribe the 'leader of 700 men'. It would not be correct to think of the king having a standing army in the strict sense, although mercenary troops are attested in the annals. It was his ability to call

Plate 1. Clogher. The mound (to the left) and the ringfort from the east. The 'funnel' can be seen running down the hill towards the foreground. Copyright Ulster Museum.

on his nobles and clients for military service which gave him this title. With such an army the king could undertake a major hosting inside or outside his territory, after a formal announcement at the tribal assembly. On a smaller scale the king's habitation reflected a martial aspect not to be found in lesser habitations. The early tales describe the storage of arms around the royal house, and the king was expected to have an armed bodyguard when in his house and an armed retinue of clients when outside it. It is therefore of some significance that weapons, almost unknown from contemporary sites, were found at Lagore and Clogher.

While, then, we must expect fine and exotic objects from royal sites, we must not expect their presence alone to allow us to distinguish royalty from other nobility. Nevertheless, particularly with regard to exotica, it seems likely that a level of wealth would be expected at a royal site that was unlikely to be reached at sites of a lower status, and the levels found at Clogher and Lagore might be taken as measures of this. The ornament assemblage, for instance, at both sites is larger than would ever be found at the average ringfort. This serves to confirm our belief that Beal Boru, although part of a unified defensive strategy, was not in our sense a royal site. Can any artefact types, then, distinguish a royal site? I can think of two examples from our proven royal sites that might serve us in this way. It would seem to be a reasonable supposition that a symbol of office would be a unique indicator of kingship. There is a possibility that fragments of some such thing were found at Clogher – small iron ox-heads reminiscent of those on the 'standard' from Sutton Hoo. The kings of Clogher had an ox epithet, and were symbolised as oxen in a hagiographical text. For the second example, Byrne (1973, 88) believed that the neck-irons with chains from Lagore were hostage-chains and I am inclined to agree with him. The king was the only member of society entitled to hold and bind hostages.

Houses

The literary descriptions of royal houses have been collected and discussed by Murray (1979). The descriptions in some sagas are clearly of heroic dwellings and therefore exaggerated, but they give us a model. The king's house in his fortress was large (*tech mór*, 'great house'), '37 feet' across according to the lawyers. Its main function was for feasting and hospitality, when it housed a galaxy of guests and functionaries in their appointed places. The dominant literary royal house seems to have been circular, with concentric partitions of large posts. None of the excavated royal sites have produced enough information to reconstruct the house, but we do have circumstantial archaeological support for the literary building. At the prehistoric royal/ritual site of Navan a great circular wooden structure of concentric post-rings built around 100 BC exactly parallels the literary descriptions and stands as a paradigm for the as yet undiscovered later royal houses (Mallory 1985). That the form was used in reality as well as in fiction is shown by the multiple-post house completely filling the interior of the eleventh-century univallate ringfort at Lissue, Co.

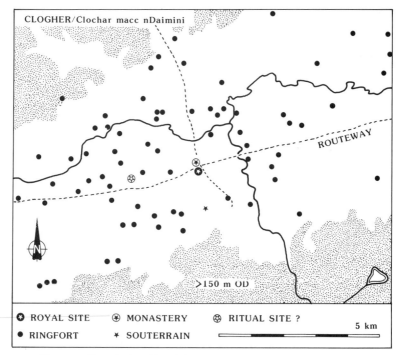

Figure 4. The relationship of Early Historic sites to the royal settlement of Clogher.

Antrim (Bersu 1947). The status of the site is unclear, but there is some genealogical evidence that it was the residence of a rather minor king. Nevertheless, and again it must be stressed, although a large house may be necessary for a royal site it would be equally necessary for the hosteller, whose obligations were similar.

Industry

The active presence of 'men of skills' at a royal site is described in a tale relating the visit of the god *Lug* to the king of Tara. The gatekeeper would not let *Lug* into the fort, despite his many skills, because men practising those skills were already present. Garranes, Lagore and Clogher produced extensive evidence for industrial manufacture, particularly bronzeworking. The probable products of the Clogher penannular brooch factory have been found widely distributed (Kilbride-Jones 1980, 63–7). Unfortunately, while we might expect a high level of industry at the residence of a king, we would also expect it at the residence of an artificer. However, the variety of industrial practices found at Clogher (iron, bronze, gold and glass, see figure 2) would only be expected at a royal site (as in the tale) or at one of the monastic centres.

The potential trapping of skills in this way, as well as the sheer status of the site, would predict to a geographer a location satisfying the 'central place' theory. An early tale describes how a royal fort had benches for the nobles who lived around the fort, suggesting a clustering of clients' residences around their lord, as we might expect. The Clogher site lies within a cluster of ringforts, about six kilometres across. Each has an area of about 80 hectares associated with it, whereas the Clogher site itself has a clear zone of over 250 hectares, and the main route through the valley runs past the royal site. Clogher seems then to satisfy 'central-place' theory, but I am unaware that any other royal sites have been shown to do so. Furthermore the neighbouring monastery at Clogher shares the same central location within this extended zone (and the same cattleway to the hills) and equally justifies, on any theoretical argument, 'central place' status.

Conclusion

The historical and archaeological evidence for kingship is substantial, and the two sets of information mostly compatible. There are problems in the search for unique archaeological indicators and it is clear that Irish kingship is not amenable to simple archaeological generalisation. It is also of interest that only the last two of Wailes' five hypothetical expectations of a royal site (see p.52 above) apply generally, partly because of the separation of ritual and residence. As generalisations are possibly required, and perhaps even useful, I shall make some, but they will tend to be negative rather than positive.

1. Signs of ritual, such as a mound, would be strong positive evidence of royalty, but they are not necessary.

2. The site is likely to be internally small but defensible. It might be a ringfort, crannog or stack-fort and might well be indistinguishable from others in the locality.

3. Complexity of earthworks, unless some are of a ritual nature, is not necessary, but multivallation might be a good pointer.

4. On excavation evidence of wealth, a very large house and mixed industrial waste would be good pointers.

It may well be that demonstration of a royal site stands or falls only on the historical evidence for that site, but clearly a combination of some of the indicators I have listed will be useful both in the search for royal sites and in the discussion of potential or claimed royal sites. For the reasons that I have given for not drawing on non-Irish sources I would not expect these conclusions to be applicable outside Ireland, except in the case of Irish colonies. They may, however, be a warning to those engaged in similar studies to beware of hypothetical or inappropriate models of kingship and the archaeological expectations based on them.

NOTES
1   Early Historic period. The period between the start of reliable documentation, say the sixth century AD, and the intense social changes around 1100. Equivalent terms are: dark age, early Christian, early medieval, later iron age (which I prefer) and later Celtic.

2 For a general combination of both disciplines for early historic
   Ireland see M. and L. de Paor (1958), and for a more specific
   example Warner (1980). A fine model of source combination is
   Alcock (1983).

3 Emphatic hypothesising: i.e., what response might *logically* be expected to a particular situation? Criticised by Binford (1982, 163).

4 This illustrates the argument about the appropriateness of models,
   for if the epic tales are not to be used as evidence for the *Irish* early
   iron age, how much less wise is their use as models for the interpretation of archaeological sites belonging to the Scottish or British early
   iron age, as by Hamilton (1966) and Avery (1976). I believe that they
   are appropriate to the early historic period in a general way.

5 For the general historical background see MacNiocaill (1972), Ó
   Corráin (1972), Dillon (1954) and MacNeill (1921; the 1981 reprint
   with notes by Ó Corráin). For the historical evidence for Irish
   kingship Binchy (1970) and Byrne (1973) are essential.

6 The laws of status and franchise are readily accessible in MacNeill
   (1923), but must be read in conjunction with the more recent authors
   in note 5.

7 To the sources in notes 5 and 6, and the further references therein,
   Gerriets (1983) is an interesting addition to the study of clientship.

8 *Derbhfine*: the pyramid of male lineage running for four generations,
   i.e., all male descendants of a king, down to his great-grandson,
   would be eligible for kingship.

9 My 'high' dating for the start of many of these site-types is at odds
   with some recently published views. For justification see Lynn
   (1983).

10 McCormick (1983, 264) notes that the female, though not the male,
   adult cattle bones from the two royal sites he studied (Knowth and
   Lagore) came from significantly larger animals that did those from
   the three non-royal sites.

11 The largest early dogs yet excavated in the British Isles were found
   at Lagore (Harcourt 1974, 168).

Northumbria :
the archaeological evidence

Although over the last decade considerable attention has been paid by historians and archaeologists alike to the explanation of the nature and progress of the Anglo-Saxon settlement of North Britain, much of the coherence of their conclusions depends on literary evidence. The towering testimony of Bede, whether in his *Ecclesiastical History, Lives of St Cuthbert* or the *Lives of the Abbots* of Wearmouth and Jarrow, is impossible to ignore. In recent years other *Vitae* such as Eddius' *Life of Wilfrid*, and the *Life of Guthlac* of Croyland, have also been analysed to explain the social and economic life of the seventh century Anglo-Saxons; but Bede's writings are more comprehensive and wide-ranging and the sites mentioned in his works can provide us with a possible framework for settlement hierarchy (Campbell 1979). But the visible appearance of such sites is less clear to us than that of the individuals he conjures up in relation to them. Paulinus, who had baptized for thirty-six days in the River Glen in Northumberland was remembered by Bede's informants, when he later baptized a multitude in the Trent, as 'tall, with a slight stoop, black hair, a thin face, a slender acquiline nose' (*HE* 2, 16). Vivid also are the pictures of Hild with a number of learned men listening to the account of Caedmon's dream and debating the nature and origin of his gift (*HE* 4, 24) or Wilfrid standing triumphantly on the steps of his new church at Ripon reading out the names of the territories he had acquired which formerly belonged to the British Church around the River Ribble, and thereby trying to explain to the uncomprehending laity the differing claims of canon and customary law. Yet of what race were the multitudes who flocked to be baptized by Paulinus, how had land been allocated to the *gesiths* whose proprietary churches Cuthbert consecrated, or what was the nature of the faith that Edwin had to struggle so hard to cast away? All these questions remain unanswered. According to Bede, Edwin found it easier to give up pagan practices than to adopt Christianity formally; and it seems likely that he realised not only the social implications of Christianity, but also that, as king, his acts would influence his entire following. Such literary evidence precludes the need to search for parallels from other cultures in order to inform ourselves that in creating, as well as maintaining, the small independent kingdoms of Anglo-Saxon England, the charisma and energy of individuals were all important. Such leaders had to attract warring bands in order to acquire wealth by which to cement alliances and to create a stable system in which crop production and craft production could flourish and develop.

All of this is difficult to detect by archaeological means alone, as indeed

Renfrew found in using Anglo-Saxon England as an example of post-collapse resurgence (Renfrew 1982, 113–16). In discussing his model he says, 'The political units in Britain which emerged in the sixth and seventh centuries, although ruled by kings, are comparable in size and in some cases in actual territory to the polities of the first century BC.' The 'analogous scale' is 'based on the texts of *The Tribal Hidage* and Cunliffe's inferences from the distribution of the coins of the Celtic kingdoms.' This strange amalgam of evidence produces a very imprecise hypothesis, in which the nature of the evidence provided by the *Tribal Hidage* is not critically evaluated. Despite the scholarly effort expended on trying to define the boundaries of Bernicia and Deira from early documentary evidence, these boundaries never coincide with the presumed locations of the tribes first known to the Romans in that region, such as the Brigantes or Parisii. They may nevertheless have been the same as those defining the territorial blocks created by the British in the sub-Roman period, but no evidence is forthcoming to support or to refute this hypothesis. We have throughout Northumbria major linear earthworks which are undated and one day it may be possible to see them as post-Roman territorial markers, but not yet.

Renfrew's third point ('(c) the possible peripheral survival of some highly organised community still retaining several organisational features of the collapsed state,') is probably not determinable from archaeological evidence alone. In a rather confusing paragraph which ranges from Ireland to Visigothic Italy he does not substantiate his summary conclusion: 'From the European standpoint as a whole the events of the fifth century were less of a collapse than a transformation, and it was only in the northern and eastern provinces of the former Western Empire that urban society for a while disappeared.' Whether that implies that rural society was unchanged or transformed I am not sure, but certainly for northern Britain it is questionable whether even in the Roman period a truly urban society existed outside York. One begins to feel that to forward the argument there must be a deeper analysis of the semantic field of terms used. The problem of social transformation is huge and dominating enough. Nevertheless, the information which is provided by the early Laws or even Theodore's *Penitential* is arguably of greater value for understanding the process than any archaeological evidence – which is better adapted to demonstrate economic or technological transformations. I return to this point later. Renfrew's point (d), 'Survival of religious elements as "folk" cults and beliefs', raises interesting problems, but Renfrew makes his 'Dark Age' analogy brief: 'There is some evidence for the survival of Christianity in Britain after the Roman withdrawal (Biddle 1976, 110–11).' This statement is indeed archaeologically verifiable but the evidence is not without ambiguity; the maintenance of Christian dogma transformed by folk beliefs is not easy to determine, nor yet whether there may have been amongst the Britons a revival of interest in pre-Christian folk cults. The transformation of the beliefs of Britons and immigrant Germanic peoples alike is difficult to resolve from archaeological evidence alone, and later Christian writers had every reason to ignore the subject. Brian Hope-Taylor made a courageous attempt to explain the post-Roman history of the royal Vill of *Gefrin* (Yeavering) in these terms, and others have considered the burial evidence for this period in relation to religion, but the difficulties of distinguishing social from religious custom are formidable.

Renfrew's next criterion, (e) that craft production would operate at a local level with 'peasant' imitations of former specialist products, is clearly more detectable by archaeological means than any of the other categories of evidence proposed as illustrations of 'post-collapse resurgence', although the picture is complicated by the inexplicable total collapse in some areas of certain crafts such as wheel-made pottery.

I will now examine further some of the categories of evidence noted above and discuss how political groups are identified, and their organisation and development charted. Most people would consider that, in the present state of archaeological knowledge, the fullest evidence for determining the presence of the Anglo-Saxons is provided by their graves. First, though, it must be remembered that no graves of those leaders, whether lay or religious, who according to literary sources shaped the fortunes of the Northumbrian people are known. Sutton Hoo mound 1 produced the only burial that is plausibly that of a tribal ruler or king; but where are the bones of Ida, of Aelle or Ecgfrith or even of royal martyrs like Oswald? For the latter we do know that his bones were already distributed to various centres soon after his death (*HE* 3, 6; 3, 11) and then redistributed later (Rollason 1978, 87). The process of identifying a community by joining the dead to a notable ancestor, which can perhaps be seen in the layout of some Germanic (and Anglo-Saxon) cemeteries, would no doubt easily marry with Christian cults which focussed cemeteries and also settlements on the burial place or shrine of a saint (Bullough 1983, 194–201).

Considerable discussion has recently been expended on the possibility that territorial claims were supported by burial rites and burial *loci* which provided a linking point of reference to ancestors of the group or leaders (Shephard 1979, 77; Charles-Edwards 1976, 83–7). Bullough has countered these suppositions by the statement that this idea 'has no obvious support in early English (or Frankish) texts; nor has the idea been found in other societies that burial on a boundary is itself a safeguard of descendants' rights' (Bullough 1983, 194).

The invading English may not have been as anxious as the Goths or Franks to establish their title to rule by conforming to the customs of their new territories, but certainly the acceptance of Christianity and the establishment of stable states often coincided. One could explore further the idea that one of the social differences which distinguished the emergent groups of the heptarchy could have been religious and that there were sects in both the pagan and Christian religions, which might account for distinctive modes of burial. In the last textual records of Christianity in sub-Roman Britain it is clear that there were doctrinal divisions amongst the Christians. The pagan 'religions' of the newly settled English could have been equally sectarian.

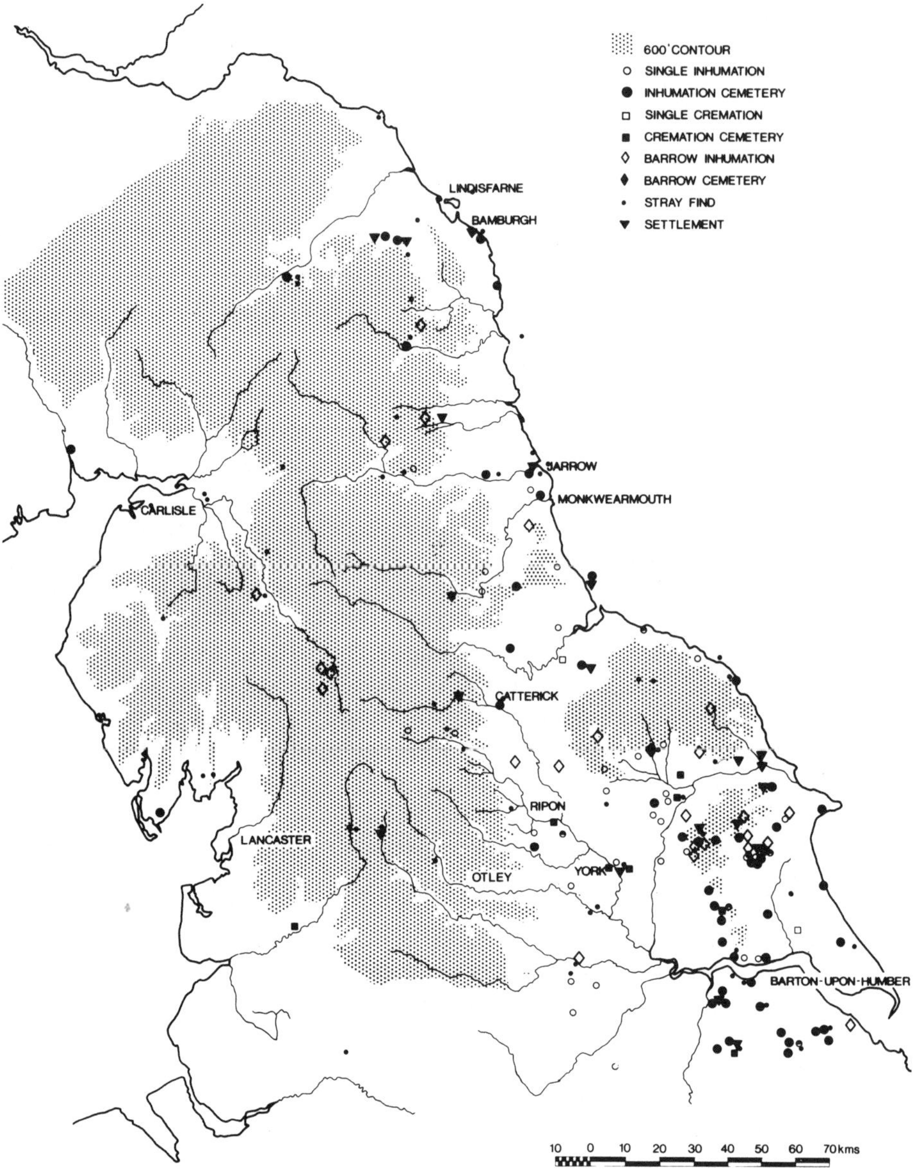

Figure 1. Early medieval Northumbria.

If one considers the generalised pattern of cremations and furnished inhumations which conform to continental Germanic practices, then the difference
between Deira and Bernicia or Cumbria is immediately apparent (figure 1).
The total lack of cremations north of the Tees and west of the Pennines is
remarkable, and has been frequently mentioned; but before one decides either
that few Anglo-Saxons penetrated those areas, or that they only did so in

detectable numbers after they had become Christian, we must remember the lack of other types of burial evidence in those areas, whether Iron Age or Early Christian. The factors which can diminish the archaeological burial record, such as specific soil conditions or erosion, destructive ploughing, economic forestry, extractive agencies, or even the custom of shallow burials are not demonstrably more prevalent in Northumberland and Cumbria than in Yorkshire or Cambridgeshire. It seems more reasonable to suggest either that the Anglo-Saxons were not present, or that they adopted the burial practices of the indigenous population rather as did the Scandinavian settlers in England two hundred years later. It is indeed possible that the English occupied Bernicia in smaller numbers than Deira, since even in the latter some elements could have conformed to local practice. But, what were local practices? It is usually assumed that they were Christian, and burials in a few oriented cemeteries south of the Forth-Clyde line have served to illustrate this; but it is possible that some people did return to Iron Age practices (Faull 1977, 5). The dense scatter of discovered habitation sites of native type which have been mapped for Northumberland by Jobey, and for Cumbria by Jones and Higham are not matched by burial sites. The people who lived in these homesteads seem to have vanished without trace. The scanty evidence for Iron Age burial practice in Britain includes burial in ditches, and in pits within living areas, but could also have included deposition in rivers or bogs which obviously would leave no trace. The Germanic peoples likewise had a long tradition of bog burials. A rather obscure reference to such burial interestingly occurs in Hutchinson's *History of the County of Cumberland*, and although it is related to the Danes, the traditional rites could have been practised by other settlers in the region. Hutchinson, in describing the manor or townships of Cardew in the Barony of Dalston, derives the name from some 'Fenny Ground at the head of the river Wampol, which is by interpretation God's fenn or God's bogg' (Hutchinson 1794, 448–9). Such despositions could help to account for the archaeological invisibility of the post-Roman, and indeed pre-Roman peoples of Cumbria.

Margaret Faull, who has specifically concentrated her scholarly attention on the problem of British survival in Northumbria, has listed those burials which could be considered 'anomalous' in an Anglo-Saxon context, and concludes that 'The grave-goods with burials in the British tradition indicate British survival at the highest as well as the lowest ranks of society' and supports this view by literary references to royal marriages between Anglo-Saxons and their Celtic neighbours (Faull 1977, 22, 26–36). Nevertheless, the task of distinguishing ethnic groups by their burial rites remains full of difficulties, not the least of which are chronological. Most graves are dated by the style of the grave-goods, which in its turn depends on a lengthy and tenuous chain of argument, and some collagen dates for well excavated cemeteries would be infinitely preferable.

Broad trends in Anglo-Saxon funerary practice have recently found acceptance; first that it is difficult to distinguish by their grave-goods named ethnic groups of the English, so for example the Deirans are not distinguishable from

the *Lindisi,* secondly that there is the appearance of increasing social distinction in the wealth which finds its way into grave deposits between the sixth and
seventh centuries. It is relatively easy to see where graves reflecting recognisable Anglo-Saxon burial practice are, or are not, to be found. It is more
difficult to find acceptable criteria of wealth which can sort them into social
hierarchies. For Faull, 'The most striking feature of the Bernician burials is
the undistinguished nature of the grave goods of all but the Castle Eden site'
(Faull 1977, 10). For Alcock the distinctive nature of the few recognisably
pagan burials of Bernicia is their high status (Alcock 1981c). I have elsewhere
said that I believe the picture is much more complex than his simple alpha,
beta, gamma rating implies (Cramp 1983, 269–70).

There is indeed a difference in the archaeological evidence for Deira and
Bernicia, but if one accepts the view that the Tees Valley is the dividing area
between the two kingdoms then one should perhaps accept that the whole
valley, and not the North or South bank, would fall into Deira or its sphere of
influence. This cultural division is reflected also in the styles of Viking Age
sculpture (Cramp 1984, 28–31). In that case the Darlington cemetery, or the
recently discovered and very richly endowed cemetery at Norton-on-Tees,
could be subtracted from Alcock's group. The Cumbrian and Bernician
mound burials, which significantly include horse-trappings, could be seen as
reflecting different criteria of wealth or status, even though the burials of
groups of lesser status such as those found at Milfield are similar to Anglo-
Saxon burials elsewhere (Miket 1980; Cramp 1983, 268–71).

Bede, in his summary of significant dates in the history of the English
people, notes that in AD 547 Ida began to reign (in Bernicia) and the history of
his successors and those of his contemporary, Aelle of Deira, is one of constant
warfare not only between the two kingdoms but between these and the neighbouring British, Pictish or Anglian kingdoms. Deira and Bernicia were not
peacefully united, according to Bede, until the reign of Oswald (AD 633–42).
Many of these wars were perhaps to establish territorial rights, but others no
doubt were, within that non-monetary economy, to obtain moveable wealth
with which to support a warband or to buy friends. Oswald's successor Oswiu,
when pressurised by the Mercian king Penda, attempted to buy him off by:

> an incalculable and incredible store of royal treasures and gifts as the price
> of peace, on the condition that Penda would return home and cease to
> devastate, or rather utterly destroy, the kingdoms under his rule (*HE* 3,
> 24).

According to Bede, the Mercian king did not accept the offer, and after
Oswiu had defeated him he presumably had the wealth to redistribute to his
own followers as well as land to donate for the benefit of the Church; six estates
in Deira and six in Bernicia for the provision of monasteries. These monastic
institutions were later to bring about enormous social changes in Northumbria, first by stabilising the economy and later by impoverishing it. First,
however, we should consider how during the seventh century Northumbrian
kings consolidated and developed their resources.

Since we have no evidence for the use of coinage in seventh century North-umbria, except gold for major transactions, taxes and tributes must have been collected and redistributed in kind. A centre, which seems to have been a tribal gathering place with religious associations and perhaps serving as tax collection and 'market' centre from the sub-Roman period to that of the period of full Anglo-Saxon supremacy, is the site excavated by Hope-Taylor at Yeavering in Northumberland (Hope-Taylor 1977). Here, the massive en-closure which preceded the establishment of the amphitheatre and impressive Anglo-Saxon halls, has its origins in native North British 'forts'. The timber halls and the careful layout of the site are a powerful testimony to the desire of the Anglo-Saxon kings to impress their own culture and their authority on traditional centres of power, while the building constructions illustrate well the resources in raw materials and labour which a seventh century North-umbrian king could enjoy. The difference between this site and those fortified centres of the Celtic world (cf. Alcock, Nieke and Duncan, Warner in this volume), is the lack of evidence for craft production at Yeavering. If royal tribute was extracted here it was consumed on the spot in the form of food rents, and the production from other forms of surplus took place elsewhere. It is possible of course that the fortified capital of Bamburgh, 'the city' as Bede calls it (Campbell 1979, 52), sheltered a group of craftsmen who operated under royal patronage and control; but so far, from what is known of the unpublished excavations on that site, the only hint as to possible craftsmanship is a small gold foil mount of an animal. Nevertheless, the lack of evidence for large- or even small-scale industries in early Northumbria is a major gap in our understanding of the early economy. The crucibles, moulds, motif-pieces, metal-working and wood residues that are found on Irish sites such as Clogher, Garryduff or Garranes, or on Scottish sites such as Dunadd and the Mote of Mark, are entirely absent from Northumbria. One might say of course that also absent are the quern-stones which are a common occurrence in Celtic sites, and that all of these lacunae are explained by the fact that Roman technology survived, and production whether of flour or of decorative metal-work continued on a larger scale than that in the Celtic world. That does not seem very likely however, at least for small rural settlements. In the North Germanic home-lands, large-scale production centres, presumably organised by regional leaders or kings, have been excavated at Helgö and Birka; but for Anglo-Saxon England only small-scale cottage industries have so far been discovered for the sixth to eighth centuries – the pre-urban phase. A mould for making a square-headed brooch, as well as residue from a shaft furnace, has been discovered from the inconspicuous settlement of Mucking in Essex (Jones and Jones 1975, 161–2); and it is possible that some of these sunken-featured buildings, such as are a dominant feature on this site, served as craft workshops for groups who were retained by a local ruler. Most of such settlements as have been excavated so far came to an end by the eighth century, which seems to have been a time of tighter political organisation in Anglo-Saxon England. The timber buildings so far excavated in Northumbria

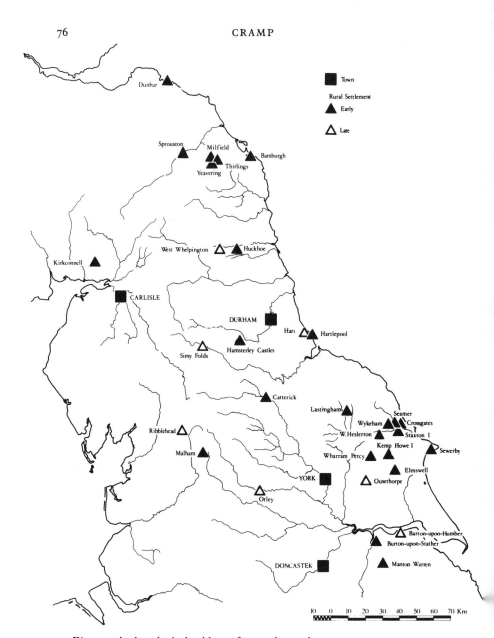

Figure 2. Archaeological evidence for secular settlement.

(figure 2), whether of royal status as at Yeavering, or of lesser status as at Thirlings, do not differ materially from structures in other kingdoms (Millett 1983) and it seems reasonable to suppose that sunken-featured buildings which occur sparsely in Yorkshire (Rahtz 1976; Powlesland 1981) could be found in Bernicia also.

Indeed, if one accepts that the marks shown on recent air photographs of

Milfield as drawn out by Tim Gates, are sunken huts, then such clusters of dwellings did exist in Bernicia. These potential huts cluster thickly round the enclosure of the large porched hall and its ancilliary buildings which is tradi- tionally identified with the palace built by the Northumbrian kings to succeed Yeavering (Knowles and St Joseph 1952, 270–1). The site is laid out, as is the similar if somewhat smaller settlement at Sprouston, with what seem to be two interrelated enclosures – the inner one housing the major hall. It is possible that in these sites we have archaeological support for the concept of planned development of stable client settlements planted by the Northumbrian kings around their palaces. The segregation of the central hall with its own enclosure could be paralleled at a later date by the fortified burghs with their suburbs of craftsmen which occur widely in Europe in the Early Medieval period.

It is possible that Celtic craftsmen could have worked under the patronage of the Northumbrian kings, just as Anglo-Saxon craftsmen may have worked on sites such as the Mote of Mark to produce metal-work in which Germanic and Celtic motifs occur together. If we had more evidence like the Bamburgh foil mount, which is so like the animals in Hiberno-Saxon manuscripts or those on the Franks Casket, it might well be apparent that the distinctive art of Northumbria, reflected alike in manuscripts and ivories, was not solely a creation of the Irish and Anglo-Saxon Churches, but also of royal workshops.

The Church had a considerable part to play in shaping the role of the Northumbrian kings, and informing them of new responsibilities. Perhaps indeed the king's role as law-giver and as the convener of all assemblies whether lay or religious was slowly diminished by the authority of the Church. Certainly as Bede himself was aware in his latter years, the rooted framework of the Church's land-holdings diminished the kings' powers to reward their followers with land grants as well as moveable wealth, thus diminishing also their powers to command the support of the hereditary nobility.

Northumbria on the eve of the Viking invasions did not share a common currency and possibly not even the developing urban economies of the other kingdoms, but however meagre the resources of a community, its rulers could find the means of distinguishing themselves from their subjects. Bede's depic- tion of Oswiu's attractive but short-lived rival Oswine is often quoted as the paradigm of an early ruler:

> King Oswine was tall and handsome, pleasant of speech, courteous in manner and bountiful to nobles and commons alike; so it came about that he was beloved by all because of the royal dignity that showed itself in his character, his appearance and his actions; and noblemen from almost every kingdom flocked to serve him as retainers (*HE* 3, 14).

Such kingly virtues are undetectable by the archaeologist but are seemingly widespread amongst many societies. This point was well illustrated recently in an article, 'An Rí (The King): An example of Traditional Social Organisation' which was concerned with discussing the custom of electing a king in remote parts of Ireland in the eighteenth and nineteenth centuries. Such kings were elected 'by making a choice of the strongest, most handsome, most intelligent, well-read person, and also of least blemish and reproach' (O'Danachair 1981, 21). Kings were apparently expected to maintain traditional laws, to adjudicate in disputes and quarrels, to receive complaints, to apportion fishing and shore rights, and to allot tillage and pasture land. All of these roles we could perhaps assign to our early Northumbrian kings, whose appearance and personal charisma, as I stated at the beginning of this chapter, are now so indistinct to us. In considering the much fuller data for the Irish 'kings' it is possible to see the subtle distinctions which separated such persons from their subjects. Power conveys privileges as well as responsibilities and both promote a gloss of self confidence which is apparent in the surviving photographs of these 'kings'. A tradition recorded as late as 1940, tells of a past king in Port Urlainn whose life-style may serve to illustrate the nature of power whether in Bede's Northumbria or in Early Modern Ireland. It is recorded that when he was made king:

> Then he had every power; everything he ordered had to be done. Everyone of them gave him a present on the day he was made king; some gave him cows, others sheep, others fowl and things of that kind. The result was he was the richest man in the place, and not only in the townland. It is nice to be a king you know (O'Danachair 1981, 19).

Power and exchange
in Middle Saxon England

> *. . . the world of humankind creates a manifold, a totality of interconnected processes, and enquiries that disassemble this totality into bits and then fail to reassemble it falsify reality. Concepts like 'nation', 'society', and 'culture' name bits and threaten to turn them into things. Only by understanding these names as bundles of relationships, and by placing them back in the field from which they have been abstracted, can we hope to avoid misleading inferences and increase our share of understanding.* (Wolf 1982, 3)

There can be no doubt that until recently the analysis of the 'bit' has been the dominant mode of archaeological and historical study of early medieval Europe. This is certainly true of students of Anglo-Saxon history and archaeology. These latter have, almost without fail, taken an insular and arguably nationalistic approach to their work and as a result we believe they have 'falsified reality' (but see Levison 1946; Campbell 1982; Brooks 1984). Analysis usually consists of descriptions only, with change (almost always seen as happening for the better) being portrayed as organic, and almost divinely ordained. As a result the history of Anglo-Saxon England is presented as a sort of moral success story. There have been few attempts to examine the deeper processes and mechanisms that cause change, and where such attempts have been made the society under study is still regarded as a 'single isolated unit and as containing within itself the mechanisms that bring about its transformation' (Giddens 1980, 23). An example of such 'unfolding' models of social change is that provided by Arnold in his recent work on the early English state (1982a, 1984). Although he recognises the existence of connections between England and the Continent, archaeologically manifest as imported artefacts, he feels that such connections played little part in effecting structural change in the contemporary social system. Instead, population pressure leading to warfare is regarded as the principal reason for the coalescing of the various small sixth and seventh century Anglo-Saxon polities, and the subsequent development of the state – 'The integration of early state modules in early Anglo-Saxon England takes place as the result of aggression for the control of resources' (Arnold 1984, 281).

To move beyond this dangerously myopic view we must, as Wolf contends in the quotation above, examine the bundle of relationships that make up any social system. We must identify those structures necessary for the reproduction of society. Almost invariably this will necessitate a real understanding of a society's interactions with those polities around it, and an appreciation of the way these interactions or contacts articulate with local and regional production and exchange (Kristiansen 1982). It is the aim of this chapter to make a start in this direction.

We will first discuss two of the major ways of analysing these interconnections, and then attempt to show the nature of the contacts between England and the Continent in the late eighth and early ninth centuries in the light of this discussion. We shall try to show how this relationship is reflected in aspects of the material culture of the period, and finally propose how this relationship and the material culture might have been used to create and maintain relations of power, especially kingship, in Middle Saxon England.

The two modes of analysis we shall look at are Immanuel Wallerstein's 'World Systems Models', and Colin Renfrew's 'Peer Polity Interaction Model'. In both cases the single society is not regarded as the best unit of analysis for looking at past socio-political change. Wallerstein's is perhaps the major theoretical approach currently used to study the interconnections between polities. Following the work of Braudel and other historians of the 'Annales' school, Wallerstein has developed what he believes to be an all encompassing typology of social systems (see Wallerstein 1974, 1979, 1980, 1984). Social systems are characterised by the fact that life within them is largely self-contained, and the dynamics of their development largely internal. 'If the systems for any reason, were to be cut off from all external forces . . . the definition implies that the system would continue to function in substantially the same manner' (Wallerstein 1974, 347). Wallerstein believes there have only ever been three such systems:

1. Small scale, reciprocal mini-systems.

2. Large scale world empires containing many different socio-political and ethnic groups united by an overarching and centralised political structure.

3. World economies which, like world empires, contain within their bounds many different units, but here without any political cohesion. Politically all the polities are independent, the world system interconnections being created through economic ties.

These categories have been adopted recently by a number of archaeologists and have been applied widely (see Hingley 1982; the contributors to the volumes by Spriggs (ed.) 1984; Brandt and Slofstra (eds.) 1983). Wallerstein, however, was primarily concerned with tracing and explaining the development of European capitalism from the fifteenth century onwards. A close reading of his work shows that, as a result, he treats world empires only briefly, and that when he describes world economies he is referring only to the modern capitalist world economy (1979, 159). This being so, we must question the all encompassing nature of his typology and the validity of using the concepts of the world economy and the mechanisms that Wallerstein outlined as being central to its operation, in analyses of pre-capitalist social systems. Thus the concepts of unequal exchange, dominance and exploitation, while they may be appropriate for the study of world systems connections in the immediate pre-capitalist period, need to be re-examined and re-defined before being used in contexts where they may have played a lesser role, i.e. most pre-capitalist social systems. Here the usefulness of these concepts must be demonstrated, not asserted.

It was perhaps in part as a response to the crude economic determinism of this kind of world systems analysis, and its application in inappropriate contexts, that Renfrew was induced to define his concept of Peer Polity Interaction (Renfrew 1982; and fully developed in 1986). Renfrew sought to explain the simultaneous development of state societies on several small islands in the Aegean during the late Bronze Age. He rejected both the idea that this 'civilisation' was imposed by an outside hegemonic power, and the possibility that similar features developed independently on all the different islands at the same time. Instead he proposed that the move to statehood in the area was generally the result of a series of interactions between polities of the same status – 'peer polities'. The interactions form the basis of Renfrew's model and can be subsumed under three headings:

1. Competition and competitive emulation.
2. Symbolic entrainment and the transmission of innovation.
3. Increased flow in the exchange of goods (see Hodges 1986).

The details of these interactions cannot be discussed here; suffice it to say that the connections were many and varied, and that it was through these inter-actions that peer polities 'pulled themselves up by their bootstraps'.

The peer polity model had been published only recently, so critical appraisal has not yet been formulated. Some salient points can however be raised. These concern Renfrew's virtual rejection of the notions of inequality and dominance in the development of his model, and the peculiar circumstances for which the model was developed – small islands in the Aegean. While the model may satisfactorily explain the move to statehood on a small scale in the Aegean, its wider application must be considered carefully. For example, would the same kind of interaction be possible in a non-maritime environment where transport costs rise rapidly with distance, and continuous communication of the kind envisaged by the model would be prohibitively expensive? Also, since rela-tions of power and dominance, arising from and reinforcing inequality, are present in virtually every human relationship, the explanatory power of a model which underplays such a concept is diminished.

In all fairness, however, Renfrew has never claimed that the Peer Polity Interaction model is a general one for explaining social change. It was de-veloped to explain a particular anomalous situation and its further validity has yet to be demonstrated (see Bradley 1984 for an attempt). However, it might be useful to look at the model as a kind of temporal adjunct to a revised form of world systems analysis, helping to account for structural change in polities which are not yet vastly different in socio-political terms. Perhaps the most useful aspect of the Peer Polity Interaction model is the range of interactions that are seen to take place between polities, and which are fundamental in effecting change. Economic relations are not seen as the only, or even the dominant, inter-societal connections. Political, cultural and ideological links are also recognised and taken into consideration.

Given the belief that there was 'no economy in pre-capitalist societes – in the sense that this presupposes an institutional separation from other sectors of society which only happens in capitalism' (Giddens 1980, 88; Godelier 1975, 1977), and our resultant picture of such societies, we would argue that a similar range of interactions to those proposed for the Peer Polity Interaction model, took place between England and the Continent in the Middle Saxon period (Hodges 1986). We would also argue that the 'super-structural' elements of these relations – ideological, political, and cultural – were at least as important as whatever economic relations there may have been. We would suggest, however, that the nature of the connections, and of the societies involved, can be more adequately explained by incorporating notions of inequality into the relationships.

Archaeologically the connections between England and the Continent in the late eighth and early ninth centuries are best appreciated in the range of imported, often prestige, artefacts found on large emporia (or 'gate-way communities') like Hamwih (Saxon Southampton) or Ipswich. The functioning of these communities, and their relationship with both their own region and the larger area that makes up the complete trading network, have been described elsewhere (see Hodges 1982; Hodges and Whitehouse 1983). What we would like to do in this chapter is to emphasise that these artefacts are only one dimension of the relationship between Anglo-Saxon England and Carolingian Europe, and to argue that their strictly economic significance has perhaps been over-emphasised.

This over-emphasis is readily appreciated since archaeology's 'primary data, being composed of material things' lend themselves to economic and ecological perspectives, especially to the idea of trade (Helms 1979, 174). However, we feel that here it is possible to widen the scope of the enquiry. Following Hodder's (1982a, 1982b) work on symbolism and non-verbal communication we wish to propose that aspects of the material culture of Anglo-Saxon England are indicators of exchange in information and ideas, and also embody and symbolise those ideas in some way. The ideas themselves, and their material cultural correlates, are actively used to effect change in the structure of society. As Helms points out (1979, 128) ideology (or esoteric knowledge as she calls it) is just as much a prestige good or scarce resource as gold, pearls or other items of display, and is 'as important for the operation of society as are the material products of the economy' (1979, 176).

Western Europe in the late eighth and early ninth centuries consisted of a series of socio-political units ranging in complexity and scale from the disjointed mass of the Carolingian Empire to the small British chiefdoms on the periphery of the Anglo-Saxon kingdoms. The Carolingian Empire was, however, very different from the kind of imperial system envisaged in Wallerstein's world empire model. In the Carolingian case the overarching political superstructure was weak, and centralisation incomplete. Local aristocratic power and authority were forces to be reckoned with, and were possible causes of disintegration.

Following the military campaigns of Charlemagne and his father Pepin, many formerly independent, and previously non-Christian 'nations' were incorporated into the Empire. With the modest military resources of the traditional Germanic warband it was a great challenge to maintain control over these far-flung and disparate territories, and to ensure the loyalty of diverse lineage heads. Charlemagne rose to this challenge by patronising the Church in general and scholarship in particular to effect a cultural and spiritual *renovatio* (Ullmann 1969). The Church, both through its ubiquitous physical presence, and through its development of a unitary ideology which portrayed Christian society as one and indivisible and the king as the 'Lord's Anointed', was to be the binding force which, in the absence of coercion, was to ensure the continued integration of the Empire.

England at the time was dominated by three kingdoms; Northumbria, Mercia and Wessex. Northumbria's importance, however, was probably on the wane, and Mercia and Wessex appear to have vied for control of England south of the Humber. Mercia, especially under kings Offa and Cenwulf, expanded rapidly at the expense of the smaller kingdoms, though in the course of the ninth century Mercian dominance was checked and overturned by Wessex. These kingdoms were all Christian; and throughout the eighth century English missions went to the Continent to assist in the conversion of the pagans, and those who had fallen from the faith, along the Carolingians' eastern border. Some of these Englishmen became influential at the Carolingian court – especially Alcuin of York (see Wallach 1959) – and are regarded as among the principal architects of Charlemagne's *renovatio*. Thus '. . . the English stream flowed into the great river that is usually called the "Carolingian Renaissance". The stream gave the river its direction, other tributaries reinforced the movement' (Levison 1946, 151). However, Levison also points out that there is evidence to show that 'the current of the early eighth century was reversed at its end' (1946, 107). Thus in the ninth century, he argues, the importance of English missionaries and their ideas decreased. They had played their role, the Empire's eastern border was now more secure, the people Christianised and a new dominant ideology, based on the Bible and the writings of the spiritual Fathers of Late Antiquity, had been developed to emphasise unity in the face of diversity and division.

We would argue, with Levison, that in the late eighth and ninth centuries the dominant ideas and ideologies emanated from the Continent and were accepted and used to a certain extent in England. The connections between England and the Continent, illustrated both by the archaeological record and this flow of ideas and information, may be seen as similar to those which Eric Wolf believes form or generate 'civilisations'. In this context 'civilisations' are 'cultural interaction zones pivoted upon a hegemonic tributary society central to each zone. Such hegemony usually involves the development of an ideological model by a successful centralising elite of surplus takers, which is replicated by other elites within the wider political-economic orbit of inter-action' (1982, 82). In the case of early medieval Europe the relationship was probably not as deterministic as is implied by the phrase 'pivoted upon a hegemonic tributary society'. Nevertheless, this concept moves beyond the purely economic relations central to Wallerstein's World Systems Models and still preserves the essence of the kind of core/periphery relations we believe were important in pre-capitalist societies.

Charles, by the grace of God king of the Franks and Lombards, to his dearest brother Offa, king of the Mercians. (Quoted in Campbell 1982, 101)

It seems apparent from the short description in the previous section that the Carolingian community had become the dominant partner in the north-west European 'culture interaction zone' in the late eighth and early ninth centuries. We would, therefore, suggest (following Wolf 1982) that the 'ideological model' developed as the foundation of the Carolingian Renaissance should be replicated by Middle Saxon elites. Can we show that this was the case?

Perhaps the best evidence for the extent of the cultural interaction zone is provided by the archaeological evidence from the emporia on the North Sea and Channel coasts. In England recent excavations at Hamwih and in the centre of Ipswich have uncovered the remains of large Middle Saxon trading stations. Hamwih flourished from the late seventh century to the 820s and for much of the time covered an area of about 40 hectares. The history of Ipswich is broadly similar, though the settlement may have been smaller. These great nucleated emporia boldly contrast with the smaller royal, monastic and rural settlements which are barely more than a hectare in size. Hamwih and Ipswich were points where long-distance trade was controlled by royal households. In anthropological terms prestige goods were exchanged at these points. The prestige goods were then used, generally in ceremonial contexts (as gifts, bridewealth, grave goods, etc.) to maintain and enhance the status of the lineages that controlled the system (see Charles-Edwards 1976). In inter-national terms they helped to establish links between different groups and so enabled the exchange of other 'ordinary' products (see Gregory 1982). The Anglo-Saxon kings were involved in a form of exchange, within a core/periphery relationship, which precluded direct 'exploitation' in the formalist economic sense.

The archaeological evidence is discussed here only in summary form. It has been dealt with more fully elsewhere (Hodges 1982) and is in a sense peri-pheral to the main theme of this chapter, the direct transfer of ideas and information. Thus, as we have said already, although the material culture embodies aspects of the prevailing 'mentality' in the form of symbols, and these symbols not only reflect but are active in forming and giving meaning to social behaviour (Hodder 1982a, 12), different levels of information and different concepts will find more explicit expression in certain material culture forms. It is here suggested that the level of information with which we are concerned – the replication of aspects of ideological and theological thought – did not find direct material expression in the imported artefacts found in the emporia.

In contrast to this archaeological evidence, the documentary sources tell us little about the extensive contacts between the Anglo-Saxon courts and their Carolingian counterparts. The chronicle writers, as well as modern historians and archaeologists, appear to have been equally unaware of the wider core/ periphery relationships. Laconic references in the chronicles to intermittent pilgrimages by the secular and ecclesiastical elites to Rome, the Holy Land, or the German missions do no real justice to the complexity of the interactions. The best documentary sources are the letters exchanged between Offa and Charlemagne (see the quotation above). The best known example deals with the problems of pilgrims, traders, the exchange of gifts and the harbouring of Anglo-Saxon exiles by the Carolingians. This letter demonstrates contact and mutual respect but tells us little about the nature of the ideas and information flowing within the 'cultural interaction zone'. In itself it is an example of how such ideas may have been transmitted, and it obliquely refers to others, the returning pilgrims and the exiles. Of the latter, many subsequently returned to England, often to positions of power, and may have brought with them and put into practice the ideas they had seen in action at the Carolingian courts (Loyn 1984, 10).

We can, however, use the range of documents available (chronicles, charters, saints' lives, etc.) to glean some information relevant to our question, and then look for patterns within that information. Accordingly, we can propose that aspects of the Carolingian Renaissance in general, and modes of administration in particular, were consciously borrowed and used in England in the late eighth and early ninth centuries. As mentioned above, a fundamental aspect of Carolingian ideological reform was the central role of the king in a united Christian society. Charlemagne consciously manipulated the Church to change the structure and basis of society (Ullmann 1969, 7). Christianity was to be the basis of this 'reborn' society, and the legislation necessary for effecting the change was produced at great reforming synods attended by the important bishops as well as the king. The king's position as a Christian ruler was formalised through his ritual anointing with oil. This gave a 'sacred' aspect to his rule and directives. He was now the Lord's Anointed and refusal to follow him could be treated as sacrilege, punishable by excommunication (Ullmann 1969).

In England perhaps the most striking use of renaissance concepts is the consecration of Ecgfrith, son of Offa, in 787. There can be little doubt that this idea was borrowed from the Continent. In 781, Charlemagne had sent his sons Louis and Pippin to Rome to be anointed by Pope Hadrian (Brooks 1984, 11; Loyn 1984, 22). Nelson (1977, 60) has cast some doubt on the importance of the consecration ritual for the actual functioning of kingly authority in Francia in the late eighth and early ninth centuries, though her views might well be challenged. Whatever the case, Offa saw anointing as supremely important for his son. After the death of Ecgfrith, Alcuin wrote, 'Truly he has not died for his own sins; but the vengeance for the blood shed by the father has now reached the son. For you know very well how much blood his father shed to secure the kingdom on his son' (Campbell 1982, 115). We also know that Offa was frequently in conflict with Archbishop Jaenberht of Canterbury and it has been suggested that Jaenberht refused to anoint Ecgfrith. This may have induced Offa to set up another metropolitan see at Lichfield close to the Mercian royal centre at Tamworth and in opposition to Canterbury. It is significant that once this see had been established, and Hygeberht was chosen as archbishop by Offa, Ecgfrith was consecrated king. In other words 'it was only when Offa had obtained a compliant archbishop that he was able to have his son anointed. Against the background of Kentish resistance to Offa and of Jaenberht's hostility to him, the fact that the royal consecration and the division of the province of Canterbury were carried through at the same stormy council (Chelsea) can be no coincidence' (Brooks 1984, 118). The effort Offa expended in securing the consecration of his son shows its import-ance, and like Charlemagne it was part of his strategy 'to secure and legitimise the claims of a new dynasty to an expanded kingdom' (Brooks 1984, 117). After 787 the idea of consecration caught on. In 796 the consecration of kings started in Northumbria (Levison 1946, 119), and in 822 king Ceolwulf (Cen-wulf's successor) was consecrated by the Archbishop of Canterbury at the royal vill of *Bydictun* (Brooks 1984, 135), while 'a tradition of West-Saxon royal consecration rites, including anointing [was] continuous from the first half of the ninth century' (Nelson 1977, 66).

The consecration of the king was obviously of great importance in these uncertain times. Of more direct significance for the administration of the kingdom and for the formulation of laws were a series of 'grand councils' held between the Mercian kings and the ecclesiastical elite. They were almost certainly based on the Carolingian reforming synods referred to above (Campbell 1982, 125). The first council was held at Brentford in 781 and the main participants were Offa and Jaenberht (Brooks 1984, 113). There followed several other such Church/State councils which, as Wormald says, are a much neglected feature of the reigns of Offa and Cenwulf (1983, 127). Perhaps the most important of these councils was held at Chelsea in 786. This was on the occasion of the visit to England by two papal legates, George bishop of Ostia and Theophylact bishop of Todi, and consequently is known as the Legatine Synod. The degrees of this synod were mostly of an ecclesiastical nature but there was what amounted to some secular legislation. The content of this legislation mirrors that produced earlier in the Carolingian core. Thus the king is specifically referred to as 'the Lord's Anointed' and the sacro-sanctity of his position proclaimed (Campbell 1982, 125). The decrees condemn conspiracies against, and all attempts to kill, the king (Levison 1946, 119). Again reflecting Carolingian attempts to provide for the existence of their Empire through the Church, this council laid down that tithes should be paid by all men. As we saw above it was at this council also that Offa created the conditions necessary for the consecration of his son.

Another important council was held at Chelsea in 816, and was presided over by Archbishop Wulfred of Canterbury. Again the decrees of this council show the direct influence of the Continental synods, and the adoption of Carolingian thought (Brooks 1984, 175). This influence on the Church is most clearly seen at Canterbury in the early ninth century. Wulfred is known to have reformed the community there at this time, and to have based his reforms on the mid eighth-century *Rule* of Chrodegang of Metz and the decrees of the Frankish synods. He also rebuilt the monastery to facilitate conformity with the new ideas. As a charter of 813 states, he 'revived the holy monastery of the church of Canterbury by renewing, restoring, and rebuilding [it] with the aid of the priests, deacons, and all the clergy of the said church' (Brooks 1984, 156).

The examples quoted above clearly show the influence of Carolingian ideology on the Middle Saxon elites. It is possible that these are mere indicators of a more general use of Carolingian concepts. The closer relationship between the Church and the emerging state is indicative of a realisation, especially on the part of the secular elite, of the potential importance of the Church for maintaining their power and position. The king's initiative in creating this relationship is shown by Offa's insistence on the consecration of his son, and by the numerous gifts of land and other resources given by the various Mercian and West Saxon kings to the Church. Although it may not have been on the same scale as Carolingian patronage, it was patronage nevertheless. Church/ State relations in England appear not to have been as harmonious as on the Continent, and suggest a realisation of the value of a good relationship with the Church, but also a fear of its potential power, and a consequent uncertainty of how to handle the situation.

Offa's relations with the Church were evidently somewhat strained through the consecration of his son and his division of the archiepiscopal see; yet his concession to Canterbury of the right to mint its own coins shows he realised its potential. His successor, Cenwulf, appreciated this potential also, and went to great lengths to ease the strains created by Offa. He returned to the Church those lands confiscated by Offa, and donated many other gifts of land, until the year 817 when a rift arose between him and Archbishop Wulfred over control of the monasteries of Reculver and Minster-in-Thanet in Kent (Brooks 1984, 129–36, 180–97). The flow of benefices to the Church resumed under king Ceolwulf, but was sporadic after the West Saxon conquest of Kent between 825 and 827. Indeed the West Saxons initially seized some church lands, and the archiepiscopal coin series at Canterbury was interrupted for several years. The flow of royal charters granting lands and concessions to the Church also dried up (Brooks 1984, 137, 145–46). By 838, however, the patronage restarted on an unprecedented scale. 'It is clear . . . that in the years 838–9 Egbert and Aethelwulf were willing to settle disputes with the archbishop and to make grants to Christ Church with a generosity that was singularly lacking in their successors' (Brooks 1984, 146). It was not just Canterbury but the

whole Church which benefited from royal generosity. Thus, similar benefices
went to Winchester (Brooks 1984, 147) and we are told in the Anglo-Saxon
Chronicle that king Aethelwulf gave one-tenth of his lands to the Church
(Loyn 1984, 59).

The gifts to Winchester and Canterbury had conditions attached which
show that the motives behind this generosity were overtly political. These
kings were 'seeking to secure the support of the [Church] for their dynasty'
(Brooks 1984, 147). It appears that such support was indeed granted, and by
839 'Archbishop Ceolnoth and the Church of Canterbury had come decisively
off the fence and had tied themselves to the fortunes of Egbert's dynasty'.
After this the benefices stopped, though this probably had more to do with the
unprecedented ferocity of the Viking attacks on England at the time (Hodges
and Whitehouse 1983, 165–7; Randsborg 1981) than with Church/State
relations. State patronage of the Church was only resumed under King Alfred,
though his initial dealings with the Church were just as uncertain as his
predecessors. It is indeed surprising to find Alfred referred to as an enemy of
the Church in the first years of his reign (Brooks 1984, 150).

> *Since the Renaissance it has become customary to consider architecture as being deter-*
> *mined by 'commodity, firmness, and delight' . . . by function, construction, and design.*
> *. . . The validity of such a view appears rather doubtful where medieval architecture is*
> *concerned . . . no medieval source ever stresses the design of an edifice or its construction.*
> *On the other hand the practical and liturgical functions are always taken into consider-*
> *ation; they lead on to questions of the religious significance of an edifice and these two*
> *groups together seem to stand in the centre of medieval architectural thought. . . . The*
> *religious implications of a building were uppermost in the minds of its contemporaries.*
> *Questions of the symbolic significance of the layout or of the parts of the structure are*
> *prominent. . . . The 'content' of architecture seems to have been among the most*
> *important problems of medieval architectural theory; perhaps indeed it was the most*
> *important problem.* (Krautheimer 1971, 115)

We stated at the outset of this chapter that aspects of the material culture
would embody or symbolise ideas and information of the kind we have just
detailed. We also suggested that information of this kind would find explicit
representation in particular artefacts. It is here suggested that, since Christianity was at the heart of the ideological model from which this information was
derived, it should be most explicitly represented in those structures immediately connected with it – ecclesiastical complexes. These buildings were probably the direct focus of English as well as Carolingian royal patronage, though
the evidence for this is slight (see Levison 1946, 111). More importantly,
however, it is now clear that in the early medieval period changes in aspects of
religious ideology and performance directly affected the architecture of the
Church (Krautheimer 1971; Wallace-Hadrill 1983, 178–9; Brooks 1984,
155–7). This is something we shall now consider in more detail.

Richard Krautheimer's seminal paper intentionally sought to redirect the
attention of architectural historians from treating medieval buildings as artefacts barely related to their historical context, towards a position in which the

buildings represent a major source for the histories of their age (see also 1980, 1983 for an illustration of his work on a large scale). This is of course an archaeological issue: to study the objects/sites for their own sakes is to adopt an antiquarian approach, to study the objects/sites as data with which to analyse their content is to adopt a historian's approach (see Hodges 1982). However, Krautheimer's thesis has had few exponents in early medieval studies. The result is a patchy, regionally oriented impression of early medieval architecture (see Conant 1978), and the unhealthy rarity of studies relating architectural history to the broad stream of European history. In this respect Anglo-Saxon architectural history is like much general history of the period. Despite a few preliminary sketches investigating the 'content', most historians and archaeologists have concerned themselves only with descriptive analyses (classically Taylor and Taylor 1965; Taylor 1978).

Krautheimer's thesis is well borne out by a brief examination of architecture and church construction at the time of the development of the Carolingian Renaissance ideology. The Carolingian abbeys were vastly enlarged and their fittings were refurbished and aggrandised with images befitting the spirit of the new age. The increased size of these churches is ample reflection, both to us and to contemporaries, of the new role the church had been given. More specifically the design of parts of these aggrandised monasteries were affected directly by the changed liturgy and religious practice. Thus Wallace-Hadrill refers to the impact of the *Rule of Chrodegang* on the design of the late eighth-century cathedral at Metz, and elsewhere in Francia. He suggests that 'the layout of the church and monastic buildings round the quadrangle that appeared at Lorsch in 763 . . . was (clearly) influenced by Chrodegang. It was to be the classic shape of the medieval monastery' (1983, 179). He then shows the influence of the new ideology on the construction and design of the church and particularly of the crypt at Jouarre. The new churches and monasteries reflect not only the designs of the new spirit, but in the form of the abbeys themselves and the buildings around them, the content (as Krautheimer calls it) of the age. In these buildings the liturgical, as well as the productive and distributive capabilities of the complex were embedded.

This phenomenon was not restricted to the Carolingian heartlands. The contemporary accounts reveal a chain of monasteries in the hinterland of the emporia from which traders set out to England. Wandrille, near Rouen (Horn and Born 1979), St Riquier (Parsons 1977), St Josse close to Quentovic, St Bertin at Omer all appear to have embodied elements of the cultural revolution engineered by Charlemagne. The current excavations at San Vincenzo al Volturno, just inside the Lombardic territory of Benevento in central Italy, have illustrated the kind of changes enacted in this period. The small monastery of the eighth century covering about half a hectare was transformed in the early ninth century into a monastery nearly ten times as large; then again in the 820s or 830s it was enlarged once more. Aspects of the design and decoration of the monastery, especially the re-use of late Imperial motifs and sculpture, are a clear echo of similar changes further north and are a reflection of the new ideology (Hodges, Moreland and Patterson 1985). The planning and scale revealed by archaeology at San Vincenzo can be used as some sort of index of the developments attributed by historians to the monasteries of the Carolingian core as well as those overlooking the English Channel.

In England on the other hand, the Carolingian ethos is traditionally thought to have been introduced by Archbishop Dunstan and his associates Ethelwold and Oswald. Their later tenth-century 'reformation', so it appears, invoked a 'Golden Age' (Blackhouse, Turner and Webster 1984). Architecture and all the arts were radically reinterpreted and in many cases transformed to become expressions of this movement, as these had been more than a century and a half previously in the Carolingian kingdoms. Taylor has led the search for Carolingian parallels for tenth-century buildings in England (Taylor 1975). Thus poorly dated alterations on some scale at Canterbury, Glastonbury and Sherbourne are all provisionally attributed to the late ninth or tenth centuries (Taylor and Taylor 1965). Following this, systematic excavations at Canterbury (Saunders 1978) and Winchester Old Minster (Biddle 1975) have revealed enigmatic pre-late tenth century remains which have also been assigned to the Alfredian period or to the tenth century.

Yet at odds with these somewhat anachronistic interpretations are three important factors. First, despite Dunstan's exile in Flanders, cross-channel relations reached a remarkably low point in the tenth century (Hodges 1982). The west European economy had fragmented into a patchwork-quilt of self-motivated regions, which only after the turn of the millennium became interconnected once more. Secondly, most continental monasteries and abbeys were experiencing a period of recession after the zeal of the ninth century (Herlihy 1961). It may be that while Anglo-Saxon England enjoyed a period of political stability (Wormald 1983) many continental kingdoms were in a state of some turmoil. In this turmoil landowners like the Church were apparently finding it difficult to sustain the momentum and conditions of the ninth century. Social ethics were in a phase of transition, and the Church was suffering the lasting humiliation of the Vikings and the Saracens while attempting to retain its ninth-century power. The socio-political situation on the Continent was not a straightforward model for Anglo-Saxon England. Thirdly, following the last point, Anglo-Saxon England had undergone its own revolution in the first half of the tenth century. Scarcely noted by its chroniclers, many new towns had been created, with craft specialists and all the paraphernalia of an emergent urban community (Hodges 1982). Consequently rural society experienced comparable change, and the social fabric of Anglo-Saxon England was altered. The Anglo-Saxon state, with its monarchy derived from a single lineage, secured by military forces funded from taxation, had now arrived (Hodges 1982). It is in this context that the tenth-century reforms must be seen. But to what extent reformers looked to alien ideas, then more than a century out of date, and to what extent they looked towards enhancing an earlier ninth-century cultural movement in England depends on our approach to the interpretation of the archaeology of the ninth century.

The history of ninth-century culture suffers from chronological imprecision. Anglo-Saxon buildings are notoriously difficult to date (Taylor 1978,
735–55). The fragments of paintings (Dodwell 1982; Wormald 1983) and
sculpture (Cramp 1978) associated with the major buildings are equally difficult to assign with accuracy to a quarter-century, let alone a decade, before the
tenth century. Similar problems arise for manuscripts, fine metalwork
(Wilson 1964), and bone and ivory carvings. This lack of chronological
precision has created a good deal of academic vacillation when assigning
buildings and objects to particular periods. It has also tempted many scholars
to use well known historical horizons. As a result the reputation of King Alfred
has been enhanced, with many buildings and objects being assigned to his
reign, as Asser in his biography claims the king to have been benevolently
disposed towards the arts and the Church (see Keynes and Lapidge 1983,
101). The temptation, however, to seek continental influence for a ninth
century Anglo-Saxon cultural movement has mostly been eschewed.

   If we reject the historical reductionist approach which assigns all pre-tenth
century buildings to the reign of Alfred, there does exist some evidence for just
such an influence. Thus, untypically, Taylor has emphasised the continental
design of the Middle Saxon crypts at Repton (Derbys) (1971) and Wing
(Bucks) (1979). He places both crypts into the late eighth–ninth century
tradition of crypt building, arising from the increased esteem given during the
renovatio to relics and their public presentation (Krautheimer 1971; Wallace-
Hadrill 1983, 179). Fernie, in a recent review of Anglo-Saxon architecture,
draws attention to the evidence from Brixworth and Cirencester, where large
pre-Alfredian abbeys seem to have been constructed. Fernie also expresses his
doubt that Biddle's historically deterministic interpretation of the Winchester
Old Minster sequence can be upheld (Fernie 1983, 99–100).

   Biddle, it should be recalled, contends that the tiny seventh-century minster
remained substantially unaltered until the 970s when he argues a great westwork (of Carolingian form) was constructed to accommodate the tomb of St
Swithin (Biddle 1975). He seeks to make the archaeological evidence compatible with the late Roger Quirk's interpretation of the written sources (Quirk
1957). However, this initial enlarged minster with its archetypical Carolingian
westwork might be better assigned to an earlier period, as Biddle in fact
suggested when the excavations were in progress (Biddle 1975). If we project
Nelson's suggestion that westworks like that at Winchester 'were the settings
for special kinds of imperial liturgical performance' (1977, 70) back into the
ninth century then the direct impact of Carolingian ideology on English
architecture becomes clear. The role of the state also becomes apparent when
we remember Egbert's patronage of Winchester with political strings attached.

   A pre-tenth century date for this phase of the minster is to some extent
reinforced by the discovery of a fragment of wall painting in an apparently
pre-903 context. The painting shows some continental influence, and clearly
comes from a major building within the complex. At present it is associated
with the tiny seventh-century minster. Such ornament, an indication of high

quality architectural painting before 903 (Blackhouse, Turner and Webster 1984, 44) is not the only illustration of major changes in the decoration of ninth-century monasteries. Medhamstede abbey (Peterborough), long associated with Bishop Ethelwald's well-recorded restorations in the tenth century, also boasts an important assemblage of decorated monumental sculpture from the pre-Viking period (Taylor and Taylor 1965, 491–4; Cramp 1977, 210–11). There are strong continental parallels for these pieces, and the pre-Viking date can probably be narrowed down to the early ninth century (Cramp 1977, 211). The monastery at Breedon on the Hill (Leics) was similarly decorated with sculptured stonework on an impressive scale, showing continental influences in the years before the Viking attacks (Cramp 1977: 206–7), while remains at Bakewell (Derbys) also suggest a period of intense cultural activity in its monastery. The evidence, slight as it is, begins to indicate a pre-Alfredian architectural expansion by certain monastic communities, in some cases clearly reflecting the dictates of Carolingian ideology. Perhaps the best example is the rebuilding of Canterbury to conform with the *Rule of Chrodegang* and the ordinances of the Frankish synods (Brooks 1984, 155–7).

Increased architectural sophistication and elaboration is also evidenced in secular elite sites. At Northampton a Middle Saxon long hall, built in stone and generally associated with the Mercian royal household, has recently been uncovered close to the remains of the Middle Saxon monastic complex (Williams and Shaw 1983). The hall reveals that the gifted builders of the timber halls had mastered stone versions by the late eighth century. Possibly more astonishing is the discovery of several stone-built mausolea of Middle Saxon date in the grounds of the minster at Repton (Youngs, Clark and Barry 1983, 172–3). These tombs suggest a burial ground for the Mercian royal household which owes part of its genesis to mound cemeteries like Sutton Hoo, and part to the renewed fascination for Roman burial forms in late eighth to early ninth century Carolingian Europe (Krautheimer 1980). Here the interaction of Church, State and Carolingian ideology in Middle Saxon England starts to come into sharper focus.

> . . . *nations are made not just by conquest and political manoeuvre, but by shared ideals.*
> (Wormald 1983, 128)

We must now consider the part these interactions played in the reproduction of society. Middle Saxon English society was undoubtedly more complex than that of preceding centuries. The area south of the Humber was now dominated by two great kingdoms, Mercia and Wessex, in contrast to the many mentioned in the seventh-century *Tribal Hidage*. Social distance and inequalities in wealth were increasing, and administration was probably much more complex (Runciman 1984). This process was accelerated in the period of Mercian hegemony when Offa tried to move beyond 'the traditional powers of the overlord, by systematically suppressing the kingdoms subject to him, and ruling them directly himself' (Brooks 1984, 111; Yorke 1981, 183). With this increased complexity the king became more distanced from the people, and from this distance would have made increased demands on their labour and time to service the enlarged polities. This would have applied to both Wessex and Mercia (Brooks 1971). In such a situation the king had to secure support for his rule and his demands. In other words his rule had to be 'legitimated' (Kurtz 1984, 301; Drennan 1976; Loyn 1984, 18). In Anglo-Saxon England two factors had to be overcome before such support could be ensured. Firstly, the fact that father-to-son succession was the exception rather than the rule meant that the position and standing of the new king was always uncertain. Thus in Wessex there is not a single case of father-to-son succession from 672 to 839, while in Mercia 'succession moved somewhat erratically between 654 and 823' (Loyn 1984, 16). The second hurdle was the lack of any structure enabling the king to secure his position and have his directives followed through the application of physical coercion. At this time 'coercion was not viable as a primary mechanism for ensuring predictability in people's actions' (Drennan 1976, 347).

With this move to increasing complexity, and the existence of such obstacles to ensuring support, we would expect the implementation by the king of a series of strategies designed to win people over to him, and away from local lineage allegiances (Kurtz 1984, 301). This applies both to individuals and large organisations. One way of obtaining the support of both local lineage heads and corporate organisations would be the giving of gifts, perhaps the prestige items imported into England through the emporia at Hamwih and Ipswich. Thus the gifts of land and other goods given by the Anglo-Saxon kings to these groups were probably to gain their support. As in other early states the Anglo-Saxon elite 'gave gifts, awarded titles, and granted rights to individuals who served it well, subventions which served to co-opt their local allegiances' (Kurtz 1984, 304). If we remember Archbishop Jaenberht's hostility to Mercian rule, and his continued support for the local Kentish kings, we begin to see the generosity of Cenwulf and his successors in a new light. There were always political reasons for this patronage but they only became explicit late in Egbert's reign (in 838).

A further aspect of the search for support and authorisation in times of change can be found in the construction of the royal genealogies. This had been common practice for even the earliest English kings (Loyn 1984, 13–14), but seems to have become more important in the late eighth and ninth centuries (Campbell 1982, 116). Offa in particular made great efforts in this direction. Thus he traced his lineage back to an earlier Offa, a hero of the Anglian homeland, and in a charter of 764 he is referred to as 'King of the Mercians, sprung from the royal stock of the Mercians.' In having these genealogies drawn up, the kings aimed at asserting the ancestry of their lineage, the nobility of their blood and their right to rule.

Anthropologists have shown that in societies like Anglo-Saxon England, where physical coercion was not a viable means for ensuring support, closer ties with the Church and the eventual sanctification of the king and his directives was a good functional alternative (Rappaport 1971a, 72; Drennan 1976, 348; Kurtz 1984, 306). They show that the need for such sanctification becomes greatest 'when the arbitrariness of the social conventions was increasing, but it was not yet possible for the authorities to enforce compromise' (Rappaport 1971b, 38). By becoming more closely connected with the Church, helping and encouraging the state religion and the development of state values and ideology, early medieval kings were seeking the support of the Church for their rule and legitimisation for their decrees. This phenomenon was most clearly seen in the Carolingian heartlands, but is also shown to have occurred in England. The culmination of the process was the anointing of the king with holy oils. Through this ritual the king was seen to have divine authority for his rule. His rulings, which might otherwise have lacked force, take on an air of sanctity. To sanctify such things, or at least to give them such an aura, is to place them 'beyond criticism and [to] define recalcitrance as sacrilege' (Rappaport 1971b, 35).

In a more general sense the overall relationship between the Church and State, epitomised in the grand councils and their legislation, served to present existing social conditions as fixed and as being a reflection of the supernatural order (Wolf 1982, 83), even when in reality these conventions were becoming more fluid. As Rappaport says, 'to invest social conventions with sanctity is to hide their arbitrariness in a cloak of seeming necessity. Conventions, to the extent that they are sanctified, are likely to be taken by those subject to them as 'natural'. . . . Indeed, they seem not to be mere conventions, but reflections of human nature, and those who flaunt them seem less than human' (1971b, 36). In Anglo-Saxon England the king and his rulings may not have been sanctified to this degree, and therefore were not so effective. Nevertheless, we suggest that the relationship between Church and State was yet another strategy by which the kings sought to maintain their position of dominance and to preserve the existing power relations in larger and more complex polities where these relations were in a state of flux (see Runciman 1984). Thus the adopted Carolingian ideology emphasised the unity of Christian society and the inviolable nature of the king's office. Everyone was to respect their secular lord and all men were to pay tithes to the Church (Brooks 1984). A similar concept of unity, English unity, was nurtured at Canterbury at this time. Again the importance of Kent, and Canterbury in particular, to the Middle Saxon kings becomes clear. 'It is hard to imagine a more effective way of imparting a sense of unity to diverse and feuding peoples than by reminding them that they were all, as Englishmen, represented in Heaven by the same saints' (Wormald 1983, 125).

In conclusion, we feel that sufficient evidence exists to sustain our hypothesis that aspects of the Carolingian movement, and the essence of the ideology in general made a significant impact on eighth and ninth century England. This ideology, we believe, was employed to maintain existing relations of power, and so to facilitate social reproduction. It must be emphasised that the full range of the renaissance movement was not imported and accepted *en masse*. The relationship was not so deterministic. Only those concepts considered useful to the English elites at that particular time were assimilated. There are signs of some direct replication, while in other cases traditional ideas and designs tempered continental concepts. In every core/periphery situation the recipients of ideas, information and ideologies use and adapt aspects of that ideology and information to their own ends. The flows in such relationships are amost never in one direction only, and interaction can sometimes result in changes in the core area too. It is the constant dialectic inherent in such interchange that stimulates social change (see Smith 1984).

As we have indicated before, this chapter is a preliminary attempt to examine an often neglected aspect of the relationship between England and the Continent in the Middle Saxon period in terms of a revised form of world systems analysis. However, if we are fully to understand the social reproduction of the societies involved in this relationship we must examine all the structures involved. In this chapter we have focussed on the 'ideological structures for the regulation of consensus', and to some extent its articulation with the 'political structures of dominance' (see Li Causi 1975). What we have been unable to do, since it is beyond the scope of this chapter, is to examine the interconnections between these structures and those production and distributional structures which form the base of society. Only when this is done will we properly understand society in Middle Saxon England.

Early Scottish towns :
their origins and economy

The origin of European medieval towns is a long-standing topic of debate which, until the advent of archaeology, was the preserve of documentary and geographical historians. The arguments are numerous and complex but may be crudely summarised as falling under two main headings. The first is often described as the 'Romanist theory' and emphasises the continuity of urban life from Roman times through to the advent of medieval chartered towns. An adjunct to this theory was that medieval towns located beyond the Roman Empire were believed to be planted or new towns, the organisation of which had been derived from Roman examples. The second, and largely conflicting theory, was propounded by Pirenne who believed that, no matter whose the soil or what the previous history, the medieval town was essentially a trading settlement. The results of archaeological excavation have tended to bolster the more economic, and therefore materially recognisable, theory of Pirenne. This is particularly true for those towns beyond the Roman Empire. The 'Romanists' have, however, been able to demonstrate a significant degree of continuity of urban settlement in the greater towns of Roman Europe. Both schools have considerably influenced thinking on the definition of medieval urban settlement in Europe. In brief, the requirement is to demonstrate a distinction between an urban community and its surrounding rural community. For the larger and later cities of medieval Europe this is relatively easy, but for smaller and earlier settlements the differences between town and country can be slight. A simple solution adopted by the 'Romanists' was to recognise only legally defined towns – chartered burghs – as urban. This does not, however, allow for either pre-charter towns or unsuccessful chartered towns. It is necessary to borrow from the Pirenne school certain economic elements so that a town may also be defined as a permanent settlement in which 'a significant proportion (but not necessarily a majority) of its population lives off trade, industry, administration and other non-agricultural occupations' (Reynolds 1977, ix–x). Unfortunately, this leaves the problem of deciding what qualifies as a 'significant proportion', especially when many specialised crafts would have been seasonal activities. Ideally, contemporary opinion should be the source of that decision, hence the value of burgh charters; but for pre-charter towns we must rely on archaeological evidence for trade, industry and social structure.

Scottish historians, both documentary and archaeological, have recognised the existence of earlier settlements on or near the sites of many later burghs. However, for mainly legalistic reasons they have tended to attribute the earliest recognisably urban settlements in Scotland to the twelfth century. During David I's reign (1124–1153) the term 'burgh' was introduced to describe a number of settlements and it is these that are generally cited as the earliest discernible Scottish towns. The twelfth century was a time of considerable economic, legal and political development in Scotland, as it was for many parts of north-west Europe. Hand in hand with these developments went the major advances in urban organisation which are documented across much of Europe. Scotland was very much a part of that movement with the adoption of the *Laws of the Four Burghs* and, during the later part of William I's reign (1165–1214), the introduction of individual burgh charters. Both the Laws and charters were comparable to those on the Continent and were largely borrowed from English boroughs, while foreign merchants, especially Flemings, were a prominent feature of major Scottish port burghs. Such documentary evidence, although regrettably sparse, provides invaluable glimpses of the economy and life of these early burghs. In recent years archaeology has begun to make its contribution to this picture of Scottish medieval towns, particularly with regard to their economic and industrial functions. The extent of Scottish urban excavation has been more limited than similar work in England and parts of the Continent. There has been little chance to excavate in the areas which urban topography suggests are the oldest parts of David I's burghs. As yet, therefore, there is little direct evidence of pre-burghal urban life although it seems likely that, for instance, at Perth there was a substantial and active urban community prior to David's first references to it as his burgh. Many of these burghs were in the vicinity of major early medieval and even Late Iron Age settlements and the possibility that they represent a continuity of settlement pattern and perhaps also political and economic function should be born in mind.

In Britain the majority of Roman towns were concentrated in south-east England, or Fox's Lowland Zone. Northern England and Wales were primarily military districts. The Roman occupations of Scotland were no more than temporary extensions of that military district. The construction of the Antonine Wall across the Forth-Clyde isthmus marked the principal boundary of that military extension, although various campaigns took the Roman army and navy much further up the east coast of Scotland. The question of continuity of Roman urban life therefore only applies to England. It has been widely argued that even for England the transition from Roman to early medieval town was so troubled that little or no continuity can be demonstrated (Wacher 1974, 418–22). It is thought that only at York, Canterbury and probably London can any continuity of urban life be demonstrated (Hill 1977, 293–5). For Scotland the question is instead one of continuity and development of native urban settlement, whilst cautiously judging the effect of temporary Roman military occupations.

There are a handful of Late Iron Age hillforts in central and southern Scotland which reach dimensions and perhaps also densities of occupation indicative of highly organised community life. Unfortunately, little excavation has been carried out on these forts and their dating, economy and function are poorly understood. However, in a number of cases field survey has indicated the existence of complex settlement histories. The two largest were Eildon Hill North in Roxburghshire and Traprain Law in East Lothian. Both of these forts enclosed at various times up to 16 hectares of ground. Field survey has identified some 300 house platforms at Eildon Hill North with room for a further 200 in areas of the fort now disturbed. Even if only a small proportion of these houses were occupied at the one time this represents a site of considerable economic and social organisation. In northern Britain these two forts were only exceeded in size by that of Stanwick in Teesdale, which at a maximum of 300 ha was one of the great settlements in Celtic Europe. Of the other large Scottish hillforts most were in the range of 4.5 to 8 ha, with three others between 8.1 and 12 ha. The majority of these larger hillforts were located south of the Forth-Clyde isthmus. North of the isthmus the main hillforts were betwen 2.5 and 4 ha with the exceptional unfinished hillfort at Kinpurney Hill in Angus of 6.6 ha.

It has been argued that the geographical regions within which these larger forts lie may be related through Roman documentary sources, such as Ptolemy's *Geography* and the *Ravenna Cosmography*, to named tribal groups, and that such forts were the walled towns or 'oppida' of these tribes. Eildon Hill North has been seen as the principal *oppidum* of the Selgovae, and Traprain Law that of the Votadini. To the west, Walls Hill in Renfrewshire (7.5 ha) may be equated with the Damnonii, while Burnswark in Dumfriesshire (6.9 ha) was probably the *oppidum* of the Novantae. Generally these forts were distinguished from other settlements of their area on the basis of their unique size. In south-east Scotland there were, however, a number of other large forts. In addition to the major hillforts of Eildon Hill North and Traprain Law there are some eleven other substantial Late Iron Age forts including North Berwick Law in East Lothian (11.4 ha) and Hownam Law in Roxburghshire (8.9 ha). Near Edinburgh are found Salisbury Craig (10.1 ha) and Arthur's Seat (8.1 ha) (Feachem 1966, 77–81).

The description of these sites as *oppida* has been strongly contested since the adoption of the term in Scotland during the 1950s and 60s (Steer 1964, 15). This is principally because they are not seen as the equivalent of the great southern English hillforts, which indeed they are not. However, they are of major significance in the settlement history of northern Britain, indeed they represent a scale of occupation comparable to many later Scottish burghs. Lack of excavation makes it impossible to discuss the detailed economy of these sites although they clearly demonstrate a considerable concentration of agricultural resources. The processing of agricultural produce in any quantity would tend to have resulted in a specialisation of skills such as brewing, butchering and skinning. Once reputations of excellence were established the exchange of crafted produce would have followed. Excavations at Traprain Law have demonstrated the work of more specialised craftsmen through the recovery of various pin, ring, ingot and spear-butt moulds (Burley 1956, 219–21).

The social organisation that existed both within and between these forts is largely unknown, although it seems likely that political control lay in the hands of a warrior elite. Through the writings of Tacitus and Caesar, the hierarchical nature of Late Iron Age society is well attested. Moreover, prestige finds such as the gold and electrum torc from Netherurd in Peebles-shire and various La Tène Group III and IV swords from south Scotland would suggest that Caesar's general descriptions of Celtic society are valid for Scotland (Cunliffe 1974, 281–3). The larger Scottish hillforts fit well with this pattern, indicating as they do a substantial organisation of economy and labour. Recent excavations at The Dunion, Roxburghshire, one of the minor *oppida* (5.3 ha) of southern Scotland, have uncovered an example of a planned laying out of street and houses (Rideout 1984). Without better dating of these larger forts it is impossible to detail their geographical, economic and political interrelationship. Nevertheless, outwith south-east Scotland, the widely scattered distribution of these sites has been seen to suggest the existence of regional economies under political control. If so, then there may well already have been a recognition of the political advantages inherent in the control of an urban economy. In south-east Scotland the concentration of large forts is such that even if only crudely contemporary there would seem to be a higher degree of both political and economic activity. In this area at least there appears to have been a significant trend towards urban settlement prior to Roman invasion and long before the documented towns of medieval Scotland.

The Roman occupation of Scotland raises the question of Rome's effect on any native trends towards urbanisation. The larger hillforts of southern Scotland would seem in the main to have been abandoned either before or during Agricola's invasion. The picture is, however, far from complete, and Traprain Law at least survived and prospered. On the other hand provisioning of Roman garrisons and the construction of roads, forts and ports must have stimulated any existing interest in trade and manufacture. The use of the Antonine and Hadrianic Walls as trade barriers illustrates extremely well the exchange of goods that went on within Scotland and between Roman and non-Roman Britain (Hanson and Maxwell 1983, 164; Frere 1978, 332–3). Although specific 'client' kingdoms such as the Votadini may have been supported and, it seems, funded by Rome it was mainly the economic rather than social or political development of urbanisation that benefited from contact with Rome.

The withdrawal of the Roman army behind Hadrian's Wall and ultimately from the whole of the British Isles progressively left the inhabitants of Scotland to their own political and economic devices. It has been suggested that at Traprain Law the last refurbishment of defences may date to the fourth century AD. As a response to the troubles of that time it seems to have been only partially successful, for the dating of finds from Traprain Law indicates that occupation there ended in the mid-fifth century. It would seem that it was no longer desirable or perhaps possible to maintain what in any case may already have become an anachronism. Although the last of the larger hillforts of south-east Scotland do not seem to have continued in use, the smaller forts which rose to prominence may not have been entirely new establishments. In several cases settlement *loci* were maintained. At Edinburgh, Perth/Scone, and Haddington/Dunbar/Traprain the economic and political focus would seem simply to have been transferred to adjacent premises which were better suited to the topographic requirements of the times. In the post-Roman period the choice would seem to have been for smaller more strongly defensible sites, indicating perhaps a change in military tactics and organisation. Continuity of major settlement *loci* would indicate, though, that for purely geographic reasons, or more probably for social and geographic reasons, the general distribution of population and agriculture remained unchanged.

Excavations at a number of the fortresses of this time, especially Dunadd in Argyll and Dundurn in Perthshire, have produced quantities of cattle, pig and sheep bones and also rotary querns. It would seem that at least the upper echelons of society enjoyed the fruits of mixed and especially pastoral farming. As with the Late Iron Age hillforts the slaughter of so many animals for the one site has implications for more than just diet. Hide, horn, gut, sinew, tallow and so forth would have been removed from carcases and processed for use in the fortress and perhaps the wider community as well. Likewise grain gathered to the fortress would have been stored and processed into bread, malt and ale. Purely through the concentration of a wealth of food there would have developed a basis for both local industry and trade.

The survival of Annals and Heroic literature means that it is possible to supplement our archaeological picture of post-Roman and early medieval society. In the absence of a money economy food, either on the hoof or in the granary, was very much the measure of true wealth. Control of agricultural produce meant the ability to house, feed and clothe a warband and thus the ability to survive attacks from competitors. Members of warbands also expected to be rewarded with wine, fine jewellery, weapons and other luxury goods. Control of such luxury goods was therefore an essential prerequisite of political power, for they were both symbols of authority and an important means of attracting retainers. Only a few sources for such goods existed; capture in war, gift exchange, purchase through trade or manufacture by specialists at home. The first alternative was the most readily recorded in the literature of the time as, for instance, the *Gododdin* informs us:

> Blaen used to raise the shout of battle returning with the booty; he was a
> bear in the pathway, it was long ere he would retreat. (Jackson 1969, 122)

Plunder, gift exchange or perhaps trade within Britain is attested on archaeological grounds by the wide dispersal of artefacts with well-defined cultural and chronological peculiarities such as brooches and hanging bowls (Longley 1975, 32–4). Various types of imported pottery have also been discovered on a number of the major settlements of this period, indicating long-distance trade with Mediterranean lands and France. The manufacture of fine metalwork at home is well attested by the archaeological record. Most notably Dunadd and Mote of Mark have provided numerous mould fragments and crucibles indicative of substantial jewellery workshops. Where this work was based upon the processing of locally available raw materials, the quantity of goods came under local political control. The major alternative source was foreign trade. Control of trade, and especially foreign trade, was therefore of prime importance for political success.

In a pre-monetary economy purchases of luxury goods and the raw materials for their manufacture must have been by payment in kind. Control of such exchanges may have been at two levels. Surplus agricultural produce and other tradable goods might be taken directly under the control of local rulers through a system of local levies. Levies in kind such as 'cain and conveth' were clearly well established in Scotland by the tenth and eleventh centuries and continued in use well after coinage had been introduced. At the same time local and long-distance trade, especially when based on barter, would have greatly benefited from fixed sites of exchange with guaranteed standards of conduct and honesty. Local rulers were ideally placed to provide such security in the form of bartering markets in or adjacent to their fortresses. Thus rulers could control the availability of purchasing materials and also the movement of visiting merchants along with the raw materials of native craftsmen. The political necessity of retaining a warband therefore explains something of the social and economic mechanics of post-Roman urbanisation. Moreover, once established, any increase in political power was part of an escalating spiral in which the warband was used to establish economic control over another district. As a result it was possible to attract yet more retainers, control further districts and so on. The pressure for both economic and political centralisation was therefore the same – the reward of what were in effect mercenary retainers.

Despite their lack of size these Early Historic fortresses had then many of the attributes of urban settlements. Indeed several were described as such by Bede in his *Ecclesiastical History* when he referred to Dumbarton as a strongly defended *civitas*, and Coldingham, Bamburgh, and perhaps Inveresk/Mussel-burgh as *urbs*. Elsewhere, Dunbar and an unidentified site 'Inbroninis' are similarly called *urbs* by Eddius in his *Life of Wilfrid* (*HE* 1.1, 12; 3.6, 16; 4.19, 25; *VW* 72, 76). In view of contemporary descriptions and their apparent economic and political role these forts would seem to be a clear step towards urban and political development.

Politically the ninth and tenth centuries are a period of gradual unification in Scotland's history. Economically, although the evidence is slight, there seems to have been an increase in trade and a greater centralisation of wealth. It was a time of considerable struggle between the various kingdoms and cultural groups that now make up the Scottish nation. These included as before the Picts, Scotti, Anglians and British. In addition there was, in the ninth century, a new wave of invader settlers, the Norse. Their reputation as warriors is assured, but it is their contribution to trade that concerns us here. Effectively, the Northern and Western Isles of Scotland became the stepping-stones for traffic between Scandinavia and the Viking towns of Ireland – Dublin, Cork, Limerick, Waterford and Wexford. The wealth generated by that trade is well attested by sites such as the Brough of Birsay in Orkney. On the Scottish mainland place-name evidence indicates that there was extensive Norse settlement of Caithness and Sutherland, with numerous small ports such as that at Freswick Links in Caithness. We know of no major ports comparable to those just noted in Ireland. However, in 870 Vikings did manage to wrest Dumbarton from the kingdom of Strathclyde and this site is likely to have provided the Norse with their own trading base in Scotland (Duncan 1975, 90). Unfortunately, we read little of the practicalities of any such trade for the meagre annals of these years are mainly a record of raids and battles. Nevertheless, it is clear that alliances were made between the Vikings and the established kingdoms of Scotland. In 937 Dublin Vikings, Scotti and Britons fought side by side at the battle of Brunanburh in an attempt to prevent Athelstan's seizure of Northumbria (Jones 1973, 237). As in England and Ireland, it would be wrong to see the Norse involvement in Scotland as altogether destructive; there were undoubtedly political and trade contacts.

The other main feature of these centuries was the amalgamation of the Scottic kingdom of Dalriada and the Pictish kingdom of Fortriu. Although there had been occasional joint rulers of the two kingdoms the first to establish a dynasty was Kenneth son of Alpin, king of Dalriada, in 842. By the end of the ninth century these two kingdoms became jointly referred to in the annals as 'Albania' (Anderson 1973, 194–8). It was this kingdom which came gradually to dominate and then, in the early eleventh century, absorb the other kingdoms in Scotland. One result of the creation of this larger kingdom was the further distancing of the king from personal control of even his most profitable lands and greatest strongholds. To supervise this enlarged kingdom Kenneth son of Alpin and his successors must have spent ever more time on the move. Even then they would have had to rely heavily upon officials who, in the king's absence, would maintain order and ensure that the wealth of the land was collected, processed, stored and marketed. The grouping of estates into larger units that this necessitated would not have been new. Even within the earlier Pictish, Scottish, British and Anglian kingdoms royal control would have depended upon the appointment, or more probably recognition and use, of local clan leaders as royal officials. Direct evidence of such organisation in these early kingdoms is lacking, however Professor Barrow has noted that the names of multiple estates north of the Forth, known from eleventh and twelfth century evidence, often incorporate the place-name element *Aber-*. Moreover, the names of many of the townships on these estates include the element *Pit-*. The elements *Aber-* and *Pit-* are both P-Celtic in origin, so that place-names involving them are likely to originate before the ninth century when P-Celtic began to be superseded by Gaelic as the dominant language (Barrow 1973, 58).

It is not until the eleventh and twelfth centuries that there is substantial documentary evidence to indicate how the wealth of these lands was organised and supervised. The terminology employed in many of these documents is predominantly that of the Anglo-Saxon thane, thanage and shire. Such terms are likely to have been original only in the Anglian districts of south-east Scotland, as for example in Berwickshire and Coldinghamshire both of which were established by the time of King Edgar's grant of 1095 (Lawrie 1905, 12–13 no.15). It is difficult to date the introduction north of the Forth of these terms. It may in part have been the result of Malcolm III and his Queen Margaret's encouragement of Anglo-Saxon institutions, while the chronicler Fordun attributed this form of land tenure to Malcolm II (Skene 1871, I, 186). It is not, however, until David I's reign that there are surviving references to Falkland and Kellie in Fife, the first known thanages north of the Forth. It may be that thane and thanage were terms first widely used if not introduced north of the Forth in David I's reign. In all, some seventy thanages are known before the term was itself replaced in the years following the Wars of Independence by the knight's fee (Skene 1890, 251–9; Muir 1975, 27–8, 126).

The original terminology for the various land units and their officers north of the Forth has therefore been largely obscured by the new vocabulary of David I's scribes and officials, many of whom may have been 'Norman' immigrants. There are only occasional references to earlier titles and lands. In the *Annals of Ulster* for the year 918 it is recorded that 'neither king nor mormaer of them [the Scottish] was killed'. Then in the *Annals of Tigernach* for the year 976 there is mention of 'three mormaers of Scotland [Alban]'. Among the first appearances of the title mormaer in a purely Scottish text are the Gaelic entries in *The Book of Deer*. The earliest of these is difficult to date, but later entries are seen as eleventh and twelfth century references to earlier property gifts. It is apparent from these and other references that a mormaer was amongst the most important men in the kingdom. The title is best translated as 'great steward', and it is clear from later association of the title with specific regions of Scotland that it was synonymous with Anglo-Saxon earl. It is probable that the mormaer was the successor of earlier regional rulers. In the case of mormaer Finnlach of Moray the royal title was slow to lapse and in three *Annals of Ulster* for 1020 he was described at his death as '*ri Alban*'. It is within the Celtic and perhaps Pictish structure of a mormaer's ancient kingdom that the office of toisech, also referred to in the Gaelic entries to *The Book of Deer*, should be seen. Toisech is readily translatable as 'leader' but it is twice used more specifically in *The Book of Deer* as toisech *clainna* meaning 'clan' or 'kin-leader'. The more usual meaning of toisech in *Deer* is as a landed official perhaps equivalent to the Anglo-Saxon thane (Jackson 1972, 102–12). During the later Middle Ages the office of Toisech survived in the Highlands in the debased form of *toschachdoracht* and *toschachdor*, 'bailies' and 'coroners'. The land unit supervised by a toisech would seem to have been equatable with that of the Anglo-Saxon shire or thanage although they would seem to have been slightly smaller that the shires of south-east Scotland. These thanages of Celtic and Pictish Scotland may have been derived from the ancient *tuath* or clan territory of Late Iron Age society (Skene 1890, 279–82).

Very little is known about the organisation and control of estates in the area of the old British kingdoms of south-west Scotland. It may be that the

Brythonic title mair or maer was used in this area. The mair has been seen as an office below that of mormaer best equated with the Anglo-Saxon thane. The office of mair frequently appears in late medieval and post-medieval Scottish texts as that of a junior legal and fiscal administrator. As with the office of toisech this may be a debasement of the original post, for there is a charter of Malcolm IV instructing his sheriffs and mairs in the diocese of Glasgow to ensure that the bishop and church of Glasgow received their due from the king's pleas and cains (Barrow 1960, 262 no.242). The post of mair is also recognisable outwith south-west Scotland. In Fife the medieval sheriffdom was divided into four quarters each having a mair (Dickson 1928, LXIII–LXIV). The only potentially early shires known in the south-west of Scotland are the royal estates of Renfrew and Mearns. Nevertheless, comparable land units may have existed at Renfrew, Strathgryfe, Cunningham, North Kyle, Douglasdale and Annandale, which were granted as recognised districts to incoming 'Normans' (Barrow 1973, 36–7).

The existence of an essentially similar, and probably ancient shire or thanage system of land division and control over much of Scotland is also reflected in a common settlement and financial organisation. Of the various estate settlements or touns within a shire, one or two would have been especially significant. These were the sites of the thane's residence and the principal church of the shire. These two elements in the community may have been adjoining, as at Dunfermline and Culross, or sited in two quite separate touns, as at Kinghorn, where the main church was probably a mile further north of Kinghorn at Abden (Barrow 1973, 42–3). In origin the principal toun of a shire or thanage is likely to be at least as old as the office of thane and probably its ancient equivalents toisech and mair. The thane's toun was the legal and economic hub of the estates and its name was usually given to them as an administrative district. The origin of kirktouns is more problematic. Documentary evidence for local churches before the twelfth century is so scarce that it appears churches were regarded as normal appurtenances which were not specifically mentioned in land grants. The main sources for the identification of early kirktouns are therefore place-names and archaeology. The east coast and central belt touns with *eccles* as an element in their place-name have been suggested as the sites of potentially early kirktouns which may even be P-Celtic in origin (Barrow 1973, 60–3). By far the most common place-name element indicative of medieval kirktouns is the Gaelic *Cell* or *Cill*, resulting in the familiar Scottish *Kil-* and *Kyl-* names. Archaeological dating of church fabric and hogback funerary monuments has further added to the list of early churches, as with the round towers at Brechin in Angus and Abernethy in Perthshire and the rectangular towers at Dunning in Perthshire, Markinch in Fife and elsewhere. Such archaeological identifications rely on surviving stone monuments which can be only a fraction of the number of timber churches that existed. It may be that the larger number of churches known from twelfth and thirteenth century sources were not entirely new foundations but reconstructions in stone of existing timber churches. This would help to explain why, when the parish structure did emerge in the twelfth century, there was a close co-ordination between thanage or shire and parish (Skene 1890, 251–70; Cowan 1961, 47–54).

Thanetouns and kirktouns, in addition to their respective legal and religious functions, were also of considerable economic importance. They were the collection points for the ancient dues payable by the estates of a thanage or shire. The Gaelic entries in *The Book of Deer* make frequent reference to the king's, mormaer's and toisech's cuit, which was clearly their share of the land's produce and probably also included labour service. In these references the king or officer concerned either donated his cuit to the community at Deer or quenched, literally 'waived', the cuit which was owed to him from lands held by the community (Jackson 1972, 119–21). Later such payments were associated with the fue ferm (English 'fee farm') status of land holdings which was prevalent through most of Scotland.

The basic payments were commonly known as 'cain' and 'conveth', which are broadly equatable to south Scottish and Anglo-Saxon cornage and waiting. Originally these payments were rendered both as labour service and produce from the land, and only later were they in part replaced by money rents. One of the clearest indications of the commuting of payments in kind to payments in cash concerns the royal revenues from Moray. In 1172–74 a teind (= tenth) of the king's revenues from pleas and cain in cows, swine, wheat, malt, oats, cheese and butter was given over to the bishop of Moray. This grant was renewed in 1187–90 and again in 1199. The last confirmation differs from the others in that it includes the phrase, 'whether the rents be paid in money or in another way by some alteration' (Barrow 1971, 51, 212 no.139, 301–02 no.273, 400 no.421). Conveth was a specialised and probably separately rendered form of these payments which originated as the obligatory provision of hospitality. Conveth from the Kirktoun of Arbuthnot in Mearns was the subject of a legal dispute in 1206. Conveth was claimed by both the bishop of St Andrews and the local thane. Local memory attested that for some forty-seven years conveth had been rendered to the bishops of St Andrews. This practice was therefore enforced by the ecclesiastical court, so that conveth plus two cows and half the bladwis (corn) and mercets (perhaps payments by unfree tenants) from the Kirktoun were paid to the bishop. The thane retained cain of the Kirktoun along with ten cheeses from each house and certain labour services from the men of the toun (Spalding Club 1841–52, v, 209–13).

With better survival of documents, especially from the archives of religious houses, references to cain and conveth become commonplace during the twelfth and thirteenth centuries. As many of these documents from religious collections refer to grants of teinds from the cain and conveth of secular estates they include considerable details of the payments rendered to both Church and State. It is apparent from these documents that there was, by the twelfth century, a very extensive organisation and centralisation of Scotland's agricultural produce. By the time of David I's confirmation charter to Dunfermline Abbey in 1128 the Abbey already controlled many shire churches with their associated kirktouns. Among the Abbey's other sources of income by 1128 were these royal revenues: an eighth part of all pleas and suits along with a teind of all food renders from Fife and Fothris; a teind of the cain of Dunfermline; a teind of venison, hides, lard and tallow from all the beasts at Stirling fair and also between the Forth and Tay; one ship free of cain; seals from Kinghorn and wood and iron from the king's supplies (Lawrie 1905, 61 no.74). Similar grants survive for many of Scotland's major twelfth-century religious centres. In each case agricultural and wild produce, along with an increasing amount of silver coinage, was being channelled from well-established districts into specific religious touns.

The diversion of such wealth from the secular economy did not always go unchallenged, as the Arbuthnot case shows, and royal confirmation of both old and new dues was often sought by the larger religious communities. The marketing of this produce also led to trade rivalries, and royal recognition of trading rights comparable to those of merchants in other market touns were also sought by religious houses. Equality was achieved by religious communities gaining for their markets the same status as royal market touns, or by their securing trading and manufacturing rights which allowed them favourable use of royal markets. The see of St Andrews is known to have had ancient control of numerous shire churches, kirktouns and teinds. Prior to 1144 the bishop of St Andrews received David I's recognition that the toun of St Andrews was an acceptable burgh (Lawrie 1905, 132 no.169). Glasgow's rights to a proportion of royal pleas and cain must pre-date an instruction from David I in 1139–41 to all his sheriffs and mairs in that diocese to ensure payment of the appropriate dues to the bishop and church of Glasgow (Barrow 1960, 262 no.242). The toun of Glasgow was recognised as a burgh in 1175–78 (Barrow 1971, 245 no.190). The Tironensians of Selkirk gained considerable privileges from Earl David, which as king he confirmed in 1120 (Lawrie 1905, 26–8 no.35). In 1237 these monks gained burgh recognition for Kelso, their new toun of residence.

A more complicated example of a well-endowed religious centre gaining burgh status is that of the Abbey lands at Dunfermline. Despite a very considerable income the presence of the adjacent king's toun, and from 1124–27 burgh, of Dunfermline prevented the monks from gaining independent burgh status for their kirktoun of Dunfermline until 1303 (Pryde 1965, 430). Instead, they had their port toun of Inveresk Major accepted in 1184 as a burgh. This later developed into Musselburgh (*Dunfermline Registrum* no.239). Dunfermline was unusual; in other cases where there was a direct clash of interests between kirktoun and kingstoun, it was usually the latter which came to dominate. At Old Aberdeen/Aberdeen, Scone/Perth or Cambuskenneth/Stirling the royal burghs were in effect used as the religious communities' trading centres. In many cases the religious houses were gifted tofts within the royal touns. One of the clearest examples of this close connection between income and trading rights is David I's confirmation charter to Holyrood Abbey. This is a complex document which appears to be a summary and confirmation of several earlier charters. Included were gifts of land in a number of royal touns which were to be, or had already become, known as burghs: Stirling, Edinburgh, Berwick and Renfrew. There were also gifts of money from ship cain at Perth and, if this was deficient, Stirling and Edinburgh as well. The Abbey received a teind of all the king's pleas and fines from Kintyre and Argyll as well as from the income of several royal mills. Amongst the agricultural produce they received were various payments of grain, a seventh part of all the grease and skins of animals slaughtered at Edinburgh, a teind of all the skins of sheep, goats and lambs slaughtered at the Castle and Linlithgow, and a teind of all the whales and sea-beasts due to the king between the Avon and Cocksburnpath. This then was the economic basis of the Abbey, the free working and marketing of which was ensured in the final part of the charter. There the abbey's merchants were granted equal status with the king's burgesses in Edinburgh and elsewhere (Lawrie 1905, 117 no.153).

This wealth, which formed the basis of the development of these religious touns, was only a small part of that which was being channelled into royal market touns. The wealth and industry of royal centres such as Dunfermline, Edinburgh, Linlithgow, Stirling and Perth is implicit in the gifts of various fractions of hides, tallow and other partially processed produce from animals slaughtered in these places. Similarly, gifts of grain and malt made from royal touns and toun mills should be seen in the light of the industrial investment and organisation needed to construct and run mills, malt houses and granaries (Lawrie 1905, 61 no.74, 117 no.153; Barrow 1960, 154 no.35, 164 no.57).

The importance of royal market touns is further illustrated by the presence in them of foreign merchants such as Berowald the Fleming, who in 1160 held a toft in Elgin and land in the surrounding district for the service of one knight in Elgin Castle (Barrow 1960, 219 no.175). It may also have been foreign merchants who established a trading community amongst the burgesses of Aberdeen, the Moray Firth and north of the Mounth. William I confirmed to these burgesses, who enjoyed his full protection, their free '*hanse*' or guild as in the time of David I (Barrow 1971, 223 no.153). The nature of this *hanse* has been much debated and is generally believed to be either a trade guild or, from similar usages in the Low Countries, a trade tariff (Duncan 1975, 476–7). Whatever its exact meaning, this confirmation was specific to a number of royal burgesses acting in partnership; and other than the principal burgh of Aberdeen their burghs of residence were of secondary importance to their status as royal burgesses. For the major religious communities the need was to gain entry to this type of trade and industry, and to do so with royal protection. Thus the canons of Scone ensured royal permission for their own smith, skinner and tailor, and equal status with the burgesses of Perth (Barrow 1960, 263 no.243). Likewise, when the bishop of St Andrews gained burgh status for his toun of residence and main market, he also ensured that there was a leading royal burgess from Berwick, Mainard the Fleming, with the necessary foreign contacts and experience (Lawrie 1905, 132–3 no.169). As the king's own burgess, Mainard's activities would have been as protected as the times permitted, but he was also subject to the king's command which sent him to St Andrews. Similar royal control is demonstrated in the case of Aslach, a king's burgess in Newcastle, who was given to St Bartholomew's priory there (Barrow 1960, 152 no.32).

The introduction of privileged royal burgesses was a logical result of royal control of luxury goods and trades. Such goods as wine and cloth retained their significance as gifts to supporters, but were now also a source of taxation in either kind or cash. Royal protection and taxation of shipping appears amongst the earliest records of royal government in Scotland with Alexander I's grant of the cain of one ship to the church of Scone in 1124. The charter makes specific mention that merchants using the ship would be protected by the king (Lawrie 1905, 43 no.143). The port for this ship was almost certainly Perth, the highest tidal point on the Tay. Identification of a few other ports, Aberdeen, Stirling, Edinburgh (? Leith) and Inveresk is also possible from similar grants made during the first half of the twelfth century. By their appearance as named sources of trading income these were clearly important ports. They are, however, only known as such through their use to fund religious houses; and no doubt other coastal touns, not least Berwick, were also active ports. These touns were normally under royal control, and the limited transfer of port duties at Inveresk from the king to Dunfermline Abbey around 1130 emphasises this:

> . . . to the Abbot and monks serving God there all rights from all ships which touch at the port of Inveresk and anchor on their land, reserving my toll, if the merchants of the ships sell their goods there or if they buy other goods within my land to take with them. (Lawrie 1905, 71, 334 no.87)

It was, then, royal market touns which, through their greater protection and agricultural wealth, were most attractive to merchants and craftsmen. Prominent amongst these businessmen would have been a small number of foreign merchant burgesses who brought with them the terminology and traditions of the Continent. The succession of David I, who was already familiar with burghs and burgesses from management of his English lands, resulted in the adoption of such terms in Scotland much as with the more general use of terms such as thane, thanage and shire. The use of 'burgh' for important Scottish market towns does not seem immediately to have replaced the traditional toun or villa terminology. The majority of early usages were in the form of grants of tofts and teinds from the king's 'burgh of X', as with David I's grant to the church of Dunfermline of houses in his burghs of Dunfermline, Stirling, Edinburgh and Perth (Lawrie 1905, 53 no.62). Occasionally towns such as Haddington were referred to during David's reign as both burghs and towns (Lawrie 1905, 101, 103, 164, 183, 208 nos.134, 135, 203, 227, 260). Even the burgh of Perth was referred to as a 'toun' in royal charters as late as 1161 (Barrow 1960, 223 no.182). In the case of St Andrews, Bishop Robert, after David I's permission, referred to the town as both burgh and toun in the same charter (Lawrie 1905, 132–3 no.169).

In contrast to the sometimes vague distinction between toun and burgh, at least in these early years, royal burgesses were from their first appearance carefully defined in right and function. The title 'merchant' appears in Alexander I's charter to the church of Scone. Here specific reference to foreign traders – '*mercatores extra regionem*' – indicates by inference, perhaps, the existence of Scottish merchants (Lawrie 1905, 43 no.48). In David I's reign the few references that are made to merchants (for instance in the *Laws of the Four Burghs*) concern foreign traders, while royal merchants were referred to as burgesses (Innes 1868, 6–7 nos.8, 9). The spurious charter of David I to Sallork (Montrose) includes the phrase 'merchants and burgesses within the area of Sallork' (Barrow 1960, 143–4 no.19). If, as Barrow has suggested, this charter has some basis in fact, then it would seem that both foreign and royal merchants were active around Montrose, and indeed that these formed the basis of a burgh community on this site. The careful definition of burgess rather than burgh status also appears in the *Laws of the Four Burghs*. Amongst the first twenty-two of these laws, which may represent that part of the collection of 119 laws which can actually be attributed to David I, the burgh appears as a physical entity only five times (nos.6, 7, 9, 10, 16). In all of these cases the concern was with the area covered by the special jurisdiction of these laws and also, in two cases (nos.9 and 16), the sale of goods. The other seventeen of these early laws were concerned not with the burgh's physical or intellectual status but with the rights and duties of burgesses. The first and second of the laws stipulate that an individual burgess had to hold a plot of land from the king, to whom he paid rent and swore fealty. The earliest known example of communal renting or fue farming of a burgh was not until 1329, when Edinburgh was allowed to pay a fixed *reddendo* to Robert Bruce.

The majority of these early laws were concerned with regulating transactions between king's burgesses and either upland men or foreign merchants. A small but significant number of manufacturing privileges were also confirmed to burgesses who, for instance, held a monopoly over the weaving, dyeing and shearing of cloth as a result of the twentieth Law of the collection. Some indication of the physical extent of such monopolies is gained from later references to David I's definition of the districts controlled by burgesses. The spurious charter to Sallork has already been mentioned as a possible example of a statement of regional monopoly, and the establishment of a similar monopoly is also attributed to David I in William I's charter to his burgesses of Rutherglen. That such references were not more common is likely to be a reflection of the traditional control of such market touns over the agricultural produce from specific shires and thanages.

David I's image as the founding figure of Scottish urban settlement has developed from his energetic introduction of new terminology and supporters. His reign was one of considerable organisation and standardisation. However, many of his activities were the result and continuation of economic and social developments the course of which can be traced back over many centuries. Earlier rulers had maintained their political authority through their control of marketable agricultural produce and hence luxury goods. There had therefore long been a royal interest in supervising the work of craftsmen and merchants. David I, in his turn, continued to keep control of much of Scottish foreign trade and, as ever, the king rewarded his retainers and supporters with gifts of cloth, wine and food. David more carefully defined existing regional organisation and monopolies, and in so doing confirmed his control over merchants and craftsmen. His adoption of the terminology of his age, both burgess/burgh and thane/thanage, may indicate considerable administrative improvements, but they do not necessarily imply radical social and economic change. Nevertheless, the alchemy of turning agricultural surplus into luxury goods is as crucial an aspect of urban growth as it is of political power. Kings, along with powerful churchmen and nobles, had under their control a considerable proportion of the produce from their lands. With limited processing this might feed and clothe them and their retainers, but further working would be sold for the desired trappings of power: the fine cloths, jewellery and wines that distinguished a lord from his servants. Both processes, the preparation and preservation of agricultural produce as well as its exchange for foreign goods and raw materials, were most suitably carried out in the trading workshops that were the early towns. Add to these economic considerations the administration necessary to ensure that a lord's dues were paid, then there exist most of the elements associated with urban society. More importantly there exists the mechanism whereby towns and states prosper. Once trade and manufacture had begun, further surplus produce would have been sought, leading to an ever wider economic hinterland. At the same time the landed controllers of these markets would have attempted to bring new lands and resources under their political sway. Both effects tend therefore to the creation of larger states centred economically on towns and politically on local and ultimately national rulers. Eventually, with the amalgamation of kingdoms, it became the king not the craftsman who became peripatetic. As a result of absentee kings, some form of urban government had to be organised. It is as a result of this stage of economic and social development that towns were first legally defined. Initially in Scotland the concern was to establish control over the burgess tenants of these burghs, and only in William I's reign did the burghs take on a separate legal identity. The granting of urban law codes and charters was, however, only a step in this process of developing urban government.

Acknowledgements

I would like to thank the editors of the volume for their many constructive criticisms and corrections to my paper. My thanks go also to Bill Lindsay, Liz Slater and Eric Talbot who read through my earlier drafts.

Territories and leadership:
frameworks for the study of emergent polities in
early Anglo-Saxon southern England

The opinion that archaeological and historical data of the post-Roman centuries have rarely been succesfully integrated is frequently expressed, yet
there has been far less discussion of why this should be. One solution put
forward is that 'the two disciplines should use their own techniques on their
own material and only then see what measure of agreement there is' (Sawyer
1983b, 47). What is not suggested is the techniques in each discipline that are
appropriate, and there is always a colourful spectrum from which to choose. I
wish to propose reasons why this goal of integration has rarely been achieved,
and to examine those reasons using the very pertinent case of the development
of the southern English kingdoms; pertinent, because that is one of the
principal themes of the historical sources.

It could be asked in what form the archaeological data should be presented
for integration. Often it is the rapidly changing interpretations of the archaeological data, and not the data itself, whatever the extent to which it has been
manipulated, that are offered for integration. At the same time the questions
asked of the respective data sets, however limited, are very rarely compatible;
if research aims were the same for each discipline and there was a conscious
effort made to analyse the available data to those ends, there would be a greater
chance of integration. But in some multi-disciplinary studies of the early
Anglo-Saxon period the level of attempted integration rarely goes further than
the direct linkage of historical events to archaeological features, with any
interpretation confined to chronology and identification, requiring great
imaginative leaps between the two sources of data. Much of this work is
carried out in a vacuum with little or no debate about the fundamental issues
pertaining to the societies in question, that is, concepts concerning the development of human societies. On the other hand, there are attempts being made to
generalise from all the available sources with a view to understanding human
processes. Also taking place is the detailed manipulation of data, aimed at
understanding the structure of such societies.

Much of the most recent work on early medieval documentary sources has
been praised for the increased effort being made 'to make all the unwritten and
. . . unconscious assumptions and pre-suppositions more explicit and precise'
(Stone 1977). At the same time there is a trend towards generalising about
societies from the documents, to the extent that at times it may be felt that
greater reliance is placed upon the generalisation than the details which allow
it. This approach finds much sympathy with those archaeologists who are
unhappy with early medieval archaeology and seek a similar solution, which

may hold a greater possibility of the two disciplines working together. This will remain difficult for as long as scholars continue to use the chronologically disconnected fragments to write a continuous narrative history.

The archaeological data require controlled manipulation into a form capable of analysis and, if necessary, interpretation. The aim of much research on the period has been to make historical statements about the progress of early Anglo-Saxon migration and settlement based on the archaeology. This type of research can be traced back to 1913 when E. T. Leeds published *Archaeology of the English Settlements*. Too often the questions being asked of the archaeological data are the same as those asked directly of the historical, despite their being generated by entirely different processes. What is required are frameworks to which the archaeological data can be related; the data cannot be studied in a vacuum, or through an individual's 'impression' of the period. One such framework is the political and social organisation of post-Roman society. The documents may give us the names of kingdoms and kings, even dates, but this information is also in a vacuum without additional information, such as the spatial controls. If the framework of the development of political and social groups in early Medieval England was better understood, more imaginative questions could be asked of the archaeological data. More specifically, if the leaders and territories of the sixth and seventh centuries could be isolated using the archaeological data, placing the patterns in a long-run time series, a direct comparison could be made with generalisations derived from the historical sources. It is doubtful, however, whether it would also be possible to pursue the 'Redwald School of thought' and relate such patterns to the specifics of political history (Bruce-Mitford 1975a, 683–717; Chadwick 1940), as that requires a degree of confidence in the historical sources which is rapidly being eroded and, again, is expecting the archaeology to 'speak' the details of political history to a level of accuracy which is not yet possible.

Models for the nature of the development of the early Anglo-Saxon kingdoms which explore the various factors which may have controlled the change from a large number of small political units to fewer, larger examples have been examined (Arnold 1980, 1982a, 1984; Hodges 1978, 1982). These are general theories, but at a level of generalisation which also appears to be acceptable to a number of early medieval historians. A critical approach to the sources has led to scepticism about the accuracy of details, but it is now more common to find generalisations about the processes involved. A general model for the earliest phase of political developments has been put forward by Dumville: 'there may have been a general lack of tribal homogeneity, each major group comprising the leader and his immediate relatives with a motley rag-bag of racially mixed followers' (1977a, 78 n39), which may serve as a model for the archaeology also. Wallace-Hadrill (1971, 15–16) thought it necessary to distinguish between the levels of leadership, *dux* and *rex*, although he was not proposing an evolutionary model; rather a pattern which Hodges describes as 'cyclical' leadership (1982, 27). Sawyer uses a similar model in suggesting that some or all of the kingdoms of the Heptarchy had been 'created by the fusion of smaller kingdoms which preserved traces of their former independent status in still being described as kingdoms or sub-kingdoms under the rule of *reges, reguli* or *subreguli*' (1978, 21). Much of the confusion in the historical sources over the earliest leaders (see Dumville 1977a, 101) may have arisen, as Sawyer suggests, because a later kingdom originated by the amalgamation of smaller groups each with their own leader. While earlier historians have been more concerned with the nature of the offices, others have thought in general terms about the concentration of power. Anderson, for instance, has suggested that following the migrations, state formation was 'ineluctable', 'and with it coercive central authority over the free warrior community' (1974, 115). Local chiefs and lords strengthened their personal power and 'by the time of the seventh century, a legally defined and hereditary aristocracy was consolidated in Anglo-Saxon England' (1974, 124). Similar distinctions, evolving levels of leadership, are proposed by Nelson; the absence of any barbarian inauguration ritual exclusive to kingship suggests that 'the *rex* was a household-lord writ large, whose succession to his inheritance was thus aptly signified when he took his place on the high seat in the paternal hall or beat the bounds of his paternal property' (1976, 102). Nelson argued that 'Christian clergy were responsible for the formulation of a clearly-defined ideology of kingship as office, so they created . . . rituals to inaugurate the officers' (1976, 103). This is viewed, in parenthesis, as the outcome of an evolutionary process, for some of the ingredients of such inauguration ceremonies were 'ready to hand'.

All this leaves this writer in no doubt that there is a desire for constructive generalisation, to varying degrees, about the process of kingdom formation, and justifies the claim that archaeologists and historians are beginning to produce generalisations which may usefully be compared. The writers assume or state that human groups have a desire for leadership and that in the fifth and sixth centuries such groups had a smaller membership and territory than those larger and more easily defined units of the seventh century and later. That process of amalgamation continued, by various means, resulting in a unified English state in the ninth century. The aim here is to examine the development of leadership and political territories in the sixth and seventh centuries as proposed in the general model, against the archaeological data. These are the principal areas in which the archaeological and historical data could be integrated, but careful consideration must be given to the manner in which this is achieved.

Leaders are named in the early medieval documentary sources although the nature of the leadership is rarely defined; the labels used in such sources do not necessarily imply a particular form of leadership at the given time. Leaders are generally only observed in the archaeological data by making a number of assumptions. These are implicit in expressions like 'royal palace', 'great wealth' or 'high status'. Given the absence of stated views to the contrary, it could be said that there is a consensus amongst early medieval archaeologists that richer graves are the burials of the more important (presumably in terms of decision-making) members of society, although fewer are prepared to extend this assumption about the relationship between power and possessions to include all graves (Alcock 1981c, 175–7; Crowfoot and Hawkes 1967, 65–6; Dickinson 1974, 35; Evison 1963, 61; Hills 1980, 92; Wilson 1976, 3). There is also the benefit of support from the documentary sources (Cramp 1957). Thus the correlation is not merely an assumption, nor is it dependent on modern analogy. It is, however, a very limited correlation as it tells us nothing about the means of acquiring power or wealth, nor anything of what that wealth actually symbolised to contemporaries. The suggestion that there is no such correlation, and that the various combinations of grave-goods represent the social identity of the deceased (Richards 1984) is a narrow one, for there is no insurmountable reason why social identity cannot be symbolised in particular combinations of artefacts whose value is a reflection of status in society. Inadequate as they may be, there is no obvious reason for rejecting such theories yet, within this chronological context, whatever the problems they may pose to students of other periods.

A number of attempts have been made to bring greater precision to the question of wealth, status and political development (Alcock 1981c; Arnold 1980, 1982a; Shephard 1979). Such research has indicated the manner in which sixth and seventh-century society was hierarchically organised. Within regions in which pagan Anglo-Saxon period cemeteries are found, the grave-goods suggest that the majority of the population was relatively poor, and the greater the various sub-sections' wealth, the smaller their membership. In general terms sixth-century society was organised in fewer hierarchical levels than in the seventh century. The majority of cemeteries of the early Anglo-Saxon period contain less than fifty individuals and, making allowance for time and life expectancy, represent the cemeteries belonging to individual farmsteads. Kinship and lineages may be more powerful here than later. It is generally in larger cemeteries that wealthier graves are found, although even there the size of the population at any one time rarely represents more than five to ten families. This must be taken into account when considering the scale of the early polities. Given the range of wealth deposited in graves it might be assumed that the families were not all farmworkers. Thus leaders in the sixth century, represented by graves in which there is a relatively large quantity of grave-goods including exotica imported from the Continent and non-utilitarian items, may be individuals who were more successful than the average on their own achieved efforts. They were local leaders who offered services to the community (decision-making, warfare) as well as providing the products of craftsmen at their own direct expense. Any attempts to define the relationship between the grades of society at this time would merely be an expression of personal prejudice, or would necessitate the use of later sources.

During the seventh century such wealth was extended, and its owners increasingly distanced themselves from the rest of society as their power and territorial control increased. Polities evolved by relative success in economic activities or by the forceful incorporation of territory; success by the former method encouraged the attentions of other polities in enlarging their territories by the latter.

Broadly speaking, on the basis of the current limits of accuracy in dating, the richly accompanied graves of the period belong to three chronological phases – the mid and second half of the sixth century, the later sixth and early seventh centuries and the later seventh century (corresponding to groups a, b, c in the tables below). Defining the relative wealth of these graves in any more detail than 'rich' or 'very rich' poses problems, and so far attempts at objective assessment have had to rely on techniques of analysis based on quantity rather than quality. Subjective though it may be, it is generally true to say that the quality of the grave-goods increases with the quantity.

Male, rich graves of the sixth century cannot yet be dated as accurately as female because there are fewer datable items. It would be dangerous to assume that both groups represent the same phase of social and political development. The male, rich graves (table 1a) are characterised by an extensive array of artefacts, always including weapons and some form of container. There is nothing in these graves that is obviously non-utilitarian, but the frequency of the association marks the graves off from the remainder of the population. The sixth century women's rich graves (table 2a) form an equally clear group in most areas, although there is greater variation than with the male examples. They are characterised by richly decorated dress ornaments, as common to this group as weapons are to the men, in most cases by a key and a coin, and in a few cases by perforated spoons and crystal balls. A non-utilitarian aspect may be seen in some of these items, noting that orbs surmounted by a cross were used as royal symbols on the Continent in the sixth century. Minimally a key, like the males' containers, is a tool; but the frequency of the association may imply much more, for instance the privileges of privacy and the protection of self and property. Poorer graves which nevertheless have some of the range of items found in the richer examples, for instance Winterbourne Gunner, Wilts. grave 7 (Musty and Stratton 1964, 91–3) and Alfriston, Sussex grave 62 (Griffith and Salzmann 1914, 44–5) may represent emulation of the elite in other richer areas. Alternatively, they may represent scales of leadership on an hierarchical basis within or between areas. Graves of this type are not confined to southern England; eastern England has its own variant, for instance Holywell Row, Suffolk graves 11 and 29 (Lethbridge 1931, 4–9, 18) and Spong Hill, Norfolk graves 24 and 40 (Hills, Penn and Rickett 1984, 72–3, 91–4), and in the midlands Empingham 11, Rutland grave 73 (Clough, Dornier and Rutland 1975, 13) and North Luffenham, Rutland. No analysis of the sociopolitical context of these or later graves in midland and eastern England has yet been carried out.

In the later sixth and early seventh centuries the male graves reveal more variety than the earlier examples (table 1b) and the group is dominated by the rich three, Taplow, Broomfield and Sutton Hoo mound 1, which share so many characteristics of context, arrangement and grave-goods. The major

Table 1. Anglo-Saxon male, rich graves.

	weapons						vessels											Reference
	sword, etc.	spear	shield	buckle	axe	arrow	wooden	metal	ceramic	glass	horn	knife	tweezers	shears	comb	musical inst.	game	
a.																		
Petersfinger, 21	×	×	×	×	×		×					×	×					(Leeds and Short 1953, 16-18)
Blacknall Field, 47	×	×	×	×			×					×	×					(pers. comm. F. K. Annable)
Sarre, 39	×	×	×		×		×	×				×						(Brent 1866, 165-6)
Chessell Down, 26	×	×	×	×		×	×											(Arnold 1982b, 23-4)
Sarre, 54	×		×	×			×					×		×				(Brent 1866, 167)
Alfriston, 86	×	×					×		×			×						(Griffith 1915, 204)
Mucking, 600	×	×	×				×					×						(Jones and Jones 1975, 184)
b.																		
Cuddesdon	×	×	×	×														(Dickinson 1974)
Coombe Bissett	×	×	×	×				×		×								(Cunnington 1896, 58-9)
Alton, 16	×	×	×	×			×	×		×		×						(Evison 1963, 43)
Taplow	×	×	×	×			×	×		×		×				×	×	(Stevens 1884)
Broomfield	×	×					×	×		×	×	×						(Read 1894)
Oliver's Battery	×							×	×			×						(Andrew 1934)
Coombe								×		×								(Davidson and Webster 1967)
c.																		
Rodmead	×	×	×	×			×	×				×						(Cunnington 1896, 77)
Ford	×	×	×	×				×										(Musty 1969)
Galey Hills		×	×	×				×				×			×			(Barfoot and Williams 1976)
Lowbury	×	×	×	×				×				×		×	×			(Atkinson 1916, 15-23)

difference between these graves and the earlier examples is that they are under mounds. What remains less clear is whether such graves represent deposition in a formal burial area reserved for the exclusive use of the elite with, perhaps, close associates. Degrees of emulation may also be observable here, as a number of such graves contain only the more available items associated with

Table 2. Early Anglo-Saxon female, rich graves.

Item	Sarre, 4 (Brent 1863, 310-20)	Chessell Down, 45 (Arnold 1982b, 26-8)	Bifrons, 42 (Godfrey-Faussett 1876, 314-15)	Bifrons, 21 (ibid., 306-7)	Bifrons, 29 (ibid., 309-10)	Bifrons, 41 (ibid., 313-14)	Alfriston, 62 (Griffith and Salzmann 1914, 44-5)	Alfriston, 43 (ibid., 39-41)	Lyminge, 44 (Warhurst 1955, 28-32)	Petersfinger, 25 (Leeds ans Shortt 1953, 21-2)	Abingdon, 61 (Leeds and Harden 1936, 43)	Worthy Park, 10 (pers. comm. S. C. Hawkes)	Long Wittenham I, 71 (Akerman 1860, 343)	Gilton, 81 (Smith 1856, 26)	Kingston, 299 (ibid., 91-3)	Swallowcliffe (Vatcher and Vatcher 1968)	Sarre (Brent 1860, 533-5)	Winchester, 23 (Biddle 1975, 303-5)	Roundway Down II (Akerman 1855, 1-2)
	a.													**b.**				**c.**	
coin	×	×			×	×		×		×						×	×	×	
glass vessel	×					×		×									×		
ceramic vessel																		×	
metal/wooden vessel				×								×			×	×	×	×	
comb	×											×				×	×		
chatelaine												×	×						
weaving batten	×	×															×		
key	×	×	×	×	×	×			×		×	×				×			
knife	×	×	×	×	×	×	×			×	×	×	×	×	×			×	
crystal ball	×	×	×					×											
spoon	×	×	×			×		×								×			
pin	×				×						×					×		×	
ring	×	×	×	×	×	×	×	×		×	×	×	×	×	×			×	
gold thread	×	×		×	×	×		×											
buckle	×	×	×		×	×		×		×	×	×			×	×			
necklace	×	×	×	×	×	×	×	×	×	×	×	×	×	×	×	×		×	×
brooch	×	×	×	×	×	×	×	×	×	×			×	×	×	×	×	×	×

the elite; or the items are much cruder pieces, for instance at Lowbury, Berks. (Atkinson 1916). This may represent the extension of the hierarchy, or the necessary extension of the range of symbols of leadership by the uppermost echelons in certain areas because of emulation. Again, therefore, there is the possibility of grades of leadership, but the unknown circumstances of death should not be overlooked, and the interesting but problematic possibility that items may be deliberately excluded from burial. Here also there is a consistency in weapons and containers amongst the males, but rarely anything potentially symbolising leadership except the particular combination itself. Sutton Hoo mound 1 and the female Swallowcliffe, Wilts. are the notable exceptions in having a number of non-utilitarian items in addition to their great wealth. The women's rich graves of this phase (table 2b) are not only difficult to find, they also lack consistency. Graves of this general type also occur elsewhere in England, and their associated grave-goods have been examined in a similar fashion (Vierck 1972).

The rarity of rich graves, both male and female, as the seventh century proceeds (tables 1c, 2c) has been viewed as a reflection of the increasing frequency of christian burial for the elite, as reported by Bede at Canterbury (*HE* 1, 33) and which archaeology is beginning to demonstrate as the pace of church archaeology increases. A recent case is that at St Paul-in-the-Bail, Lincoln (Gilmour 1979). The suggestion that conclusions on the 'social plane' cannot be drawn from the seventh-century rich burials 'since contemporary christian men of equal standing, no doubt lie unrecognisably in findless graves of west/east orientation' (Evison 1963, 61) probably overstates the strength of Christianity in the seventh century and is unconvincing. Here again there may be a symbolic factor in the combination of artefacts, but amongst the latest of the rich pagan graves there are also some utilitarian objects which might, subjectively, seem out of place in the hands of such a person, and others which are more obviously non-utilitarian; in the former category could be placed weaving equipment and in the latter so-called 'regalia'.

The Sutton Hoo mound 1 items were labelled regalia very soon after their discovery and presumably the implications of insignia of office, and more precisely insignia used by royalty at coronations, were fully appreciated. The sixth and seventh centuries are pre-documentary so far as the details of inauguration rituals are concerned, and we may have to be content with probable identification of such symbols. It would help to have an understanding of the meaning behind the symbols of office, but as Nelson has shown, the sources dictate that our study focuses on the development of rites, especially anointing. A greater problem here is that the sources connected with inauguration rituals are concerned with the installation of leaders, whereas the archaeological data are concerned with their funerals. It is nevertheless interesting that heirlooms, relics and regalia are rarely found absent from installation ceremonies in anthropological studies (Fortes 1968) and the possession and use of such objects as vehicles for the continuity of office is common; after each generation the rites may be redefined, but for periods they may remain fixed. If the objects being buried in rich graves of the sixth and seventh centuries are complete sets of items symbolising leadership, it is very important to note that they were indeed being buried with the individual. The mound burials with few lavish items might, in this light, be seen as those in which the 'regalia' were passed on. The problem here is the question of completeness, which cannot be demonstrated in either case.

A potential area for integrating the historical and archaeological data exists in early medieval inauguration rituals, and especially regalia. Nelson points out that the date at which a fixed inauguration ritual was introduced is unknown, but a case can be made for elements of West Saxon usage earlier than AD 856 being preserved in later forms: 'the relatively early introduction of a fixed rite in England may be explained in terms of the precocious political and ecclesiastical centralisation already achieved by the eighth century (1980, 48). Nelson's research has brought to our attention 'the sceptres of the Saxons, Mercians and Northumbrians' included in a fourteenth-century coronation out of respect, it is argued, for earlier ritual tradition (Nelson 1975, 45, 1977, 56). The use of a helmet rather than a crown until *c*. AD 900 (1980, 45) and of weapons in general are common features (1975, 59). Bede describes how Edwin set up bronze drinking cups for the refreshment of travellers beside highways; his majesty was such that banners (*vexilla*) were carried before him in battle, in peacetime his progress was preceded by a standard-bearer, and when walking along roads a standard (*thuf*) was carried before him (*HE* 2, 16; Bruce-Mitford 1974, 7–17; Deansley 1943). An important distinction emerges between earlier and later Anglo-Saxon leadership: 'the significance, political and symbolic, of inauguration rituals arose largely from the fact that no early medieval king succeeded to his kingdom as a matter of course. . . . In no kingdom of the early medieval West was there quickly established a very restrictive norm of royal succession' (Nelson 1977, 51). Without forcing a connection too strongly for the reasons already given, we are again reminded that symbolic items were buried in some graves; this could be taken to suggest that the nature of leadership was changing rapidly and/or there was at times a lack of hereditary succession. The more worrying alternative is that we may more frequently be dealing with heirlooms at this level of society in funerary contexts than can ever be demonstrated, despite a number of writers' suspicions. It is only when there is a great quantity of diagnostic items that the objects which were already antique when buried can be isolated.

With such rich pagan graves we are not dealing with a long time-span, perhaps 150 years at the most, and if there was a continuous succession of leaders in any single area we may only be dealing with up to five generations. It is therefore interesting that Dumville suggested that in the genealogies 'only that extent (perhaps four or five generations) which is essential to the smooth running of the social structure will be remembered, while more distant ancestors . . . are not recalled in the context of exact genealogical relationships' (1977a, 87). Perhaps they only go back to a point at which those societies' forms of leadership existed or could be identified, prior to which the genealogy is a figment. It is of relevance for this purpose to know when the genealogies were recorded. Often they were Christian recordings of the seventh century; the same pivotal period as suggested by this assessment of the archaeological evidence. Of equal relevance to the sequence of rich graves is Dumville's observation that 'there comes a superior limit of immediate credibility and in each case this is somewhere in the second half of the sixth century', and more precisely c. AD 550–575. This is also fully in accord with the archaeological data, as it is then that the sequence of rich graves begins; and by the same set of assumptions it is the earliest stage at which leaders are represented in the early Anglo-Saxon archaeological record. Such leaders may have existed earlier, but at this time it was felt to be appropriate to represent a person's status in an observable (and durable) form at death. It is also suggested that pedigrees expressing political or dynastic links are presented in genealogical terms because that is what was involved, whether by blood or marriage (1977a, 80). While the very strong similarities between the grave-goods in some of these rich graves might tempt us to think in terms of a blood relationship, as with Chessell Down, Isle of Wight, grave 45 and Sarre, Kent, grave 4 (table 2), until the distinction can be made between the mobility of the objects and people, it is a subject which extends no further than pure speculation. It would be preferable to have family relationships demonstrated independently of the artefacts by physical anthropology.

A case can be made that early Anglo-Saxon archaeology provides evidence of a class of leaders represented by richer burials; the historical sources indicate the names of leaders and their territories. Given the changing configurations of the early kingdoms the names applied to regions in the sixth century need not refer to the same areas in the seventh. While a link can rarely if ever be made between the two data sets, there is one element in which they could at least be seen to overlap, that is with political boundaries.

In the introduction to the Ordnance Survey's map of *Britain in the Dark Ages* it was explained that 'the names of large regions and provinces have been written across the areas covered, but the precise boundaries have not been shown because they are rarely if ever known, and because they were constantly changing through the period' (1966, 33). There we have three important elements: the boundaries, the areas bounded, and time. There is no point in dwelling on how we know that boundaries 'were constantly changing' when they are 'rarely known'. In an attempt to give a geographical perspective to the evidence, Leeds made a distinction between the cultural divisions c. AD 550 and the political divisions at the end of the sixth century' (1913, fig.4), that is, 'the boundaries of the early kingdoms as accepted by historical writers (1913, 37). Later, Myres took the more cautious approach of only giving the names because he knew that the historical writers very rarely described boundaries (Collingwood and Myres 1936, map VI). The use of names alone has generally been the practice ever since (Alcock 1972, map 1; Wilson 1960, fig.2; Brown 1978, 13; Blair 1970, map 3), although boundaries have occasionally been drawn in recent years, either as dotted or solid lines (Laing and Laing 1979, map 2; Morris 1973, map 23). The one course of action is perhaps an acceptable level of generalisation, the other requires more justification. Whether actual boundaries are marked or not, both practices tend to fossilize two or three hundred years of political development in one image, at a time when they are thought to have been constantly changing. It is necessary to break this image down into smaller chronological units.

If the model for political development in the sixth and seventh centuries, as stated by archaeologists and historians, is to be tested we need both to see the political territories and know the manner in which they were changing through time. This may be achieved experimentally by reconstructing the frontiers using Theissen Polygons constructed around the rich graves, sub-divided by the phasing given above. Time is still being telescoped and a number of assumptions need to be made which may reduce the expectation that the resulting maps reflect the general pattern of political development and, in particular, demonstrate the merger of small groups into the larger ones. The data are very unlikely to be strictly contemporary and each phase represents up to thirty years' duration; given the necessity in pre- and proto-historic studies of considering material spanning hundreds of years as being contemporary, a lapse in methodology here by such a small time-range seems comparatively minor. The funerals of the members of the societies in question would not have occurred at the same time, although the periods over which the locations or graves may have been venerated would be more likely to overlap. The polygons are not so much constructed around graves as around states of affairs; the three identifiable phases represent periods of stability in an otherwise changing political world. Naturally some rich graves await discovery, but arguably they are more likely to be found in those areas which already possess them than in new areas. Some areas of England already do possess more than one such grave in the same time brackets, but how far apart they must be before a line can be drawn between them is arbitrary; solid lines have not been drawn between burials of the same phase less than 5 km apart. Centricity of burials may seem logical on the basis of veneration of the dead, residence patterns and security, yet it must be noted that we know little of the decison-making processes that governed the choice of site for burial of an individual. Reconstructing such territories also tells us nothing of the details of the organisation of the society within them, which are the principal concern. In dividing the rich graves from the remainder of the population and treating them as having similar social identities it is assumed from the outset that such graves represent a uniform social plane. The method assumes maximum political control of the landscape, and all the maps suffer from the 'boundary effect' caused by the edge of the study area.

The results of the experiment can be described briefly. During the mid to later sixth century (figure 1a) a number of regions of roughly equal size are created incorporating, to use modern terminology, Kent, Sussex with parts of Surrey, Hampshire excluding the southern coastal belt which forms a separate unit with the Isle of Wight, the upper Thames valley, as well as a series of smaller units in west Hampshire and Wiltshire. Many of the hypothetical frontiers correspond with natural features, particularly rivers. By the late sixth and early seventh centuries there has been a marked change (figure 1b). The Kent region has lost ground on its north-west frontier, but expanded

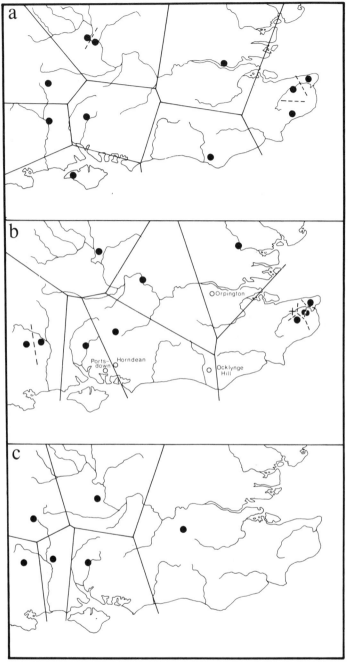

Figure 1. The distribution of early Anglo-Saxon rich graves in southern England in three phases (dots). Hypothetical political territories are suggested. Circles represent cemeteries mentioned in the text.

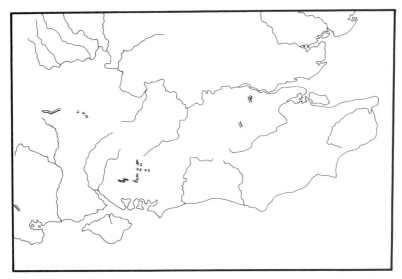

Figure 2. The location of post-Roman and undated linear earthworks in southern England.

westwards; Essex appears as a distinct zone, incorporating part of the area south of the Thames; Sussex remains as a separate unit extending further westwards with a new region to the north lying astride the Thames. The Hampshire zone now incorporates the Isle of Wight, while Wiltshire and the upper Thames valley remain divided into small units. Finally, in the later seventh century (figure 1c) Kent, Sussex and Surrey are now one with the region to the north; one region remains in the upper Thames valley looking northwards, leaving a large zone comprising Hampshire and the Isle of Wight and, again, the smaller regions in Wiltshire, extending further westwards.

In the second and third phases the territorial frontiers correspond less with natural features, and it is more likely that as the political map of southern England became more artificial, there would be a greater need felt to construct artificial boundaries, such as linear earthworks. Few such earthworks are closely dated, although some are demonstrably post-Roman. A number have been seen as reflecting early Anglo-Saxon political history, notably the eastern section of Wansdyke (Fox and Fox 1958), the east Hampshire complex (Coffin 1976), Bokerly Dyke (Rahtz 1961) and those on the borders of Surrey and Kent near Westerham (Clark 1960) and Crayford (Hogg 1941). It is the absence of close dating which tends to leave such testimonies of human territoriality floating amongst the details of political history, and it is of little value to correlate them speculatively either with historical events or with the hypothetical frontiers generated here, despite there being a number of apparent matches (figure 2). Far worse would be to use such correlations to date the earthworks (see for example, Wheeler 1934). The linear earthworks may, at least, be a reflection of the existence of territories requiring physical definition.

An area for further research may be those zones which appear to be frequently disputed, frontier zones lying between the core areas of regional groups. Studies of ornamental metalwork emphasise that many forms of artefact and their styles of decoration are regional. Evidence for the movement of such regionally distinct artefacts to other regions is rare. If the structure of society permitted the free exchange of metalwork and decorative styles between such regions a mixing of stylistic traits might be expected on frontier zones. However, cemeteries located close to such zones which appear to change frequently are notable for their indistinct, amorphous nature, and for the problems they have posed in being fitted to a particular regional assemblage. Contenders for this category may be Orpington, Kent (Tester 1968), Portsdown (Corney *et al.* 1967; Bradley and Lewis 1968) and Horndean, Hants (Knocker 1957), and Ocklynge Hill, Sussex (Welch 1983, 334–40) (figure 1). They seem to emphasise that the mechanisms for the distribution of diagnostic artefacts owe more to the social structure than to economic reasons for much of the period. Residents living and dying in frontier zones may have had no allegiance to either side, or may have been excluded from participation in the distribution system. The movement of frontiers in the volatile political state of early Anglo-Saxon England may also have changed the configurations of access to material possessions.

These maps are not the material for a history of the English kingdoms, just as a correlation with Bede and the *Anglo-Saxon Chronicle* would be of dubious value when they rarely mention boundaries. At a general level it could be claimed that the results support the original hypothesis; at the specific level of historical detail the maps are at least stimulating. It is interesting that it is the regions that are generated by this method for the sixth century (figure 1a) whose names are most commonly placed on maps of Dark Age Britain and which form the vocabulary of the early kingdoms; there are units in Kent, Sussex, the Isle of Wight with the Meon valley. Hampshire is divided from the Thames valley which is a feature, in general terms, of most studies of the origin of the West Saxon kingdom. The numerous small groups to the west remind one of multiple kingship within a larger unit (Biddle 1976). Kent can be divided into three very small regions reflecting the administrative regions postulated by Hawkes (1979).

At the level of more specific historical interpretation we may observe that the East Saxons are interpreted as having relieved Kent of the London area by the early seventh century (*HE* 2, 3), but eventually lost it to Mercian control before AD 700 (*HE* 3, 7). The political history of Sussex is not at all clear, but it is generally assumed that its independence was under threat by both Mercians and West Saxons. The giving of the Isle of Wight and the Meonware to the South Saxons by Mercia in the seventh century raises interesting strategic implications *vis-à-vis* the position of the West Saxons. In the late seventh century Kent was apparently very unsettled as it was disputed by the West Saxons and Mercia, the latter being the dominant force by the middle of the century.

At such a level there is perhaps no problem and it comes as something of a relief to find some agreement. But to attempt to go further would be to fall into the trap that has been so carefully laid by historians! 'Many texts that archaeologists cite with great confidence are the subjects of debate' (Sawyer 1983b, 46). It is, however, only when a very detailed level of integration is attempted that problems arise. Some of the changes observed in this analysis occurred before the earliest suggestion that they were taking place in the documentary sources. In part this is due to the inevitable imprecision of archaeological dating, 'missing' pieces of evidence and the various problems that can be found with the historical sources. But to say that would imply acceptance of a correlation between the two types of evidence at even the most general level. A typical example is that of Sussex and the Isle of Wight which are to be seen as disappearing as independent units on the basis of the archaeological analysis *c.* AD 600, and which have little or no seventh-century archaeology. Historically, they are described as being annexed in the second half of the seventh century in conflicting accounts in Bede and the *Anglo-Saxon Chronicle*.

One area which may, in part, bring together leadership and territories is the question of the burial of supposed symbols of leadership. Within the area of study the only graves with such items are female, of the sixth and early seventh centuries; one context in which a set of regalia is claimed as being associated with a male is Sutton Hoo mound 1. Special attention has been drawn to Edwin's 'standard' of AD 632 which has been compared with the Sutton Hoo iron stand (Bruce-Mitford 1978, 403–31), despite the problem of Bede suggesting that various types existed. While the Roman world has been raked through for similar paraphernalia, attention might be drawn to the 'six pronged instrument of iron, in shape much like an ordinary hay-fork' from Benty Grange, Derbys. (Bateman 1861, 31). Similarly we could point to the object from a grave within hall A4 at the royal 'palace' of Yeavering identified as a surveyor's *groma* but which could have been a standard (Hope-Taylor 1977), and the pronged, almost rune-like, symbol beside the diademed portrait on the obverse of the seventh-century WITMEN gold coinage and its copies (Sutherland 1948, 46–50, 88–94). This is a more convincing parallel than the crosses held by the figures on the reverse of the early *sceatta* coinage (Bruce-Mitford 1974, 11–17) which is out of step chronologically. A ceremonial significance has also been attached to the whetstone from Sutton Hoo, which has been described as 'an emblem of kingly office' (1974, 6), and which most commentators refer to as a sceptre, linked with examples from other cemeteries (Bruce-Mitford 1978, 311-93; Evison 1975; Reynolds 1980a). If it is assumed that symbols of office such as these always existed once this form of leadership had become formalised, their almost total absence from male graves might imply that they were passed on through the male line but not through the female. In terms of succession, whether hereditary or not, this is easy to understand when the effective, documented leaders of the sixth and seventh centuries were male. The absence of such items from the majority of the wealthier male graves might also indicate the increasing number of ranks in society, in which those sub-leaders were able to emulate the elite in many personal items, but not the symbolic ones. That all of an individual's personal possessions (if indeed that is what they are) were buried, can never be demonstrated. The other possibility, that such burials did *not* contain all such possessions, can at least be considered though hardly tested. If it is assumed that symbols of office were buried at a point of dislocation in a line of leaders, and given male succession, we may be impressed by their presence in female graves of the sixth century at least.

Whatever the merits of considering grave assemblages in this way, the one cemetery where this idea might be particularly germane is Sutton Hoo. It has been argued that despite mounds 2 and 4 having been looted they were not rich deposits in the first place (Arrhenius 1978, 194). Yet if the site is a royal cemetery why does mound 1 contain such a rich array of supposed regalia compared with the others? Does this represent a dislocation, permanent or temporary, in a royal line? Bruce-Mitford offers two reasons for the deposition of the sceptre: that it was not the sceptre of the East Anglian royal house and did not require to be handed on; and that its pagan assocations were unacceptable to a Christian kingdom (1978, 377).

If the assumptions concerning the identification of symbols of leaders are valid, it may be permissible to suggest that during the sixth century wealthy males were buried with a regular assemblage of items, none of them overtly non-utilitarian, whereas females were accompanied by the latter. During the seventh century there are fewer richly accompanied burials, but there is both a higher probability of males being accompanied by symbolic items and a greater incidence of the annexation of territory.

At this stage the thread becomes very frayed and the large number of unknown variables makes speculative reasoning of little value. It has been necessary to explore various levels of integration to identify that which is most suitable. The concern here has been with testing aspects of a model for the development of complex societies as a means of experimenting with levels of integration, and not with the generation of an all-embracing interpretation of the political development of pagan Anglo-Saxon England. If the methodology used is unsatisfactory then it will be necessary to design better tools or to reject the possibility of integration. At the start it was argued that if the archaeological data could be presented in a form that was at least comparable with the historical evidence, it should also be compatible; for that reason I have not pursued the questions, however interesting in themselves, of what shape of buckle Edwin would have worn, nor on which day of the week Wansdyke was built. Compatibility is difficult, if not impossible, actually to verify. But if the goals of the disciplines are the same there should be ample room for collaboration in those subject areas which are shared by both sources of data. Much archaeological research is now concerned with aspects of society about which the sources are silent. By this I do not mean the description and study of the archaeological data only to provide interesting details and dates, valuable as they are, to be blended with historical detail in an uncontrolled and untestable manner; rather I mean the manipulation of that data to indicate patterning which aids our understanding of the organisation and development of societies in the past. Early medieval archaeology can do more than locate 'things' and correlate them with historic kings and kingdoms existing only in name.

Style and sociopolitical organisation :
a preliminary study from early Anglo-Saxon England

The central issue in archaeology is the nature of the relationship between material culture and culture itself. Because material culture is structured according to a set of standards, variation in the archaeological record has meaning.

A concern with relating archaeological cultures and groups of people may be traced in the archaeological literature back into the last century (Hodder 1982b, 2–7). A reappraisal of normative approaches to the interpretation of artefact variability during the 1960s and 1970s led to the development of the 'social interaction' hypothesis of stylistic variability. According to this hypothesis, similarities in the material culture of different groups are a measure of their interaction. The material culture of groups which interact intensively, therefore, is more alike than that of groups which associate infrequently. Under this assumption, residence (Deetz 1965; Hill 1970; Longacre 1970), rates of trade (Engelbrecht 1974; Fry and Cox 1974) and population movements (Cohen 1977, 82; Washburn 1978, 105–6), for example, have been related to variability in ceramics.

In contrast, Wobst (1977) has argued for a functional rather than deterministic relationship between style and social interaction. Stylistic variability, according to this 'information exchange' hypothesis, summarises and transmits messages about an individual's social role, stimulating both the integration of that group's members and the recognition of distance from their behavioural norms. Personal and group identification and external differentiation may thus be economically marked by stylistic variation. As a corollary, Pollock (1983, 357) argues that stylistic messages will become more elaborate as an increase in sociopolitical complexity results in more social units between which information must be exchanged.

Although the 'social interaction' and 'information exchange' hypotheses have been criticised for the passive role in which they cast stylistic variability (Hodder 1982b, 9), an active role is implicit in arguments of adherents of the latter hypothesis, who propose that style helps to maintain and further differences between groups. Recent analyses of style in material culture have indicated that such differences have a strong affective as well as reflective quality (Hodder 1982a, 214, 216; 1982b, 214; 1982c, 10; Wiessner 1984, 194). As these ethnographic studies have demonstrated, stylistic variability is not necessarily an accurate indication of the amount of social interaction between individuals or groups. It is the character of that association, rather than its frequency, which determines the degree to which the participating parties are alike. Thus, not only does stylistic variation serve as a tool for the transfer of information, it also acts as a channel through which social relationships may be manipulated: 'in the process of presenting information about similarities and differences . . . [style] can reproduce, disrupt, alter, or create social relationships' (Wiessner 1984, 194).

Because of the contrastive character of stylistic variability, ethnographic studies have been directed to the identification of those conditions under which style plays an important role in distinguishing an individual or group of people from others. Wiessner turns to social psychology to argue that much of 'the formal variation in material culture which has been called style by archaeologists has a behavioral basis in a fundamental human cognitive process, that is, personal and social identification through comparison' (1984, 191).

The comparison between self and others 'can be made at very different levels of consciousness and intent, ranging from purposeful signaling to feelings transmitted by insinuation and can involve referents of varying degrees of specificity, from conscious messages of specific group affiliation to those that are employed subconsciously, supporting but not directly symbolizing social relations' (Wiessner 1985, 161). The intensity of this conceptualisation of personal or group identification and external differentiation changes with circumstances and events. One response an individual or group may exhibit to social or economic stress is the demonstration of personal identification or group cohesion on the one hand, and external differentiation on the other. Hodder's (1979) ethnographic study of tribal groups in the Baringo district of western Kenya indicates that the likelihood that material culture will distinguish between groups competing for scarce resources increases as access to those resources decreases. In densely populated border areas inhabited by groups which employ identical economic strategies to procure the same limited resources, differences in material culture will be more clearly marked than they are between neighbouring groups in less stressful environments. Conkey, discussing the tempo of stylistic diversification among early *Homo sapiens*, argues that the ability to distinguish between oneself and others assumes importance 'under conditions of increasing social complexity' (1978, 67).

This differentiation between self and others may be marked either vertically or horizontally. Not all stylistic variability refers to the same axis or level of differentiation. Different objects may be used to project messages to different audiences. Hodder (1982b) demonstrates that in Baringo stylistic variation referring to relationships within and between tribes involves different objects. Likewise, Wiessner (1983; 1984, 210, 227) documents that, among the Kalahari San, the boundaries of tribal or linguistic groups are maintained by stylistic differences in projectile points while beadwork designs on headbands are used to negotiate individual identities and relationships with kindred members and affinal kin irrespective of linguistic group membership.

Mortuary variability

Reference to mortuary data in the analysis of socio-cultural behaviour was made by nineteenth-century ethnographers (Bartel 1982, 32–7). However, modern studies of mortuary data are set within a conceptual framework elaborated by Binford and Saxe in the 1970s and developed subsequently by other archaeologists. Fundamental to this approach is the recognition of a relationship between aspects of the living society and the ways in which its dead are disposed of. An individual will be accorded burial treatment consistent, although not necessarily isomorphic, with his role in the living society. Variability between grave assemblages and mortuary treatment, then, will be related to the individual's vertical (e.g. rank) or horizontal (e.g. political group membership) position in a multidimensional society.

Variation exists among the kinds of signals that refer to vertical differentiation and to horizontal differentiation. Pollock argues that while vertical differentiation is represented by artefacts exhibiting distinct levels of energy/labour expenditure and sumptuary items, the variations that signal horizontal differentiation will be qualitative: 'distinctions . . . will be signaled through variations in attributes in the same (vertical) level. In the case of design, one can expect such variation to take the form of differences in design elements and/or in combinations of these elements' (1983, 358). Traditionally, emphasis has been directed toward identifying and interpreting the material correlates of behaviour characterising vertical differentiation. Less interest has been shown toward horizontal variability perhaps, as O'Shea (1981, 49–50) argues, because these distinctions are manifested through 'neutral' variables which are either rarely preserved or archaeologically ambiguous. However, recent archaeological studies of groups known historically to have been horizontally related (e.g. Engelbrecht 1974; O'Shea 1981, 1984) indicate that such analysis may expand our understanding of the conditions which affect the expression of stylistic variability.

The historical setting

Written sources provide a control on the attempt to relate archaeological patterning to sociopolitical organisation. While many details of the character of early Anglo-Saxon kingship remain elusive, there is little disagreement about the development of polities by the seventh century. The structure of these units, as well as their relationships with other groups, was by no means static.

Although reference is often made to the Middle Anglian and East Anglian 'kingdoms', the political implications of this term are misleading (Renfrew and Shennan 1982, 115). Bede's mention of shared kingship in seventh-century East Anglia (*HE* 3, 18) may indicate that this 'kingdom' was not a centrally-organised autonomous unit but was composed of discrete provinces or areas which occasionally came under the control of their own leaders (Sawyer 1978, 49). No record exists of Middle Anglia as an independent unit governed by an individual leader, nor is there any evidence that those people referred to as Middle Angles held in common a sense of community identity (Davies 1973–74, 20). Judging from the nomenclature of the *Tribal Hidage*, Middle Anglia was an acephalous confederation of local groups (Davies and Vierck 1974, 227). Indeed, the modern notion of coherent political units circumscribed by recognised boundaries is anachronistic in early Anglo-Saxon England. The evidence of the *Tribal Hidage* suggests that expressions of political authority referred not to territorial units but to groups of people who inhabited an area (Davies and Vierck 1974, 228–9). Thus, any attempt to define with precision the limits of the Middle Anglian or East Anglian 'kingdoms' is doomed to failure.

Following a systems model, Arnold (1982a) has argued that the changes observable in the archaeological record of seventh-century Anglo-Saxon England, such as the increase in the wealth of male relative to female grave furnishings, the increase in the quantity of luxury goods, and the appearance of burials singled out for interment under mounds or within churches, represent responses to stress generated from both internal and external sources. With the development of political units, imbalances between the components of social and economic networks were alleviated. It is not necessary to accept the assumptions of Arnold's systems model in order to recognise the sixth and seventh centuries as a period of cultural change.

Stylistic variability, it is hypothesized in this chapter, assumes a relatively important role in identifying, negotiating and maintaining social relationships during such a period of stress. Of particular interest are relationships of group membership and differentiation. Stylistic similarity will emphasise alliances within a group and, conversely, will distinguish group members from those with other affiliations. Thus, the material culture of a group bound by political alliances will be internally similar yet differentiated from that of external groups. The observation that the early Anglo-Saxons were politically organised at more than the single level of 'kingdom' in no way precludes the material culture of this group from stylistic analysis. As mentioned above, particular stylistic messages may be directed toward particular audiences at different organisational levels. Thus, results of this stylistic analysis may indicate the presence of distinctions more subtle than those of 'kingdoms'.

Study data

Data from burials at six early Anglo-Saxon cemeteries in Northants (Wakerley I and Wakerley II), Suffolk (Little Eriswell and Holywell Row), and Norfolk (Bergh Apton and Swaffham) (figure 1) were collected for two sets of tests. Variables for the first test described mortuary treatment: the type of interment (cremation or inhumation), the position of the body (extended, flexed, or prone), the orientation of the body (head to west or head to another direction), the minimum number of individuals in a single grave, and the presence or absence of grave structures (coffin, plant bedding, stone packing, or postholes) were recorded for all graves sufficiently undisturbed to allow assessment

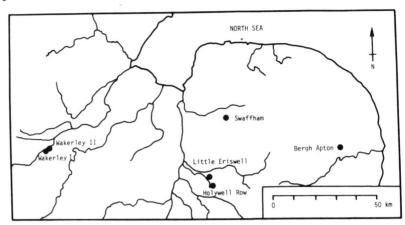

Figure I. Location of six Anglo-Saxon cemeteries used in study.

(table I). When the position or orientation of the body could not be determined, a missing value was noted. All graves were assumed to contain single
burials unless the skeletal remains of more than one individual could be
identified. Without this assumption, the samples from sites with poor skeletal
preservation, such as Bergh Apton, were so small and of such questionable
representativeness as to be useless. Similarly, in the absence of evidence to the
contrary, all burials were assumed to lack structural features.

A second data set was created from those single, closed inhumations that
contained dress fasteners. Burials were excluded if the extant objects could not
be associated with an individual or could not be assumed, given the limitations
of preservation affecting all burials, to be the complete collection deposited at
time of interment. The first restriction excluded multiple burials and the
second restricted disturbed or incompletely excavated graves from this data
set. The data collected were used to examine regional relationships as indicated
by (1) the frequency of graves containing particular types of dress fasteners
and (2) the structure of sets of dress fasteners. The categories of dress
fasteners recognised were those first-order distinctions universal in the
archaeological literature of this period: annular, cruciform, small-long,
square-headed, penannular, and swastika brooches, pins and, when worn on
the chest, large rings. A greater typological refinement was considered to be
impractical in view of the small sample size. The two diminutive penannular
brooches from Wakerley II which had apparently been used as shoe- or
garter-fittings were excluded from the data set.

The wearing of brooches, pins, and rings has traditionally been thought the
province of women. Pader (1982, 101–4, 182), in an argument weakened by
circularity, has shown a high, but not absolute, positive correlation at Holywell
Row and Bergh Apton between the presence of brooches and individuals
identified as female on the basis of skeletal and/or artefactual evidence.
Accordingly, the possibility that males also infrequently wore brooches cannot

be ruled out. This study assumes that the types of dress fasteners used and the ways in which they were worn did not differ significantly from area to area on the basis of the wearer's sex.

By combining the six sites in this study into three regional groupings – Middle Anglia (Wakerley I and Wakerley II), the Lark River area (Little Eriswell and Holywell Row), and East Anglia (Bergh Apton and Swaffham) – burials of late fifth- or early sixth-century to late sixth-century date were represented in each of the three regional groups. Seventh-century graves, comparable to those in Middle Anglia and the Lark River area, were under-represented in the East Anglian sample. It was hoped, however, that clustering the cemeteries in this way would reduce the amount of chronological distortion inherent in the selection of cemeteries as well as provide samples of useful size. It is intended that the larger study of which this preliminary analysis is a part will examine the development of early Anglo-Saxon polities in eastern England from a diachronic perspective. However, the chronological refinement desirable with a larger sample would splinter a sample of the size here into unsuitably small groups. The regional groupings used in this study are heuristic: indeed, the Lark River area is traditionally considered to have been within the East Anglian kingdom.

Wakerley I (Northants): The Anglo-Saxon cemetery at Wakerley (SP941983) is located roughly 14 km north-north-east of the town of Corby on sloping ground 1 km south of the River Welland. After discovery of the site during iron ore extraction, excavations were conducted in 1968 and 1970 by D. A. Jackson for the Ministry of Public Buildings and Works.

A total of 85 inhumations and one cremation were found in 72 graves (B. D. Adams and D. A. Jackson, personal communication). No burials are thought to have been lost to quarrying. Eighty-three burials were sufficiently preserved to allow the recording of details of mortuary treatment. Of these, 16 were undisturbed single inhumations containing dress fasteners. Adams (Jackson and Ambrose 1978, 232) assigns use of the cemetery predominantly to the sixth century with limited activity continuing into the seventh century.

Wakerley II (Northants): Another Anglo-Saxon cemetery, lying approximately 200 m north-east of the sixth-century site of Wakerley I, was likewise discovered on land quarried for iron ore. In 1975, D. A. Jackson, on behalf of the Department of the Environment, excavated eight inhumations in six graves. The mortuary treatment of all eight burials was reconstructable. However, with the exception of the two penannular brooches from grave 10, which were excluded from this analysis, no dress fasteners were found. The relationship between Wakerley II and the earlier Wakerley I cemetery nearby conforms to the 'two cemetery pattern' noted elsewhere in England at this time (Meaney and Hawkes 1970, 45–55).

Little Eriswell (Suffolk): The site (TF731803) is located on a rise approximately 1 km north-north-east of the village of Little Eriswell. In 1957, workmen at the Lakenheath airfield exposed an Anglo-Saxon inhumation burial furnished with gravegoods (Briscoe and LeBard 1960). Ditch-digging in advance of construction at the airfield in 1959 produced a quantity of skeletal material. Upon agreement by the Air Ministry, the United States Air Force, and the Minstry of Works, a restricted area was excavated under the direction of Captain LeBard with the supervision of Lady Briscoe. Thirty-two single inhumations were uncovered by trench-excavation techniques during the 1959 season, bringing the total number of burials to 33 (Hutchison 1966). Twenty-six burials were sufficiently well preserved to allow analysis of mortuary treatment. Dress fasteners were found with 10 closed inhumations. The limits of the cemetery are thought to have been established to the south, west and north, but to extend under and beyond airfield buildings to the east (Hutchinson 1966, 3).

Holywell Row (Suffolk): The inhumation cemetery at Holywell Row (TL 714765) in Mildenhall is located on a small rise adjoining an arm of the fen to the west of the Little Ouse. Although Anglo-Saxon objects were recovered from the area in the nineteenth century (*Proc. Bury and W. Suffolk Arch. Inst.* 1855, 305; Smith 1911, 344), discovery of the site by warreners led to excavations initially by the Rev. C. Wood and Dr A. B. Cook and, in the 1920s, under the direction of T. C. Lethbridge. While Wood and Cook's activities uncovered 'several skeletons' (Lethbridge 1931, 1), the greater part of the cemetery was excavated and published by Lethbridge (1931). Lethbridge recovered 101 burials in 100 graves. The mortuary treatment of all burials was analysed. Dress fasteners were found in 25 single, undisturbed graves. Despite the quality of Lethbridge's original publication and the recent reappraisal of the site by Pader (1982), the disposal of some artefacts and skeletal material by the 1940s has hampered study of the site. It is unclear to what extent the excavated graves represent the total number of individuals buried at Holywell Row: the limits of the cemetery were not determined by Lethbridge and quarrying had been conducted prior to excavation. Gravegoods from Holywell Row indicate that the cemetery was in use from the late fifth or early sixth century into the seventh century (Pader 1982, 90).

Bergh Apton (Norfolk): The inhumation cemetery at Bergh Apton (TG 306001) is situated approximately 9 km south-east of Norwich. In 1973, the discovery of Anglo-Saxon artefacts during commercial gravel quarrying on a small hill roughly 400 m north of the Well Beck led to excavation the same year by Barbara Green of the Castle Museum, Norwich, and later by Christopher Green for the Norfolk Archaeological Unit (Green and Rogerson 1978). Sixty-three graves were excavated. The original size of the cemetery is unknown, as the southern and western ranges were removed by gravel extraction. Fifty-six burials were used in the mortuary treatment analysis. Unfortunately, this study was hampered by the poor conditions of preservation at the site. Of this group, 10 undisturbed graves furnished with dress fasteners appeared to contain single inhumations.

Swaffham (Norfolk): Nineteen inhumations and a possible cremation were uncovered in 1970 after construction activity produced skeletal material and Anglo-Saxon artefacts at 'The Paddocks', Haspall's Road (TF 817084), on the

Table 1. Comparison of mortuary treatment at Anglo-Saxon cemeteries.

	MIDDLE ANGLIA		LARK RIVER AREA		EAST ANGLIA	
	Wakerley I (n = 83)	Wakerley II (n = 8)	Little Eriswell (n = 26)	Holywell Row (n = 101)	Bergh Apton (n = 56)	Swaffham (n = 11)
Type of interment	Inhumation (99%) Cremation (1%)	Inhumation (100%)	Inhumation (100%)	Inhumation (100%)	Inhumation (100%)	Inhumation (95% ?) Cremation (5% ?)
Position of body	Extended (66%) Flexed (32%) Prone (2%)	Extended (75%) Flexed (25%)	Extended (65%) Flexed (35%)	Extended (59%) Flexed (39%) Prone (2%)	Flexed (67%) Extended (33%) Prone (10%)	Flexed (60%) Extended (30%)
Orientation of body	Head to West (96%) Other (4%)	Head to West (88%) Other (13%)	Head to West (100%) Other (0%)	Head to West (95%) Other (5%)	Head to West (85%) Other (15%)	Head to West (80%) Other (20%)
Minimum frequency of multiple burials	Moderate (30%)	High (50%)	Low (0%)	Low (2%)	Low (9%)	Low (9%)
Frequency of grave structures	Low (1%)	Low (13%)	Low (3%)	Low (5%)	Low (9%)	Moderate (18%)

south-west outskirts of Swaffham (Hills and Wade-Martins 1976, 1). The excavated graves presumably represent only part of a larger cemetery now buried beneath or destroyed by standing buildings and roads. The site is placed roughly in the sixth century, although a few of the gravegoods cannot be excluded from a fifth- or seventh-century date (Hills and Wade-Martins 1976, 28). Although 11 burials were sufficiently preserved to allow details of mortuary treatment to be recorded, only two single, undisturbed inhumations were furnished with dress fasteners.

Methodology and results

Statistical tests were used to identify differences in mortuary treatment and in dress fasteners between the six sites in the three areas. All of the values scored for each of the mortuary treatment variables were added up for each site and the frequency distribution of values was compared between different sites. This approach to mortuary variability between different social groups has demonstrated utility (O'Shea 1984).

The *chi*-square test was used to measure differences in mortuary treatment. This tests the null hypothesis of randomness by comparing the observed frequency of a variable with its expected frequency. A correlation between mortuary treatment and site or area was considered to exist in cases in which the null hypothesis was rejected. The *chi*-square statistic becomes a poor measure in small samples in which any expected cell frequency is 1 or less. Most of the expected results should exceed 5 if 2 expectations are close to 1 (Snedecor and Cochran 1980, 77). When these conditions could not be met, a two-tailed Fisher exact test was substituted. The Fisher exact test has the advantage of applicability to small samples with low expected cell frequencies (Siegel 1956, 96–7). A two-tailed test, which examines association rather than directionality, was considered appropriate.

The results of both the *chi*-square and Fisher exact two-tailed tests were considered significant if the *p*-value was equal to or less than .05, i.e., if there was a .05 or less probability that the results were produced by chance. The null hypothesis of randomness was rejected in these instances and a statistically significant difference in mortuary treatment was held to exist between the sites or areas tested. The simple matching coefficient (Sokal and Sneath 1963, 133), which summarises as a numerical value between 0 and 1 the amount of similarity between paired dichotomous samples, was then calculated for each pair of sites.

The results show similarity between the pairs of sites within each of the three areas (table 2). Each of the Middle Anglian sites (Wakerley 1 and Wakerley 11) was most like the other. Similarly, the East Anglian sites (Bergh Apton and Swaffham) had the greatest affinity to each other. Although mortuary treatment of the Lark River sites (Little Eriswell and Holywell Row) did not differ significantly for any of the variables considered, unity was also observed when mortuary treatment at Little Eriswell was compared with that at both of the East Anglian sites. Thus, mortuary treatment at Little Eriswell,

Table 2. Comparison of mortuary treatment at early Anglo-Saxon cemeteries. Upper half of matrix represents number of positive matches (total = 5); lower half of matrix represents simple matching coefficient (0 = low; 1 = high).

	Wakerley I	Wakerley II	Little Eriswell	Holywell Row	Bergh Apton	Swaffham
Wakerley I	X	5	4	4	3	4
Wakerley II	1.0	X	4	4	4	3
Little Eriswell	0.8	0.8	X	5	5	5
Holywell Row	0.8	0.8	1.0	X	4	4
Bergh Apton	0.6	0.8	1.0	0.8	X	5
Swaffham	0.8	0.6	1.0	0.8	1.0	X

as measured by these five variables, was equally similar to that at Holywell Row, Bergh Apton, and Swaffham.

When the average similarity between sites from each area was contrasted with the average similarity to sites in the other two areas (table 3), it was noted that while the average within-group similarity was uniformly high for all areas, the between-group similarity was greatest for the Lark River sites and those in the other areas. The Middle Anglian sites were the least like sites in the other two areas.

The historical ascription of the Lark River area to the East Anglian kingdom was examined by comparing mortuary treatment at the Lark River sites with

Table 3. Comparison of mortuary treatment within and between areas using simple matching coefficient.

	Average similarity	
Area	Within area	Between areas
Middle Anglia	1.0	0.75
Lark River Area	1.0	0.85
East Anglia	1.0	0.80

Table 4. Comparison of mortuary treatment between areas using simple matching coefficient.

	Average similarity between areas		
	Middle Anglia	Lark River Area	East Anglia
Middle Anglia	×	1.8	0.7
Lark River Area	0.8	×	0.9
East Anglia	0.7	0.9	×

Table 5. Comparison of mortuary treatment within and between grouped areas using simple matching coefficient.

	Average similarity between grouped areas	
Group	Within group	Between groups
Middle Anglia and Lark River Area	0.87	0.80
Lark River Area and East Anglia	0.93	0.75

that both in Middle Anglia and in East Anglia. Here, the results (table 4) supported those which would be expected from historical tradition: mortuary treatment at the Lark River sites was shown to be marginally more similar to that in East Anglia (0.9) than in Middle Anglia (0.8). This relationship may be illustrated in another way by comparing the average similarity of sites within and between areas when the Lark River sites were grouped, first with those from Middle Anglia, and then with those from East Anglia. The results (table 5) showed the greatest level of within-group similarity and between-group difference when the Lark River sites were combined with those from East Anglia.

Variability among the gravegoods was more difficult to define. For this preliminary study, differences in the types of dress fasteners worn in each of the three areas were considered. Because of the small sample size, sites were not considered individually but were paired together into the three areas considered previously. These areas, in turn, were clustered into two different groupings; the Lark River was joined first with Middle Anglia in opposition to East Anglia, and then with East Anglia in contrast to Middle Anglia.

As noted above, the graves containing dress fasteners were classified in two ways. Initially, the presence or absence of particular types of fasteners were recorded for all graves in the data set. Although the absolute number of fasteners in a grave was not noted, graves which contained more than one kind of fastener were recorded repeatedly with each fastener type. Accordingly, the number of cases ($n = 93$) was greater than the number of graves ($n = 63$).

Using the *chi*-square or Fisher exact test under the conditions outlined above, the frequency of graves with each fastener type was compared between the three individual areas and between the combined areas. Because of the risk of ignoring masked correlations in a sample of this size, a p-value of .10 or less was considered significant.

In a few cases, dress fastener type could be correlated with area. The frequency of cruciform, square-headed, small-long, penannular, and applied brooches and rings did not differ significantly at the .10 level between Middle Anglia, East Anglia and the Lark River area when these regions were considered either singly or in groups. The possibility that this apparent lack of variation is a result of the small sample size cannot be excluded. An identical test with a larger sample may reveal statistically significant differences between the frequency of graves with these fastener types in each area.

In contrast, the frequency of graves with annular brooches, swastika brooches and pins did vary significantly between each of the three areas (table 6). However, the differences between areas did not demonstrate any consistent pattern. The frequency of graves with annular brooches differed between Middle Anglia and the Lark River area and between Middle Anglia and East Anglia. When data from the Lark River area were combined with those from Middle Anglia, the frequency of burials with annular brooches in this larger area differed significantly from that of East Anglia. The small sample of graves with swastika brooches demonstrated a significant difference between Middle Anglia and the Lark River area. This distinction was maintained when the larger regional groupings were compared; the frequency of burials with swastika brooches from the combined area of the Lark River and East Anglia differed significantly from that of Middle Anglia. Finally, a significant difference in the frequency of graves with pins was demonstrated between the Lark River and East Anglia. This difference remained statistically significant after data from Middle Anglia were combined with those from East Anglia. As noted above, the frequency of graves with annular brooches also distinguished the Lark River area from East Anglia. Although in these two areas a high proportion (86%) of the seven graves which contained pins were also furnished with annular brooches, a two-tailed Fisher exact test indicated this association not to be significant at the .05 level. Thus, the observation that both pins and annular brooches distinguish between the Lark River area and East Anglia cannot be explained simply by the co-occurrence of these dress fastener types in individual graves.

Not only was variation in types of dress fasteners examined, but differences in the structure of the sets which they formed were also tested. The dress fasteners from each grave were categorised, without reference to type, as belonging to one of eight sets which described (1) the absolute number of

Table 6. Association between types of dress fasteners and areas, as measured by *chi*-square or two-tailed Fisher exact tests. *P*-values less than or equal to 0.10 are underlined.

TYPES OF DRESS FASTENERS

	Annular brooches Middle Anglia = 7/16 Lark River Area = 20/35 East Anglia = 11/12 Total = 38/63	Swastika brooches Middle Anglia = 2/16 Lark River Area = 0/35 East Anglia = 0/12 Total = 2/63	Pins Middle Anglia = 4/16 Lark River Area = 3/35 East Anglia = 4/12 Total = 11/63
Fraction of total graves in each area containing type of dress fastener			
Units compared			
Middle Anglia//Lark River Area//East Anglia	$\chi^2 = 6.91$ $p = \underline{0.03}$	$\chi^2 = 6.07^\star$ $p = \underline{0.05}$	$\chi^2 = 4.65$ $p = \underline{0.10}$
Middle Anglia//Lark River Area	$\chi^2 = 0.79$ $p = 0.37$	Fisher $p = \underline{0.09}$	$\chi^2 = 2.50$ $p = 0.11$
Lark River Area//East Anglia	$\chi^2 = 4.74$ $p = \underline{0.03}$	No swastika brooches	$\chi^2 = 4.32$ $p = \underline{0.04}$
Middle Anglia//East Anglia	$\chi^2 = 6.86$ $p = \underline{0.01}$	Fisher $p = 0.49$	$\chi^2 = 0.23$ $p = 0.63$
Middle Anglia and Lark River Area//East Anglia	$\chi^2 = 6.09$ $p = \underline{0.01}$	Fisher $p = 1.00$	$\chi^2 = 2.59$ $p = 0.11$
Lark River Area and East Anglia//Middle Anglia	$\chi^2 = 2.46$ $p = 0.12$	Fisher $p = 0.06$	$\chi^2 = 0.85$ $p = 0.36$
East Anglia and Middle Anglia//Lark River Area	$\chi^2 = 0.32$ $p = 0.56$	Fisher $p = 1.93$	$\chi^2 = 4.32$ $p = \underline{0.04}$

$\star$ 50% of the cells have expected counts less than 2.

Table 7. Dress fastener sets.

---

1 = Single (e.g. annular brooch)

2 = Matched Pair (e.g. two annular brooches)

3 = Unmatched Pair (e.g. one annular and one cruciform brooch)

4 = Matched Pair with Unmatched Singleton (e.g. two annular brooches and one cruciform brooch)

5 = Matched Triplet (e.g. three annular brooches)

6 = Unmatched Triplet (e.g. one annular, one cruciform, and one small-long brooch)

7 = Similar Double Pair (e.g. two pairs of cruciform brooches)

8 = Matched Pair with Matched Triplet (e.g. two annular and three cruciform brooches)

---

fasteners and (2) the similarity between fasteners in the set following the typological distinctions employed in the first test (table 7). The number of cases ($n = 63$) equalled the number of graves containing dress fasteners. Again, the areas were compared individually and by regional groupings using the *chi*-square and Fisher exact tests as appropriate, and a p-value less than or equal to .10 was considered significant.

As with the tests correlating fastener type with area, the results of those examining the structure of the fastener sets revealed no clear directional variation. This parallel is not surprising, as the two variables are not unrelated. While statistically significant area differences could not be recognized between the frequency of sets of single fasteners, unmatched pairs, unmatched triplets, similar double pairs, matched pairs with matched triplets, and matched triplets, differences between area and dress fastener sets were demonstrated to be significant for matched pairs and for matched pairs with unmatched singletons (table 8). The frequency of sets of matched pairs of dress fasteners varied significantly between East Anglia and Middle Anglia. When data from the Lark River area were added to those from Middle Anglia this difference remained significant. The frequency of sets with a matched pair of fasteners in combination with an unmatched singleton varied significantly between all three areas. When data from the individual areas were contrasted, the frequency of these dress fastener sets was found to differ significantly between the Lark River area and East Anglia. This distinction was maintained when data from either region were combined with those from East Anglia. It should be noted that annular brooches appeared in 70.8% of the dress sets with matched pairs of fasteners. Likewise, 72% of the sets composed of a matched pair with an unmatched singleton included pins and/or swastika or annular brooches.

Conclusions

While this preliminary study seeks only to investigate a small amount of the total variability exhibited by mortuary remains in eastern England during the early Anglo-Saxon period, a few conclusions may be suggested. The statistical

Table 8. Association between types of dress fastener sets and areas, as measured by *chi*-square test. P-values less than or equal to 0.10 are underlined.

Units compared	TYPES OF DRESS FASTENER SETS	
	Matched pair Middle Anglia = 8/16 Lark River Area = 14/35 East Anglia = 2/12 Total = 24/63	*Matched pair with unmatched Singleton* Middle Anglia = 7/16 Lark River Area = 10/35 East Anglia = 8/12 Total = 25/63
Fraction of total graves in each area containing type of dress fastener set		
Middle Anglia//Lark River Area//East Anglia	$\chi^2 = 1.02$ $p = 0.19$	$\chi^2 = 5.57$ $p = \underline{0.06}$
Middle Anglia//Lark River Area	$\chi^2 = 0.45$ $p = 0.50$	$\chi^2 = 1.18$ $p = 0.29$
Lark River Area//East Anglia	$\chi^2 = 2.17$ $p = 0.14$	$\chi^2 = 5.49$ $p = \underline{0.02}$
Middle Anglia//East Anglia	$\chi^2 = 3.31$ $p = \underline{0.07}$	$\chi^2 = 1.45$ $p = 0.23$
Middle Anglia and Lark River Area//East Anglia	$\chi^2 = 2.89$ $p = \underline{0.09}$	$\chi^2 = 4.51$ $p = \underline{0.03}$
Lark River Area and East Anglia//Middle Anglia	$\chi^2 = 1.29$ $p = 0.26$	$\chi^2 = 0.15$ $p = 0.70$
East Anglia and Middle Anglia//Lark River Area	$\chi^2 = 0.12$ $p = 0.73$	$\chi^2 = 4.06$ $p = \underline{0.04}$

tests examining the mortuary treatment and dress fasteners from the six cemeteries did not consistently or reliably distinguish between regional groupings. However, the results from this analysis of mortuary treatment were relatively more effective in identifying differences between individual and grouped sites than were those from the tests involving dress fasteners. The communal aspect of ritual activity connected with burial in a shared cemetery may be a factor in this discrepancy. Within each of the three areas, mortuary treatment did not differ significantly from site to site. However, differences were recognisable between sites from different areas. Sites in the Lark River area were shown to be most like those in East Anglia. This affinity is consistent with the historical relationship between the two areas.

Of particular interest is the absence of a clear directional relationship between the variety of dress fasteners and the three areas. In the few statistically significant cases in which the frequency of fastener types differed significantly, no pattern was apparent. Annular brooches, swastika brooches and pins all distinguished between different areas. In one instance, both annular brooches and pins differentiated the Lark River area from East Anglia. The structure of the dress sets demonstrated only slight variation from area to area. While, on the one hand, the frequency of sets of matched pairs of fasteners differed significantly between East Anglia and Middle Anglia, sets of matched pairs of fasteners with unmatched singletons distinguished East Anglia from the Lark River area. For both kinds of dress sets, the combined region of Middle Anglia and the Lark River area could be differentiated from East Anglia.

The failure of the dress fastener data from the Lark River area to exhibit consistent affinity with those from East Anglia, as would be expected from historical tradition, may be read in several ways. The effects of chronological variation on material culture patterning must be recognised. More immediately, however, the relationships between groups of people living in the Lark River area and those dwelling to the east and west presumably changed during the some 150 years covered by this study. Arnold's suggestion (this volume) that anomalous cemeteries may indicate culturally fluid conditions on territorial borders is of particular interest in connection with the Lark River sites.

It is perhaps unreasonable, moreover, to expect people who lacked distinct regional identities, as Davies has argued in the case of the Middle Angles, to use style to mark and manipulate political boundaries on the scale of 'kingdoms'. The fact that each area could be distinguished from the other two in at least one case may indicate that the groups to which variability in dress fasteners in these three areas refers existed at the level not of the 'kingdom' but of the local community.

It is interesting to note that the types of dress fasteners which differed significantly from area to area are technologically and stylistically simple: the production of annular brooches, swastika brooches and pins generally did not involve the metalworking techniques of casting with complex multiple moulds, sheet or solid metal relief work, or applying secondary metals characteristic in varying degrees of cruciform, square-headed and applied brooches. These more elaborate brooches, as well as penannular brooches and large rings, which appear to be randomly distributed between the three areas studied, may have carried stylistic messages relating to larger regional concerns or may have been transported in regional exchange networks. Obviously, these two possibilities are not mutually exclusive.

These two groups of dress fasteners – those which are found equally in all three areas and those whose distribution varies significantly from area to area – may have referred to different relationships of alliance. The significant differences between the frequency of graves with annular brooches, swastika brooches and pins may indicate that these fasteners emphasised and fostered relationships within local communities while simultaneously differentiating community members from those outside the group. In contrast, the other fasteners may have facilitated interaction between the members of different communities by visually reducing the distance between them.

While past studies of mortuary practices have often focussed on the archaeological correlates of vertical differentiation, the archaeological record also contains information about horizontal differentiation. The growing body of literature on the relationship between style and human behaviour provides a context in which to examine these horizontal relationships.

Acknowledgements

The fieldwork upon which this paper is based was supported by grants from the Department of Anthropology, University of Pennsylvania, and the Wenner-Gren Foundation for Anthropological Research (Grant-in-Aid no. 4428). I am particularly indebted to B. D. Adams and Dennis Jackson, who generously allowed me to include in this contribution information about the Wakerley I cemetery in advance of publication. Barbara Green (Castle Museum, Norwich), Robert Moore (Central Museum and Art Gallery, Northampton), Elizabeth Owles (Moyses Hall Museum, Bury St Edmunds), and J. Pemble (Westfield Museum, Kettering) graciously provided access to collections. I am grateful to Bernald Wailes for comments on an earlier draft of this paper and to Susan Johnston and Lauris Olson for discussions of anthropological archaeology. Any errors are my responsibility alone.

Style and symbol: explaining
variability in Anglo-Saxon cremation burials

The traditional role of archaeology in the study of England from the fifth to the seventh century AD is not so much as a handmaiden of history but more as a low-paid domestic servant. Archaeological material has been used to illuminate events known to us through the processes governing the chance survival of documentary material. Thus Leeds (1912) has discussed the distribution of Anglo-Saxon saucer brooches in relation to the Battle of Bedford (AD 571) and Myres (1969, 114–9) has described the distribution of Anglo-Saxon pottery in relation to the known events during the ages of Aelle (477–c. 500) and Ceawlin (556–93).

Anglo-Saxon pottery has been studied as a spatial indicator of race and culture and as a chronological indicator of historical events (Myres 1969, 1977). Variability in pottery style has been regarded as being determined by variations in ethnic origins according to traditional culture historical interpretations. It has been seen as providing a passive reflection of movements of peoples. Comparing, for instance, the spread of Saxon *Buckelurnen* without feet to the spread of those with feet, Myres (1969, 101–2) comments:

> The distribution of the former seems to fan out from the Humbrensian area over the northern Midlands, while the latter appear to spread rather from East Anglia south-westward through Middle Anglia to the upper Thames valley and to have penetrated at quite an early stage as far as such Berkshire sites as Harwell and East Shefford.

The anthropomorphism is so striking that the reader is almost left wondering whether these marching pots wore jackboots.

The role of prehistoric archaeology, on the other hand, is now seen much more as a means of studying process and pattern rather than particular events (for example Binford 1962). Pottery is studied for the light it can throw on all aspects of human behaviour (for example Plog 1980; Braithwaite 1982b; D.E.Arnold 1983). It may play an active role in structuring society:

> The pottery forms can thus be related to the assimilation and ritual legitimation of the social order (Welbourn 1984, 17).

Others have stressed individual variability (see, for example Hardin 1977; Hill 1977). Style has been seen as a reflection of the techniques and 'motor-habit' variation of specific potters.

Between the particularist Anglo-Saxonist and the processualist prehistorian there has opened a great, and ever-widening, gulf of methods and objectives. It has begun to seem as if there is no common ground between the two. One reaction has been to deny completely the relevance of existing work on written sources to early Anglo-Saxon England in an attempt to reintegrate Anglo-Saxon archaeology with prehistory (see, for example, Pader 1982). Whilst this approach has many attractions, in the long run it must be counter-productive. In general, there are many unknown variables in the 'black box' of archaeology (cf. Leach 1973). In the early Anglo-Saxon period the written sources provide contextual information that may eventually allow us to give values to some of these variables, and so gain a better understanding of society as a whole. They may, in fact, illuminate the crucial relationship between material culture and human behaviour which is at the root of many problems in prehistory.

The most productive way forward, therefore, appears to lie in the reintegration of the best of the old archaeology with the best of the new (cf. Rahtz 1983). This chapter suggests one way in which it may be possible to integrate traditional interpretations of Anglo-Saxon pottery with current explanations of style.

Fisher (this volume) has described rival interpretations of the relationship between material culture and social interaction, which need not be repeated here. She follows Wobst (1977) in assigning to stylistic variability a functional role in the transmission of messages about an individual's social position. She suggests that this function becomes more important in marking social relationships at times of stress, such as may have existed in early Anglo-Saxon England; and she follows Wobst and Hodder (1982b) in concluding that different artefacts can carry different kinds of messages to different audiences. It is proposed here that the same artefacts can also carry different messages to different audiences. Each artefact consists of a large number of attributes which can vary independently of each other. Some attributes may be used to distinguish sub-types used in particular regions; others may distinguish social groups within that region. Furthermore, even the same attributes may carry different messages according to the context of use. Deetz (1977, 51) has discussed the various functions of a candle according to context; these include technological (for lighting), social (at the dinner table) and religious (in a church). The meaning of the same artefact stems from the context of its use.

It has been demonstrated elsewhere (Richards 1984) that the form and decoration of Anglo-Saxon cremation urns are used to mark aspects of the social identity of the individual(s) buried within them.[1] Reynolds (1980a) has discussed the significance of an association between a swastika design and a whetstone at Sancton, and Arnold has suggested that stamped decoration may perform a heraldic or totemic function (C. J. Arnold 1983). The symbolic potential of funerary vessels has been well studied in other contexts (for example, Rydh 1929). The style of Anglo-Saxon cremation urns is seen as making a statement about the place of the deceased in Anglo-Saxon society, reinforcing the corporate identity of the group:

> By summarizing an individual's economic and social situation, stylistic messages may play a more active role in the integration of social groups (Wobst 1977, 327).

Thus the form and decoration of a cremation vessel may signify the social role of the individual(s) buried within it on many levels. Some attributes may mark the deceased as an Angle, others may suggest that he is a high-ranking male, others may relate to clan or moiety groupings, and so on. Wobst (1977, 336) has proposed a sliding scale relating message content to stylistic form. The more widely a message is to be broadcast the more visible will be the artefact chosen to convey it. It is suggested that the more general the message then, broadly speaking, the more visible the attribute used to represent it. Thus the most gross aspects of pottery form and decoration identify a cremation urn as Anglo-Saxon, the finer details transmit finer points of social role.

It is proposed that, running from the general to the particular, the following levels may be differentiated in pottery style:[2]

'Horizontal' differentiation

   (1) culture group – Germanic cremation rite

   (2) ethnic group – Angle, Saxon, etc.

   (3) regional group – East Angle, Middle Angle, and finer regional sub-groupings

'Vertical' differentiation

   (4) age, sex, or other social group

'Motor-habit' differentiation

   (5) potter's style group

The significance of this hypothesis is that it allows that traditional and more recent approaches to artefact variability may both be valid. It promises a reconciliation between the culture historical view of Myres, and the more recent culture process (including functionalist and structuralist) interpretations, and promotes a reintegration of historical and archaeological material.

Anglo-Saxon cremation urns represent an ideal means of testing the nature of the relationship between artefact variability and social role. Being hand-made non-standardised pottery there is a considerable range of styles. In one sense every vessel is unique, varying slightly in shape, or in the use of a stamp, or in the number of lines in a chevron, from its nearest match. Yet at the same time there is considerable repetition in the range of forms and decorative motifs so that common styles may be identified. Information about the individual(s) buried in each urn may be derived from the cremated skeletal remains and the grave-goods, including items of dress cremated on the pyre as well as unburnt offerings.

Information about pottery form and decoration, grave-goods and, where possible, skeletal analyses was collected for 2,440 urns from eighteen sites (figure 1, table 1): Abingdon (Leeds and Harden 1936), Baston (Mayes and Dean 1976), Caistor-by-Norwich (Myres and Green 1973), Elsham, Illington, Lackford (Lethbridge 1951), Longthorpe (Myres 1974), Loveden Hill (Fennell 1964), Markshall (Myres and Green 1973), Mucking, Newark, Sancton (Myres and Southern 1973), Snape (West and Owles 1974), South Elkington (Webster 1951), Spong Hill (Hills 1977; Hills and Penn 1981), Worthy Park, York–Heworth, and York–The Mount (Stead 1958). These urns may be considered as a single cultural assemblage of Anglo-Saxon cremation urns

Figure 1. Anglo-Saxon cremation cemeteries providing study data.

from England, or they may be sub-divided according to site, and the sites compared against each other. There are considerable differences in the size of the individual assemblages included in the study data, and in the quality of the information. Nevertheless, the recording system applied to all the sites imposes a degree of uniformity on the material and allows comparisons to be made between sites.

All the vessels used were relatively complete, and had to have a fully reconstructible profile to be included. This should mean that the record of the grave-goods and skeletal remains is also relatively complete. If a vessel retains a full profile then there is unlikely to have been a high loss of urn contents through plough damage and other disturbance.

The aim of the complete study, of which these results represent a small part, is to examine variability in all attributes of Anglo-Saxon cremations. Present space does not allow an exhaustive presentation of these results. Rather, a few examples will be given of attributes which appear to vary at each level of social interaction.

Table 1. Mean urn heights.

Site name	No. of urns	Mean height	Standard deviation
Abingdon	36	18.67	4.48
Baston	15	21.00	4.38
Caistor-by-Norwich	227	19.09	3.88
Elsham	205	19.87	3.82
Illington	94	18.71	3.91
Lackford	286	19.17	4.18
Longthorpe	14	17.71	3.43
Loveden Hill	251	20.02	4.20
Markshall	7	18.86	3.97
Mucking	77	18.44	3.89
Newark	142	19.93	4.60
Sancton	243	20.12	4.19
Snape	5	19.70	3.07
South Elkington	91	21.13	4.11
Spong Hill	675	19.57	3.98
Worthy Park	22	15.02	3.29
York – Heworth	42	19.94	4.50
York – The Mount	8	18.38	4.02
Total	2440	19.56	4.12

Culture group: The average height of vessels at each site is compared in table 1. The standard deviation represents the spread about the mean. It is immediately clear that all the averages are very tightly clustered about 19.5 cm. For sites with more than fifty urns, there is only a 2.7 cm difference between the largest and smallest mean. This represents a high level of consistency in the production of urns. There are no functional reasons why funerary urns should be made to this height. A few individual instances are known of urns as short as 8 cm high, or as tall as 28 cm. Therefore, we must conclude that Anglo-Saxon potters were generally working to an idealised cultural type, and that this type was recognised throughout Anglo-Saxon England, emphasising the common Germanic ancestry of all Anglo-Saxon pottery.

Within Anglo-Saxon pottery the same attributes may be used to distinguish a cemetery assemblage from a domestic one. A greater variety of size and form

Table 2. Percentage of classes of incised decoration.

	Caistr	Elsham	Illgton	Lckfrd	Lovedn	Muckng	Newark	Sanctn	S.Elkn	Spong
Decoration	78.9	86.3	73.4	82.9	77.3	37.7	81.0	78.2	81.3	77.9
Incised decoration:										
Horizontal	72.7	82.0	71.3	76.2	71.7	28.6	77.5	76.1	79.1	74.5
Vertical	43.2	35.1	7.4	31.8	35.9	14.3	38.0	26.7	36.3	30.1
Continuous chevron	18.1	26.0	21.3	25.5	24.3	9.1	27.5	27.6	23.1	22.5
Single upright chevron	5.3	4.4	3.2	7.7	5.2	—	1.4	4.9	11.0	4.3
Single reversed chevron	3.1	3.9	1.1	3.1	6.4	1.3	4.2	7.8	8.8	5.3

Table 3. Percentage of of types of grave-goods at 10 major sites.

	Caistr	Elsham	Illgton	Lckfrd	Lovedn	Muckng	Newark	Sanctn	S.Elkn	Spong
Arrow head	—	—	—	—	—	—	—	—	—	0.1
Bone bead	—	0.5	—	—	0.8	—	—	0.4	1.1	2.8
Bronze shears	—	—	—	—	0.4	—	1.4	1.2	—	0.1
Coin	0.4	—	—	1.0	—	—	—	—	—	0.3
Coral	—	3.4	—	—	—	—	—	—	—	—
Cowrie shell	—	2.4	—	—	—	—	0.7	—	—	—
Earscoop	—	—	—	—	—	—	0.7	—	—	1.2
Girdle hanger	—	—	—	—	0.4	—	—	0.8	—	—
Honestone	—	0.5	—	—	—	—	—	—	—	0.9
Iron nail	3.1	—	—	—	0.4	—	2.8	0.8	—	—
Iron ring (non-toilet set)	1.3	0.5	—	—	0.8	—	—	—	—	0.7
Iron rivet (non-comb)	—	0.5	—	—	0.8	—	—	1.6	—	2.8
Large bead	0.4	—	—	—	1.2	—	0.7	—	—	0.6
Razor	—	1.0	—	—	—	—	—	—	—	3.0

of vessel is found in settlement assemblages, such as Mucking (Myres 1968). The proportion of decorated vessels may also be used to distinguish a cemetery assemblage from a domestic one. 77% of the total cremation data set are decorated vessels. At the village of West Stow the decorated pottery made up only 5% of the total sherd count of some 12,000 sherds (West 1969a, 1969b).

Silver ring	0.4	1.0	—	0.7	—	—	—	—	—	—
Spear	—	—	—	—	—	1.3	—	0.4	—	—
Bone fitting	0.4	4.9	1.1	—	—	—	2.1	4.9	1.1	0.3
Bone ring	—	1.5	2.1	—	1.2	—	4.9	0.4	—	1.3
Bronze fitting	0.4	1.5	1.1	0.7	0.4	—	2.1	0.8	1.1	1.5
Bronze ring	0.4	0.5	—	0.3	0.8	—	0.7	1.2	—	1.2
Buckle	0.4	—	1.1	—	1.2	3.9	0.7	2.9	—	0.4
Crystal	—	5.9	1.1	0.3	0.8	1.3	1.4	0.8	—	1.5
Glass vessel	1.8	2.4	1.1	—	1.2	2.6	0.7	0.4	—	4.3
Iron fitting	0.4	1.5	—	—	0.8	1.3	1.4	—	—	0.9
Iron knife	1.8	0.5	—	0.3	2.4	—	0.7	2.5	2.2	1.2
Iron rivet	2.6	1.0	—	0.7	1.2	—	—	4.1	—	5.0
Iron shears	0.9	0.5	—	0.3	—	—	—	0.4	1.1	0.3
Pin	—	1.5	1.1	0.3	1.6	1.3	1.4	2.9	2.2	0.1
Playing piece	0.9	2.9	2.1	1.0	6.0	5.2	1.4	0.8	2.2	2.4
Potsherd	1.3	2.0	—	—	—	—	—	—	—	9.0
Spindlewhorl	—	9.3	1.1	1.0	0.8	3.9	2.8	2.9	—	2.1
Worked flint	—	1.5	1.1	—	—	—	2.8	0.8	—	3.6
Wristclasp	—	1.0	—	2.1	0.8	—	2.1	1.2	—	0.4
Bronze fragment	2.2	21.0	6.4	1.4	10.0	14.3	15.5	14.8	4.4	8.1
Bronze sheet	6.2	5.4	4.3	1.0	1.6	3.9	4.9	1.2	2.2	8.1
Bronze tweezers	2.6	4.9	1.1	3.5	2.4	—	5.6	4.9	—	3.6
Brooch	3.0	2.0	4.3	3.2	3.2	1.3	3.5	4.9	1.1	7.0
Comb	9.7	25.4	13.8	9.1	9.6	—	23.9	14.0	—	13.0
Glass	0.9	17.6	3.2	—	2.4	—	18.3	12.8	1.1	3.7
Glass beads	9.3	16.1	9.6	—	11.6	11.7	9.9	18.5	7.7	23.0
Iron fragment	2.6	2.9	—	0.7	2.0	2.6	6.3	2.1	5.5	3.6
Ivory	1.8	13.7	5.3	2.8	2.8	—	11.3	1.6	—	6.1
Miniature iron blade	9.3	2.9	1.1	0.7	2.0	—	2.8	1.6	—	5.2
Miniature iron shears	11.0	3.9	2.1	0.3	3.6	—	4.9	0.8	—	8.7
Miniature iron tweezers	11.5	1.5	1.1	1.0	6.4	2.6	2.8	0.8	1.1	8.0

While even the most highly decorated cremation urn is likely to yield a large number of plain sherds upon breaking, this does not account for such a dramatic difference.

Clearly, the size, shape and general appearance of an Anglo-Saxon cremation urn would have served to distinguish it from pottery produced by any other cultural group, and would also distinguish between funerary and domestic assemblages, despite some overlap between them.

Ethnic group: Of the eighteen sites, only Abingdon, Mucking and Worthy Park are in what is traditionally regarded as a Saxon rather than an Anglian area of settlement (Myres 1970). As these only provide a total of 135 urns, it is not really valid to compare 'Anglian' with 'Saxon' pottery. However, it may be significant that at each of these sites the mean height for the site is lower than the mean for the total sample. This may perhaps indicate a difference between Saxon and Anglian potter's 'templates', with the Saxon potters favouring shorter vessels. Interestingly, Illington is also low, maybe indicating links with the Saxon rather than the Anglian area.

According to the present hypothesis, broad classes of decoration may also serve to distinguish between regional groupings. Clearly cemeteries represented by very few urns cannot provide a statistical sample for comparison. Only ten sites are represented by more than fifty urns, namely Caistor, Elsham, Illington, Lackford, Loveden Hill, Mucking, Newark, Sancton, South Elkington and Spong Hill. It was thought that each of these was large enough to allow it to be meaningfully compared against the others.

Table 2 indicates the proportion of urns which bear any form of decoration, for each of the ten major sites. With the exception of Mucking, the only Saxon site, about 75% of vessels are decorated at each site. Table 3 also compares proportions of various classes of incised decoration present. The most remarkable feature is again the high level of consistency in the classes used, indicating tightly defined cultural ideas of pottery style. With the exception of Mucking (where the proportion of vessels with horizontal incised decoration simply reflects the low number of vessels with any type of decoration) all sites have *c.* 75% of urns with horizontal incised decoration.

There is more variation in the percentage of urns with vertical incised lines, and Illington stands out with relatively few examples. Since the use of vertical lines is generally regarded as being part of an Anglian style of decoration (Myres 1977), this supports the case for a strong Saxon element at Illington, as suggested above.

The percentage of vessels with a continuous chevron design is relatively constant at all Anglian sites, ranging between 18.1% at Caistor and 27.6% at Sancton. In the case of individual upright and reversed chevrons, South Elkington stands out with a higher proportion of each than any other site. Caistor, Ellsham, Illington, Lackford and South Elkington have more upright than reversed chevrons. At Loveden Hill, Mucking, Newark, Sancton and Spong Hill, the balance is the other way round.

In conclusion, while there is a clear distinction between Mucking and the Anglian sites, further fine distinctions are apparent between sub-groupings within the Anglian area. Fisher (this volume) has already argued that stylistic analysis may indicate the presence of distinctions more subtle than those of 'kingdom' level.

Regional group: The use of grave-goods has traditionally been regarded as varying regionally. A comparison of the proportions of classes of grave-goods on each site may also help us to identify subtle regional variations. Table 3 presents the percentage occurrence of each class of grave-good for each of the ten major sites. The objects fall into two major groups: those that are unusual and only occur in small numbers on one or two sites, and those that appear to be standard equipment in cremation burials and turn up regularly on most sites. Into the first category fall arrow heads, bone beads, bronze shears, coins, coral, cowrie shells, earscoops, girdle hangers, honestones, iron nails, iron rings (not from miniature toilet sets), iron rivets (not from combs), large beads, razors, silver rings and spear heads. All the other items fall into the second category of objects whch are present on several sites. Since the first group are defined by their rarity few points of comparison can be made. For the second group it may be worth noting the relative frequency of individual classes, and discussing possible explanations. Within the second group we can further distinguish several objects which occur widely but in very small proportions. These include bone fittings, bone rings, bronze fittings, bronze rings, buckles, crystal, glass vessels, iron fittings, iron knives, iron comb rivets, iron shears, pins, playing pieces, potsherds, spindle whorls, worked flints and wristclasps. Finally that leaves the relatively common objects: bronze fragments, bronze sheets, bronze tweezers, brooches, combs, glass fragments and glass beads, iron fragments, ivory, miniature iron blades, iron shears and iron tweezers. It is generally only valid to base inter-site comparisons on this last group of common objects.

It is possible to make the following generalisations about proportions of grave-goods at each of the ten sites. Firstly, we should not allow minor differences in proportions of grave-goods to let us to lose sight of the fact that the overall impression is of a high level of consistency between sites. We may conclude that Anglo-Saxons at each site were practising a broadly similar burial rite. They were including the same general types of grave-goods and presumably these goods were used to mark the same features of social identity. Differences between sites must reflect regional variation in the use of grave-goods.

Secondly, there are some grave-goods which appear regularly in the same proportions at each site, while there are others where the proportion varies markedly between sites. Brooches are a particularly good example of the first type of object. They never occur in less than 1% of vessels, and never in more than 7%. Thus their use as identity markers seems highly consistent throughout the cremating areas of Anglo-Saxon England. In contrast, items such as combs may appear in 25% of vessels at some sites (Elsham, Newark) and be entirely absent at others (Mucking, S. Elkington). Thus there is tremendous regional variation in the use of such objects as identity markers.

Thirdly, those objects which are used in different proportions at different sites, it may be possible to distinguish between groups of sites which share the same traditions. At first sight, it may seem that there is simply random variation between sites, with continuous gradations in the proportions of grave-goods used. One should be cautious of arbitrarily creating groups of similar sites. Nevertheless, it does appear possible to isolate certain reasonably distinctive groups.

Table 4. Distance coefficient matrix.

	Caistr	Elsham	Illgton	Lckfrd	Muckng	Newark	Sanctn	S.Elkn	Spong
Caistr	0.00								
Elsham	11.83	0.00							
Illgtn	5.39	9.73	0.00						
Lovedn	4.00	10.01	2.36	0.00					
Muckng	7.36	12.19	5.48	4.63	0.00				
Newark	9.28	3.09	7.37	7.53	10.28	0.00			
Sanctn	9.04	5.92	6.51	6.50	8.73	4.46	0.00		
S.Elkn	7.04	13.97	5.46	4.94	3.92	11.57	9.89	0.00	
Spong	6.56	6.16	6.13	5.50	8.77	3.91	4.21	9.88	0.00

A hierarchical clustering procedure was applied to the information about proportions of commonly occurring grave-goods contained in table 3. The hierarchical clustering model is appropriate, for the groups are not especially discrete and each is part of a larger group of similar sites at a higher level.[3] The results are presented in the distance coefficient matrix in table 4 and the dendrogram in figure 2.

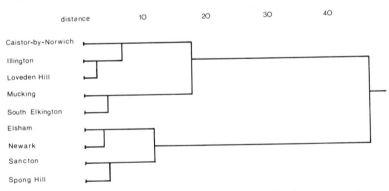

Figure 2. Dendrogram for hierarchical clustering of 9 sites by grave-goods. Cophrenetic correlation coefficient = 0.47327.

Illington and Loveden Hill clearly fit into one group of sites with relatively low proportions of combs, ivory, bronze fragments and glass beads, and very low numbers of miniatures. Caistor joins this group at a higher level because of the greater number of miniatures present. Mucking and South Elkington form another category of sites with few grave-goods, and where combs, ivory and miniatures are extremely scarce. However, all these sites are clearly distinguished from the remaining four by the clustering procedure. Elsham and Newark each have a high proportion of ivory, combs, glass beads, bronze fragments and relatively infrequent miniatures. Sancton and Spong Hill may also belong with them, especially when the number of small rivets is added to the number of combs.

The main conclusion from these groupings of grave-good assemblages is that Bede's account is a gross oversimplification:

> They came from three very powerful Germanic tribes, the Saxons, Angles, and Jutes. The people of Kent and the inhabitants of the Isle of Wight are of Jutish origin and also those opposite the Isle of Wight, that part of the Kingdom of Wessex which is still today called the nation of the Jutes. From the Saxon country, that is, the district now known as Old Saxony, came the East Saxons, the South Saxons, and the West Saxons. Besides this, from the country of the Angles, that is, the land between the kingdoms of the Jutes and the Saxons, which is called *Angulus*, came the East Angles, the Middle Angles, the Mercians, and all the Northumbrian race (that is those people who dwell north of the river Humber) as well as the other Anglian tribes. (*HE* I, 15)

At a very general level the archaeological evidence lends some support to this picture, although it is widely accepted that there was a greater mixing of peoples than allowed for by Bede (Hills 1979, 313–7). At a finer level of detail, however, it appears that there are other groupings which are not accounted for by the traditional model. There are clear groupings of cemeteries, for example, comprising sites from geographically distinct locations. One explanation might be that several groups of Anglo-Saxon newcomers, each importing their own variation of cremation burial rite, must each have split into smaller groups and settled in different areas of England where they maintained their own customs. While they may have shared the practice of cremation with their neighbours, the use of particular grave-goods may have differentiated them from their immediate neighbours and united them with related peoples living further afield. These distinctions may have been consciously maintained as a means of reinforcing social ties.

Age, sex or other social group: It is generally held that grave-goods are also used to mark vertical social role, and to distinguish between individuals of different age, sex, status, etc. That assumption will be maintained here. If attributes of the cremation urns are themselves used to mark social position within Anglo-Saxon society, then one would expect to find both positive and negative associations between pottery style and urn contents. For instance, if a particular grave-good is found in vessels bearing a particular decorative motif more times than could reasonably be expected by chance, then a positive association must exist. The decorative motif may be taken to signify the same aspect of social role as represented by the grave-good. The aspects of social role signified may include sex, age at death, group affiliation (including kinship and/or moiety or clan allegiance), status (including wealth and the number of individuals owing allegiance to the deceased), circumstances of death (including place and cause). Skeletal remains provide some means of identifying cases where we are concerned with either of the first two aspects, but at present it does not appear to be possible to distinguish between the latter three.

The *chi*-square test was used to establish whether the degree of association between particular pottery attributes and definable aspects of social role is greater than could be expected by chance. In tables 5 and 6 associations significant at levels of 10% or greater have been underlined. Cowgill (1977) has pointed out the dangers of reading too much into significance levels, and has warned against choosing an arbitrary cut-off point. Significance levels are therefore given for each association. The further the value from 1.0, then the greater the variation from a random distribution.

In order to examine vertical differentiation it is necessary to analyse the sample from one site. Spong Hill, as the largest, is the most likely to yield statistically significant results, although it suffers from the disadvantage that skeletal data was only available for a few of the cremations. Similar links are also found at other sites included in the study data. Table 5 indicates the significant links between a few common grave-goods and particular classes of incised decoration present in a random sample of 482 vessels from Spong Hill. The first column shows the total number of vessels with each of five aspects of incised or impressed decoration. The subsequent columns show the proportion of vessels with each of these aspects of decoration and also containing particular grave-goods.

Horizontal incised decoration shows no significant links, whilst vertical incised lines are more common on vessels containing tweezers and single iron blades than would be expected. Shears follow the same trend although the association is not significant at the 10% (0.1) level. The use of diagonal incised decoration (mainly various classes of chevron) displays no significant links with any of the grave-goods. On the other hand, curvilinear decoration (hanging and standing arches) are very highly correlated with iron blades and shears, but not with tweezers. Finally, dots are linked with glass beads, but not with any of the other grave-goods.

Table 6 shows which of these grave-goods are age or sex related, using all Anglo-Saxon cremations for which there is skeletal evidence. Because of the large numbers of infants, children and adolescents in multiple burials, only those vessels containing one individual were included for these cross-tabulations. The significance levels for sex-links are for a combined male versus female test.

Of the five classes of grave-goods examined, only iron shears and iron tweezers display sex-links significant at the 10% level. Both occur in male and female burials, but they are more common in male ones. The other grave-goods appear to be randomly distributed throughout male and female burials. This is particularly surprising in the case of glass beads, which are found in nineteen male burials, and may force us to revise our intuitive interpretation of these objects as items of female apparel. As the number of beads present was not distinguished it is possible that the nineteen cases may all be examples of single beads attached to sword pommels, and known as 'sword beads'. This must be an area for further research.

Table 5. Associations between classes of grave-good and classes of incised decoration in 482 urns from Spong Hill.

| | Total | | TYPE OF GRAVE-GOOD | | | | | | | | | | | | |
| | | | Glass beads | | | Iron blade | | | Iron shears | | | Tweezers | | |
Incised decoration:	No.	Col.%	No.	Col.%	Sig.	No.	Col.%	Sig.	No.	Col.%	Sig.	No.	Col.%	Sig.
Horizontal	371	77.0	115	81.6	0.16	28	87.5	0.21	38	84.4	0.29	45	83.3	0.31
Vertical	148	30.7	44	31.2	0.96	15	46.9	0.06	18	40.0	0.21	24	44.4	0.03
Diagonal	169	35.1	51	36.2	0.82	12	37.5	0.92	17	37.8	0.81	23	42.6	0.28
Curvilinear	86	17.8	21	14.9	0.34	13	40.6	0.001	18	40.0	0.001	12	22.2	0.48
Dots	82	17.0	32	22.7	0.05	6	18.7	0.98	11	24.4	0.24	10	18.5	0.90

Table 6. Associations between grave-good classes and skeletal groupings.

| | N | GRAVE-GOODS | | | | | | | | | | | | | | |
| | | Glass beads | | | Min. Fe blade | | | Min. Fe shears | | | Min. Fe tweezers | | | Ae tweezers | | |
		No.	Row%	Sig.	No.	Row%	Sig.	No.	Row%	Sig.	No.	Row%	Sig.	No.	Row%	Sig.
Total	442	118	26.7		20	4.5		31	7.0		29	6.6		32	7.2	
Male	73	19	26.0	0.39	3	4.1	1.0	8	11.0	0.08*	8	11.0	0.03*	5	5.8	1.0
Female	115	38	33.0		4	3.5		4	3.5		3	2.6		9	7.8	
Young adult	84	26	31.0	0.4	—	—	0.05*	—	—	0.01	1	1.2	0.05	8	9.5	0.51
Mature adult	82	22	26.8	1.0	4	4.9	1.0	3	3.7	0.28	1	1.2	0.06	6	7.3	1.0
Old adult	21	6	28.6	1.0	1	4.8	1.0	3	14.3	0.37	1	4.8	1.0	4	19.0	0.09*
Adult	181	52	28.7	0.49	6	3.3	0.43	13	7.2	1.0	19	10.5	0.01	14	7.7	0.88
Total	391	99	25.3		17	4.3		30	7.7		28	7.2		27	6.9	
Infant	14	1	7.1	0.2	2	14.3	0.23	—	—	0.56	1	7.1	1.0	1	7.1	1.0
Child	61	16	26.2	0.99	7	11.5	0.01*	10	16.4	0.01*	3	4.9	0.64	3	4.9	0.7
Adolescent	28	7	25.0	1.0	2	7.1	0.79	3	10.7	0.8	4	14.3	0.26	2	7.1	1.0

* 25% of the valid cells have expected cell frequency less than 5.0.

The correlations with age groupings again reveal that each of the grave-goods is found with each age-group, although some tend to be associated with particular groups. Miniature iron blades and shears are positively associated with children, but are not found once the individuals reach young adulthood, although they return in later adulthood. A high proportion of the single blades may be half of a pair of shears, so the link is really between shears and children. We do not know whether the shears were intended for personal use, but they are simply miniature versions of those used for sheep-shearing. It may be that, judging from a link between child burials and the inclusion of cremated sheep bones, children may have been associated with sheep in the Anglo-Saxon mind. Iron tweezers, on the other hand, are positively linked with the general adult category but are less common in those burials where the individual has been identified as a young or mature adult. Bronze tweezers do not display any significant links, nor do glass beads.

In summary, it is apparent that within a cemetery, pottery and grave-good attributes, which on a horizontal level mark regional and sub-regional differences, may also mark vertical aspects of social role within one area. Some grave-goods appear to be age and sex linked, but others mark some other aspect of social role about which we can only speculate, such as totemic or moiety grouping. Even groups of items frequently found together, such as miniature toilet implements, must be split into specific items each reflecting different aspects of social role.

Potter's style group: Finally, it is proposed that there is a level of microvariation of style which does not relate to horizontal or vertical roles of the deceased, but rather reflects the style of individual potters. It has long been accepted that it is possible to identify the work of potters or schools of potters (Myres 1937). Therefore, pots sharing the same stamp are immediately recognisable as the work of a specific potter or group of potters. Other detailed aspects of decoration also seem peculiar to individual potters. Table 7 compares the standard deviation in the number of horizontal incised fields per vessel for twenty stamp groups identified at Spong Hill. It also gives figures for the average number of horizontal lines per field for each of the same twenty stamp groups. The top line gives the figures for all vessels from Spong Hill with horizontal incised decoration. The number of urns in each stamp group is clearly much smaller, but nevertheless one would expect higher standard deviations unless there is a high level of consistency within the group. In all cases except one (Stamp Group 7) there is considerably less variation within a stamp group than between stamp groups. Therefore potters appeared to favour the use of specific numbers of fields of lines and numbers of lines within a field, and it would have been possible to identify the work of particular potters by the details of their pottery. On the other hand, such fine details of style are probably not used to mark any of the broader aspects of vertical and horizontal social differentiation discussed above. The number of lines in a horizontal incised band was cross-tabulated against skeletal and grave-good classes. In only one case was there a positive link (between combs and vessels with a large number of lines,

Table 7. Spong Hill: variation in horizontal incised decoration within stamp groups.

| | No. of urns | STANDARD DEVIATION | |
		No. of horiz. incised fields	Avge. no. of horiz. lines per field
Total	381	1.152	1.615
Stamp group			
1	3	0.6	0.6
4	4	1.0	0.5
5	3	0.0	0.6
6	2	0.0	0.0
7	17	2.5	0.9
8	4	0.0	0.9
10	2	0.7	0.0
11	2	0.7	0.0
14	2	0.0	0.0
15	2	0.0	0.0
17	3	1.0	1.0
19	2	0.0	0.0
20	3	1.0	0.0
22	2	0.7	0.0
26	2	0.0	0.0
28	2	0.0	0.0
31	3	0.6	0.6
38	2	0.7	0.7
41	2	0.7	0.7
42	3	0.6	0.6

significant at the 0.01 level). This may just have occurred by chance, but it does leave the possibility open that even such fine details of style may mark social role.

This chapter has sought to demonstrate that stylistic variability in Anglo-Saxon pottery can operate on several levels. Different attributes are used to mark different aspects of social role. There is a sliding scale of visibility of these attributes, according to the size of the audience to which the message is being broadcast, although there is considerable overlap between levels. The overall picture is extremely complex, with a particular grave-good, for example, representing a particular social role, according to which other attributes (both ceramic and other grave-goods) it is associated with.

The general appearance of a vessel identifies it as Germanic. The proportion of decorated vessels and of different forms allow a cemetery assemblage to be distinguished from a settlement assemblage. Differences in the proportions of vessels with particular classes of incised decoration mark an assemblage as Anglian or Saxon, whilst finer differences distinguish between regional sub-groupings. Within a single site, specific decorative motifs appear to mark age, sex and other social groupings. The use of incised arches, for example, signifies a group who are also represented by the inclusion of miniature iron blades and shears on the pyre. Some of these miniatures may be marking the burial as that of a child, but others may be representing other aspects of identity; and not all children will be accompanied by blades and shears. The actual number of arches, however, and the number of lines per arch may be used to distinguish vessels produced by particular potters, and would have no significance to a wider audience. In conclusion, one cannot fully explain the stylistic variability in Anglo-Saxon ceramics by examining one level alone. A composite model is needed, incorporating several levels of differentiation, and offering reconciliation between the culture historical and more recent schools of archaeological thought. The overall impression is of a society with a highly complex iconography and finely divided but well-defined social ranks. Archaeology allows us to build upon what we know from the written sources. It reveals that the historical picture is basically correct but that it appears to be an over-simplification of reality in the fifth to seventh centuries.

Acknowledgements

My first acknowledgement must be to those who have excavated and published the Anglo-Saxon cremation vessels incorporated in the study. They are too numerous to name individually, but one man, J. N. L. Myres, must be singled out. His *Corpus* remains the starting point for anyone studying Anglo-Saxon pottery.

A further debt is due to those archaeologists who have allowed me to draw freely upon excavated material which is currently being prepared for publication. Firstly, I must thank the Spong Hill project, namely Catherine Hills, Kenneth Penn and Robert Rickett. At Mucking Post-Excavation, Margaret and Tom Jones and their colleagues gave me every assistance. For Elsham, I am indebted to Freda Berisford and Chris Knowles; for Newark to Gavin Kinsley; for Sancton to Nicholas Reynolds; for Illington to Barbara Green and Bill Milligan; and for Worthy Park to Sonia Hawkes. In addition, I am grateful to Mary Harman and Keith Manchester for allowing me to use their unpublished skeletal reports.

The research was carried out with the support of an SERC studentship. In addition to the many individuals mentioned above who have given freely of time and information, I am especially grateful to the research supervisors, Dr Catherine Hills and Dr John Wilcock. Any errors are my own responsibility.

NOTES

1   The problem of multiple burials (Putnam 1980) means a weakening of associations between skeletal groups and grave-goods, and between skeletal groups, grave-good groups and ceramic attributes. Nevertheless, it is apparent that each individual is still marked.

2   This is not intended as an exhaustive list, and there may be other levels of stylistic variation, such as chronological variation. How-

ever, in the absence of a well-secured chronology for Early Anglo-Saxon pottery, I have adopted a synchronic approach to the material, as does Fisher earlier in this volume.

3 Lackford was excluded because of incomplete grave-good data. For purposes of comparison the values for glass and glass beads were combined, as were those for bronze fragments and bronze sheets. Excavators have been inconsistent in distinguishing between these objects in the past. Iron rivets were added to the figures for combs, as they probably represent the only surviving fragments of additional combs.

The relationship between history and archaeology: artefacts, documents and power

This chapter is about working with documents and artefacts of the Early Historic period in Britain and Ireland. It is intended for scholars who believe that their central task is to use both texts and artefacts to write histories which account for the greatest possible portion of society. Simply stated, this problem may be conceived of in two ways: as a philosophical question or alternatively as a methodological one. From the methodological perspective, the integration of various sources of information generates the major difficulties, because information about the past derives from different materials – parchment, pots, inscriptions, postholes – each drawing upon the interpretation of a specialist. This widely held view does not question the value of disciplinary boundaries, but sees boundaries as an intrinsic property of the intellectual architecture necessary for the progress of knowledge. Viewed, however, as a philosophical problem, at issue is the procedure by which we create history from documents and artefacts. Here, interpretation of the past hinges on the theory by which we understand the interrelationship of human action, society and material culture, and takes it as axiomatic that our knowledge of the past derives from the present. I will not undertake a detailed discussion of general social theory here, but the arguments which follow are informed by my sympathy with the philosophic perspective.

Conventional history and archaeology tend to view the question of integrating historical and archaeological knowledge as, for the most part, a methodological problem. This imposes specific limitations on the ability of conventional practitioners to perform the integration adequately. This chapter examines the nature of those limitations as part of the effort towards improving our ability to interpret documents, artefacts and society.

Two premises define the objectives of this chapter. First, it is beneficial to disregard the conventional disciplinary boundaries of historical scholarship; and, more importantly, it is essential to examine critically the assumptions about past society which are implicit in those boundaries. Particularly problematic is our use of literacy, a concept with a specifically modern meaning, as the organising principle governing the study of the past. In other words, the modern formulations of history and archaeology may, through their very structure, inhibit our understanding of the past. In this instance the erosion of disciplinary boundaries would be a constructive process. Second, use of social theory generated by anthropology and sociology is the means to achieve this critical vantage point. By this I do not wish to replace one set of methodological constraints by another: rather, since it is society we are studying, I suggest that we take note of the social scientist's understanding of the way in which society works. At various points, this chapter relies upon the work of anthropologists and sociologists for insights into the workings of material culture, the social construction of reality and social reproduction. These excursions into the social sciences should be judged both in terms of their coherence and in terms of the explanations these bodies of theory generate.

Accepting these premises entails acceptance of, or at least recognition of, certain philosophical attitudes and observance of certain practices. For myself, these may be summarised as a continual concern with the assumptions, goals and motives of my study. Critical theory is a term describing this concern with understanding the cultural attitudes of the analyst *vis-à-vis* the object of study. It is a recognition that we always introduce an interpretative framework or theory of society in order to make sense of disparate facts about the past. It requires that we acknowledge what theory we use and why we favour it. This is of course the position outlined by E. H. Carr in *What is History?* (1961). Scholars who fail to discuss more or less explicitly their assumptions and theory arouse suspicion and distrust because of the many possible interpretations of their silence. This silence is unfortunately institutionalised in the publication practices of medieval history and archaeology.

One possible reading of such silence on theoretical matters is as an ignorance of the historicity of our values, and is apparent in the use of contemporary values to interpret the past. In its most extreme form an image of our society is reproduced in the past, producing a history which may be termed 'Whigish'. Statements about past society found in this sort of history are of little use. Silence on theoretical issues may also indicate an empiricist outlook, which considers thought and reality as distinct entities. Assuming the existence of a single, ethically neutral, objective interpretation of those facts which constitute reality means that attention is laid upon the means by which that interpretation may be arrived at and agreed upon. It has been suggested that an emphasis on methodology is symptomatic of this perspective (Saitta 1983), which may explain why we find more written about the techniques of excavation and analysis of medieval sites than on their interpretation. A third possible reading of that silence is as an expression of the idea that knowledge flows from the accumulation of fact (naïve positivism) and that the structure of the explanation is derived unambiguously from the facts. This is perhaps best exemplified by the production of corpuses of artefacts and documents which lack any interpretation beyond date and means of manufacture.

It is important to be equally clear about why we study history as about how we study it. Historiography shows that history does not exist as some objective reality external to the contemporary world, and anthropology suggests how the past and present may be related. Henry Glassie, taking a cue from Malinowski's metaphor of myth as a primitive social charter, writes:

> History is myth because its elements are infinitely capable of new orderings and these new orderings selectively explain the present in terms of the past and guide us in the creation of the moments out of which the future witlessly unfolds. (1977, 1)

Myth here is not a synonym for fiction, but describes a means of comprehending the world. It serves to emphasise that history is a creative social process and that the 'tie between the present and the past is what the former does with the latter, not how the former grew from the latter' (Leone 1982a, 182). Moreover, if history is critical, it provides commentary on the present, if uncritical, it reaffirms the present, neither of which is politically neutral. These ideas will be useful to bear in mind when we turn to consider the relationship between writing and power.

This is a chapter in four parts, each of which is shaped with the Early Historic period in mind. Part I examines how the relationship between history and archaeology has been constructed. It consists of a brief critique of the conventional academic formulation of the distinction between documents and artefacts. It is argued that the academic disciplinary divisions impose our literate values on past cultural practice in order to claim that there exists a natural division between documents and artefacts. This is primarily because documents happen to be the cultural expressions we are most adept at reading. For the Early Historic period documents are the most complex and specific (surviving) media of communication, but writing did not (and indeed does not) have a monopoly of expression. This leads directly to Part II, which examines how political power may be mediated through the technology of writing. Establishing the link between writing and power makes it apparent that literacy must be considered as a phenomenon with unique properties derived from the specific political circumstances of its use. Moreover, since writing is just one instance, albeit a special one, of human agency creating a material record, we should be able to extend that knowledge about the link between power, human action and writing to the material record in general.

Establishing the connection between power and artefacts means first of all learning to 'read' them as we do documents: as expressive things actively involved in mediating social relations. Part III is an introduction to the methods of 'reading' artefacts which have been pioneered by American historical archaeologists working in the anthropological paradigm. This is a fairly recent development, which must be placed in the broader context of Binford's New Archaeology (Schuyler 1978; Ferguson 1977). The chapter concludes with an outline of an analysis of Pictish symbol stones which puts into practice those ideas about reading artefacts and about relating them to human action and power.

1. History and archaeology: a created relationship

The past as we know it is a cultural construction and as such the methods of its construction are constantly subject to revision. If the historical record is to be interpreted as a record of human social and political action, then a theory of historical archaeology must acknowledge two fundamental points. These bald assertions will be developed in due course; here they serve to introduce my arguments, and as a point of departure for the following discussion.

1. Documents and artefacts are both components of material culture, in so

far as both are instances of human action imposing form on nature. If we are interested in human action, then we must determine the nature of human action before examining its specific manifestations, such as pottery, charters and so on.

2. Documents and artefacts are both means by which social relations are negotiated, which is to say that artefacts, like documents, articulate social relations, are utilised as expressive media and therefore should be conceived of as socially active (not passively, as labels or markers). Understanding the socal meaning of either documents or artefacts is achieved via examination of specific contexts of use, production and discard. Here the point is that the meanings of artefacts are defined by their social context (Foxon 1982; Hodder 1982c).

The conventional formulation of the relationship between history and archaeology segregates artefact-making from writing. These activities are seen as so distinctive as to be institutionalised in separate academic disciplines. The histories of the two disciplines are well known, yet the basis of this division is taken for granted. The rare scholarly statements referring explicitly to the epistemological relationship of document to artefact emphasise that making texts and making things are different sorts of human phenomena. This emphasis on difference makes it difficult for the conventional formulation to accommodate either of my two theoretical points. The validity or usefulness of the separate disciplines is never questioned by conventional practitioners because the distinction between document and artefact is believed to be so fundamental (cf. Wainwright 1962; Dymond 1974; Sawyer 1983b; Rahtz 1983). In failing to grasp the congruence of documents and artefacts as products of thoughtful human action, we are left with investigative methods which run parallel and appear to converge somewhere on the horizon but, like railroad tracks, never really meet.

At the risk of caricaturing the conventional attitude, there are certain typical expressions which are revealing. The objectivity and reliability of archaeology is proclaimed in the maxim 'the spade doesn't lie', and in statements such as:

> Archaeological facts, because they are usually unconscious evidence not created with communication in mind, are often thought to be less prone to misinterpretation than written evidence with its conscious or unconscious bias. (Addyman 1976, 311)

The disciplinary turf once marked out is defended with xenophobic fervour by leading scholars. An historian writes:

> . . . the two disciplines should use their own techniques on their own material and only then see what measure of agreement there is, and to what extent the different types of evidence can complement each other. (Sawyer 1983b, 47)

A recent defence of archaeological independence set the model of archaeology as a natural science in opposition to the subjectivity of historical scholarship (Rahtz 1982, 1983). In presenting archaeology as a scientific test for documentary history, Rahtz not only swallows the epistemological flaws of the New

Archaeology, but at the same time robs archaeology of any explanatory power *a priori* (Driscoll 1984).

The conventional position contains two unstated and thus unexamined assumptions. First, that the division between document and artefact is natural because the mental processes at work in each instance are different: therefore the disciplinary boundaries are epistemologically valid. Second, that artefacts can only be known at the functional level, since meaning and intention are so remote from form. They are assumed to be incommunicative about social matters in sharp contrast to documents. When we turn to look at the work of certain American historical archaeologists in Part III, it will become clear that neither assumption can be sustained. Indeed, the entire endeavour of the scholars in question (James Deetz, Henry Glassie and Mark Leone) requires their rejection, since all three stress the common mental threads running through all sorts of human activity.

If the division between document and artefact is not 'natural' then it must be cultural, that is to say a product of our own culture. The origin of the division can perhaps best be understood as an imposition of our literate values and biases on the past. In Part II, I argue that it is restrictive to conceive of literacy as an undifferentiated skill which a society simply does or does not possess. The ability of writing to channel power dictates that it has specific social and political associations, in short that it has a history and a historically specific meaning. In this sense literacy is like other seemingly natural and unproblematic concepts such as time (Evans-Pritchard 1940; Leone 1978), space (Hall 1966; Goffman 1959; Kuper 1972) and gender, all of which require critical examination before they can be applied to a society other than our own. The case of gender is instructive. Scholars working from a feminist perspective have criticised the 'naturalness' of the notion of gender as it defines appropriate behaviour of the sexes, and they argue that gender is a cultural construction with political implications not unlike those of 'class' (Harris and Young 1981; Ortner and Whitehead 1981). Viewed with a critical understanding of gender serious deficiencies and distortions are apparent in the usual presentation of women in archaeological literature (Braithwaite 1982a; Conkey and Spector 1984), to say nothing of the historical literature. This suggests that a critical examination of the concept of gender must precede its use as an analytical term in historical scholarship. A similar critical analysis of literacy must precede any discussion of the role of documents in a given society.

The deconstruction of the conventional view of the relationship between history and archaeology as complementary but separate disciplines serves several purposes. The point is to recognise that documents and artefacts are the products of similar mental processes, which are to be understood by using similar analytical frameworks. Ideally such an approach helps to avoid prejudicing social analysis at the outset. Such an analytical framework must accommodate both documents and artefacts, yet be derived from a general social theory independent of the specific methodologies of history, archaeology, anthropology or sociology.

I am here asserting that the analysis of material culture should be linked to a precise notion of human action, and should be interpreted through its role in negotiating social relations. *Social reproduction* describes the continuous renewal and transformation of the social system including its institutions, patterns of social relations, values, cultural practices and its whole cognitive structure. Social reproduction is achieved through human action of all sorts and is therefore a continuous process. Both building a house and writing a charter contribute to social reproduction in that they draw upon existing knowledge about society and reassert it. In the case of building a house, the location of the kitchen *vis-à-vis* the bedroom is an expression of cultural practices associated with eating and sleeping and actively intervenes to organise those practices (Bourdieu 1973; Glassie 1982). A charter likewise seeks to create and regulate certain cultural practices associated with tenancy, ownership and production. Social reproduction is a process carried out by individuals acting more or less pragmatically. It does not function like a xerox machine; change is constantly occurring. As Sahlins says, 'At the last, all structural transformation involves structural reproduction, if not also the other way around' (1981, 68).

'Every social actor knows a great deal about the conditions of reproduction of the society of which he or she is a member' (Giddens 1979, 5). Human action is the 'continuous flow of conduct' of motivated and conscious behaviour, governed by cultural norms. This cognitive view of society as developed with specific reference to material culture is discussed in Part III. Attendant on this notion of meaningful human action are the 'unacknowledged conditions and unintended consequences' which contribute to the real outcome of any given act (Giddens 1979, 55–6). It is essential to recognise that 'People act upon circumstances according to their own cultural presuppositions, the socially given categories of persons and things' (Sahlins 1981, 67), if our model of society is not to be populated by complete dupes. One of the great tasks of twentieth-century anthropology has been to demonstrate that the cultural practices of so-called primitives exhibit as much rationality as our own when examined in the light of their own beliefs and systems of knowledge. We must expect that the societies we study will have sources of knowledge radically different from our scientifically dominated sources. Sahlins uses the term 'mytho-praxis' to refer to societies whose most valid form of knowledge is that encoded in myth (1983); might not that also be true of some Early Historic societies?

One of the achievements of Marxist inspired sociology has been to illuminate the intergroup dynamics occurring within a society. In any society, even the simplest, there exist different interest groups based upon age, sex, birth, social status and so on, each of which have distinct views on how society should work and their own means of validating knowledge. Thus social reproduction involves competition. The patterns of action or strategies adopted by groups and individuals may be termed *discourse*. The term is useful because discourse implies a more or less continuous pattern of behaviour governed by 'cultural presuppositions' which are not always conscious. It suggests an analogy with speech and its relation to grammar. In order for discourse to be useful to the archaeologist or historian it must refer not only to verbal, face to face negotiations, but to every medium by which social relations are negotiated. It must include both mundane practices such as the wearing of specific clothing (cf. Hebidge 1979) and the preparation of food, as well as exceptional activities which we might wish to label as historical, like writing a law or staging a revolt. A good example of this, involving material culture, is Mauss' *Essai sûr le don* (1954), where gift giving is studied as a means of asserting political superiority and creating social obligations. An example of the discursive properties of material culture drawn from personal experience may help to show how objects are actually involved in negotiating social relations. A trowel is not only a device for spreading mortar or scraping earth, but because of these associations it comes to signify masons and archaeologists. Thus seeing a trowel in someone's pocket is likely to guide how we address them (especially if we are archaeologists or masons).

To sum up, in this scheme, logically the products of knowledgeable action (like writing or housebuilding) are *necessarily* linked to social discourse and the strategies of social reproduction.

11. Literacy and power: the technology of writing

The advent of literacy is generally regarded as the threshold of civilisation. Historians and archaeologists have expended considerable effort documenting the major cultural transformations accompanying writing, the chief of which is the growth of extensive political entities: city states, kingdoms, empires, and so on. However, the notion of literacy normally used is a taken for granted, common sense one vaguely denoting the practice of reading and writing. Recently more precise formulations have been sought which develop from an awareness that '. . . writing is not a monolithic entity, an undifferentiated skill; its potentialities depend upon the kind of system that obtains in any particular society' (Goody 1968, 3). In other words, since the meaning and practice of literacy vary from culture to culture, our attitudes to literacy are not transferable.

The identification of literacy as the hallmark of civilisation has tended unconsciously to connect it with rational thought, self-awareness and progress. That is to say literacy, as we conceive of it, is a constructive, stabilising social force. Clearly such a notion of literacy is of little use in assessing the significance of writing in Early Historic society (or any other). To accept our notion of literacy as universal is to deny that the importance and meaning of writing stems from the particular social and political context in which it is practised.

If we are to discover the significance of writing in Early Historic society, we should approach it as a medium of social discourse. It is my general thesis that artefacts and documents should be approached similarly so as to reveal the link between power and discourse. The case for literacy is presented first because it should be easier to demonstrate this link between power and cultural expressions if we start with the familiar example of the technology of writing.

Power is a term so frequently used to mean so many things, that it is worth clarifying the specific notion of power that I wish to use in describing properties of social discourse. This brief definition is drawn from the extensive writings on the subject by Anthony Giddens and Michael Foucault (Dreyfus and Rabinow 1982; Cousins and Hussain 1984). Power is a property found in the matrix of social relations and is reciprocal, not one sided. It affects both master and slave, lord and client:

> Power relations are relations of autonomy and dependence, but even the most autonomous agent is in some degree dependent, and the most dependent actor or party in a relationship retains some autonomy. (Giddens 1979, 93)

According to Giddens, power is logically linked to human action and refers to the 'use of resources, of whatever kind, to secure outcomes' (1979, 347). Power is manifest in social relations where there is an asymmetry in the ability to command material resources (to allocate goods and facilities) and in the ability to exercise authority over others. It is important not to conceive of power negatively, as restriction or coercion. In some instances the asymmetry of power relations can be termed domination, but power may not be reduced to simple domination. The point of this elaborate definition is to suggest why power is intrinsic to all human relationships and to emphasise that power is expresssed through the various forms of material culture, in so far as material culture is a medium of social interaction. The implications of this definition for the study of the development of Early Historic kingdoms should be clear. The technical properties of writing enabled power relations to be expanded beyond the confines of kinship, either real or imagined.

In an article entitled 'The Consequences of Literacy', Goody and Watt (1963) provided what can be termed a handbook on the technical properties of writing which was, in fact, a guide outlining cultural changes which could be expected to accompany literacy. They drew upon evidence from the invention of writing in the Ancient World and, more pertinent to the Early Historic period, from the introduction of writing to traditionally oral, non-literate societies under Western colonialism and Islamic imperialism.

Goody and Watt were not concerned to examine any particular case and thus did not explore the link between writing and power in a specific historical situation. Their cross-cultural approach gives the impression that they believed the consequences of literacy to be broadly similar regardless of historical circumstances (since corrected in Goody 1968). Nor did their study allow them to consider how writing is seized as a political instrument. These reservations aside, it is a groundbreaking survey. Its influence may be judged from the number of scholars inspired to study the social contexts of literacy in specific situations (e.g. Goody 1968). Of particular relevance here is Michael Clanchy's 'Remembering the Past and the Good Old Law' (1970), which examines the changes in medieval English legal practice associated with the proliferation of writing. He recognises that '. . . the extension of writing is not in itself a measure of progress . . .' (1970, 176). And more to the point, he notes the political implications of written law, which were to make the crown (and attendant arbiters of the written word) more powerful. Clanchy's paper is a useful introduction to the historical analysis of the political impact of literate technology.

Having said that writing is to be understood from the historical and social contexts of its practice, it is nonetheless worth reviewing the general properties which may be ascribed to literacy. The special skills of reading are learned skills, and imply formal teaching if not institutionalised education. Frequently an expertise in letters precludes participation in normal food and craft production. The equipment and facilites for writing, like parchment and books, tend to be expensive. Thus in Early Historic Britain and Ireland where literacy was restricted to a tiny portion of society (Wormald 1977), literate individuals represented a significant social and economic investment. Literate knowledge tends to be the privilege of the elite, not least because the elite tend to control the material means of literacy. Not surprisingly most documents produced before the age of print reflect these social and economic facts. The close association between the written word and the powerful provides the idea of documents with authority. Restrictions on learning literate skills ensure that written knowledge is privileged. In addition, the religious context of literate education makes all writing to some extent sacred and even arcane.

In societies where very few are literate, documents are simultaneously authoritative and mysterious and those possessing literate skills stand in a special position within the network of power. With respect to the text, the interpreters are essential for the propagation of the written expression and are powerful in that they may recall details with as much accuracy as is convenient. The autonomy of those with literate skills is ensured by the production of further texts requiring interpretation. With respect to their audience, interpreters are clearly dominant by virtue of their privileged access to knowledge, which is constrained only by the extent to which their reading is believable.

As compared to speech, the written word has a more abstract and general relationship to its referent. Writing extracts the referent from its context in a particular speech community located in time and space. Objectification describes this process whereby ease and subtlety of expression are sacrificed for intelligibility. It is a necessary trade-off if the ideas represented by words are to be understood beyond the speech community.

Fixing events in ink makes it difficult to accommodate changing social and political situations; it establishes a sort of past which is alien to oral tradition. It alters the perception of time by introducing a chronology which is abstracted from the time of daily routine and extends beyond cyclical annual time.

We may shift away from these general properties of literacy to the relationship between writing and power by turning to look at the capacity of literacy to transform social relations. The transformations are not automatic consequences of the technology, but are the results (perhaps unintended) of efforts to extend power. Writing above all facilitates the expansion of social relations beyond the kin group and those which may be maintained by face to face contact. The obvious administrative advantage in political terms is the ability to transcend limits of time and space and maintain relationships in several places at once. This advantage is not without its drawbacks. The objectification of social relation freezes what was once fluid and introduces a degree of alienation. Criticism of authority becomes easier because flaws are more readily identified in writing than in speech, and are easier to voice since they may be directed against a document not *ad hominem*.

Concepts of time and the past are altered by literacy. Evans-Pritchard's famous discussion of the non-literate Nuer (1940) perhaps typifies the 'primitive' view of time which has been variously described as reversible, cyclical or unprogressive (see Goody 1977). Time reckoning for the Nuer is 'less a means of co-ordinating events than of co-ordinating relationships, and is therefore mainly a looking backwards, since relationships must be explained in terms of the past':

> Time perspective is here not a true impression of actual distances like that created by our dating technique, but a reflection of relations between lineages . . . The events have therefore a position in structure, but no exact position in historical time as we understand it. (Evans-Pritchard 1940, 107–8)

For all societies the past is an important source of knowledge about the present and writing is just one means of producing that knowledge. Sahlins describes how the Maori rely upon mythology for guidance in formulating ways of coping with the present. Mytho-praxis is the system of knowledge drawn upon by heroic societies like '. . . Maori, who think of the future as behind them, [and] find in a marvellous past the measure of the demands that are made to their current existence' (1983, 526). The distinction we make between history and myth, which both purport to explain how the present came to be, hinges upon the concepts of time characteristic of literate and non-literate societies. Not only does writing alter perceptions of time, but it can undermine the appeal to tradition as a source of legitimation, because, being less flexible, it is likely to be inconvenient at times. It does, however, introduce a new mode of legitimacy: progress. Christianity, the religion of the book, can only have encouraged a linear, progressive concept of time: it is after all a religion with a clear beginning and pre-ordained end.[1]

This review of the cultural implications of the technology of writing prepares us for a closer look at the political status of literacy in Early Historic society. If we are interested in understanding the production, interpretation and preservation of documents by the Church and aristocracy it will be profitable to consider writing as a resource drawn upon in social discourse. The advantages of controlling the medium should be apparent. We can recognise that certain documents such as annals, genealogies, Easter-tables and charters are means of summoning the past, while admitting that it is difficult to understand precisely how some of this material was used. It is attractive to argue that the use of these 'historic' documents with their implicit association with a linear, progressive concept of time was part of a conscious attempt to control the past, not just a by-product of the control of a system of knowledge. In a society with restricted literacy the literate non-reversible concept of time must have been likewise a restricted concept.[2] Indeed, written means of producing and reproducing knowledge seem unavoidably in conflict with traditional oral means of knowing about, and drawing upon the past in the same way that time would have been a contentious concept. Thus we might well expect that one area of conflicting social discourse would be over the uses made of the past. This expectation leads us to an issue of critical importance for understanding the development of Early Historic kingdoms. According to the documents, the expansion of political territory was achieved by military might, but how was the hold over formerly sovereign groups sanctioned and maintained? Is it a coincidence that the radical political reorganisations of the seventh and eighth centuries are coeval with the florescence of the Irish and Saxon Churches with their radical notions about time, the past and social destiny? Or that documents of all sorts become increasingly common then? If an opposition to this literate, progressive discourse of expansion is to be postulated it may be identified in appeals to traditional, oral and familiar values.

At this point, it is instructive to move away from the generalisations and look at a specific instance which illustrates for the Early Historic period the link between documents, discursive practice and power. Donnachadh Ó Corráin's study of the historicity of the Irish *ard-rí* (high-king) led him to consider the political context of a group of documents which purported to refer to the past:

> It would appear that the Irish had developed a sense of identity and 'otherness' as early as the seventh century and had begun to create an elaborate origin legend embracing all the tribes and dynasties of the country. This was the work of a mandarin class of monastic and secular scholars whose privileged position in society allowed them to transcend all local and tribal boundaries. (1978, 35)

Ó Corráin identifies the creation of origin legends as an aspect of the political reality of the expansion of a few tribal groups (*tuatha*) at the expense of their neighbours. He shows how writing by both ecclesiastics and laymen enhanced the credibility, if not the authority, of the created tradition. And, most importantly, he shows the conscious invention of tradition to be an authoritative discourse seeking to silence opposition. In the creation of this myth emphasising the common origins of the Irish, we are seeing the redefinition of the sphere of acceptable political activity, a redefinition which corresponds to real expansive tendencies and which pre-empted the use of tradition by weaker *tuatha* to support claims of autonomy.

This selective, synthetic use of the past is precisely what Talal Asad says we should expect of dominant groups. According to Asad, power (unequal access to resources) enables the authoritative discourse to silence or render impotent competing discourses and thereby ensures that society is reproduced according to the designs of the dominant group. In his words, authoritative discourse is:

> ... materially founded discourse which seeks continually to preempt the space of radically opposed utterances and prevent them from being uttered. (1979, 621)

Before we can go on to show that other, non-written forms of material culture are utilised discursively, it must be demonstrated that artefacts are expressive and that we can interpret them. This is the subject of Part III.

III. Anthropology and historical archaeology

In crossing the Atlantic one encounters a significant shift in the orientation of archaeology. It is most immediately recognised through spatial analysis: the archaeologists are sited in the anthropology departments. Although those interested in the historic past have not always had offices next door to ethnographers, for the past two decades anthropology has governed the research aims of historical archaeology and has elevated it 'from a discipline that regarded digging in the ground as a way of verifying historical records, and of supplementing them with otherwise unavailable data, to a social science' (Leone 1983, 2). This transition is only part of a broader trend which has seen the rise to prominence, if not predominance, of social history (Hobsbawm 1971) and the emergence of anthropology as an important influence on historical thought.

It is interesting to note the shift in emphasis which has occurred since Keith Thomas (1963) felt obliged to review the achievements of anthropology for historians, and challenged historians to learn about the Nuer. Recent reviews of the state of history have taken for granted that anthropology could be a source of insight into historical problems (Stone 1979). When anthropology has been the focus of attention in recent discussions of historical practice, the emphasis has been not on justifying the relationship, but on improving it (Cohn 1980, 1981). Medievalists have been perhaps a little slow to embrace anthropology and have required the occasional push (Davis 1981), but it scarcely needs mentioning that some of the most provocative recent studies of the early Middle Ages acknowledge explicit debts to anthropology. A casual list of topics includes kingship and inaugural ritual (Nelson 1977; Wormald 1986), oral literature and traditional law (Clanchy 1970, 1979; Wormald 1977; Dumville 1977a), non-capitalist economics (Hodges 1982) and mortuary ritual (Pader 1982; Bullough 1983).

The benefits to the early medieval historian of a working familiarity with anthropology are numerous. There are important areas of mutual interest, such as the maintenance and evolution of political systems, and ritual, religion and ideology as social forces. Anthropological concepts and analytical techniques are useful because they were developed in the first instance to understand societies that are every bit as foreign to Westerners as Picts and Saxons are to us. On the other hand, a failure to acquire a working knowledge of anthropology can have serious consequences. At worst it can permit us to impose anachronistic notions from one society upon another, as we have seen in the case of literacy. Or it can lead to the historian simply borrowing the odd ethnographic titbit to add rhetorical flair to an argument. It is in this context that the work of anthropologically trained American historical archaeologists is valuable. In the best of their archaeology we find archaeological methods employed to examine issues of historical importance through questions suggested by anthropological concepts of culture. Indeed, various approaches to American historical archaeology can be grouped into loose schools using differing concepts of culture as the distinguishing criteria.

One of these schools is best represented by the work of Stanley South (1977) who has followed Binford's programme for a scientific prehistoric archaeology, and has rigidly employed it to study colonial America. This produces an archaeology very much like Rahtz's New Medieval Archaeology: both aim to discover universal patterns of human behaviour through the scientific logic of hypothesis testing. Following Binford, the fundamental questions are generated by the concept of culture as a mechanism of environmental adaptation. As practised by South the social science of historical archaeology has two related failings. First, it sees human action overwhelmingly as a response to environmental stress. Secondly, South has been unable to integrate documents significantly into the practice of historical archaeology. The view that human nature is shaped primarily by environmental pressures relegates documents to the study of particular historical events; a similarly defective view of human nature is responsible for Rahtz's avoidance of documents. This first failing leads directly to the second fault: the inability to ask particularly interesting questions or the tendency to ask ones to which people like Sawyer already know the answers. South's work is mentioned, not because it holds the promise of integrating history and archaeology, but because it shows how a specific (in this case empiricist) concept of culture can guide research, and also because it serves to preview the potential of Rahtz's New Medieval Archaeology.

The most influential of the various schools of American historical archaeology has adopted a 'cognitive' definition of culture as the mainspring of their practice (Keesing 1974). James Deetz is perhaps the best known advocate of this approach. Deetz begins with the idea that 'culture is socially transmitted rules for behavior, ways of thinking about doing things' (1977, 25). This definition shifts the locus of human action (and therefore the focus of the scholar's attention) away from an environment objectively defined by the scholar into an environment constructed from the perceptions of its historical inhabitants. In rejecting an external empiricist view of the world in favour of an internal one, that sees the world as a coherently ordered system of meanings constructed from arbitrary symbols, Deetz is approaching a structuralist position (cf. Leach 1970, 1976). Consequently, it is inadequate to view material culture simply as a passive reflection of behavioural responses to environmental stress as Binford does. Because material culture is part of the system of meanings and is, therefore, loaded with symbolic value, material culture actively contributes to maintaining the system or to renegotiating it (i.e. 'social reproduction'). Knowing this, Deetz chooses to distinguish his concept of material culture from the conventional restrictive view that material culture equals artefacts:

> A somewhat broader definition of material culture is useful in emphasis-ing how profoundly our world is the product of our thoughts, as *that sector of our physical environment that we modify through culturally determined behavior.* (1977, 24, his emphasis)

Two important analytical benefits are derived from this viewpoint. First, it suggests that the forces which shape the patterns of social life act on all aspects of a cultural system. This Deetz has argued for colonial New England, where he found the same structural principles (analogous to a grammar) governing the form of ceramics, houses, gravestones, and concepts of individuality, privacy and afterlife (1977). The structuring principles in this case may be called 'the Georgian mindset', a term which is taken from the control and symmetry found in Georgian architecture, and which aptly expresses the link between the patterning of material culture and mental structure. This is not a static formulation. Deetz saw, in the shift from a pre-Georgian ('medieval') mindset to a Georgian mindset, that the structuring principles govern both form and change in form.[3] Second, by postulating the existence of shared structuring principles, the techniques developed for studying language can be seen to provide a way to understand the patterning and meaning of artefacts. Recalling that we construct language more or less unconsciously from a grammar, and that grammar is a set of structuring principles allowing us to order arbitrary sounds into meaningful expressions, we should recognise that material culture is no less an instance of arbitrary form being given meaning through a cultural grammar. And, of course, the meaning of artefacts, like that of speech, is entirely a matter of historical and social context.

Deetz's work consists of provocative suggestions, fascinating correlations and compelling examples, but ultimately is disappointing because he fails to satisfy the self-imposed demands of his method. Context, all important to the notion of meaning, is not under control. He does not look at the whole cultural system, but selects only a few classes of artefacts. This procedure ultimately leaves the reader in doubt as to the universality of the structuring principles. Typically, his work is as mysterious as it is provocative. It is never made clear how the structuring principles are revealed to the investigator, and more importantly, we are never offered any explanation as to *why* the particular principles embodied in the Georgian mindset were originally adopted and proliferated in these particular circumstances (Leone 1982b, 744–5; 1983, 4–5).

Closely related to Deetz's work is that of folklorist Henry Glassie. In *Folkhousing in Middle Virginia* (1975), the context is tightly controlled; the analysis follows a single class of artefact as it developed in a small region over two centuries. The project avoids Deetz's faults by selecting a less ambitious, even parochial, topic and succeeds by stressing the empirical observations and analytical technique. Glassie's idea that 'culture is pattern in mind, the ability to make things like sentences or houses' (1975, 17) resembles Deetz's concept of culture, and through it Glassie follows Deetz in linking his work directly to that of linguists like Noam Chomsky. Glassie derives an architectural grammar capable of generating the various house types found in the study area. This grammar, existing unconsciously in the mind of the builder, is articulated in the houses that constitute the empirical basis for Glassie's study of the Middle Virginian mind. Equipped with the detailed knowledge of the structuring principles (the architectural grammar), he is able to address the question of why this particular set of principles (which incidentally are part of the Georgian mindset) came to be adopted. This is precisely the question which Deetz has failed to pose. Glassie relies on the structuralist theory of Levi-Strauss to explain how the architectural decisions mediated social and environmental relations. Through the contemporary documents, he connects the attitudes he sees expressed in the architecture with the changing material circumstances of politics and economics, and thus satisfies the need to place the architectural expressions within the larger context of cultural values.

Glassie's work has important ramifications for historical archaeology. By 'reading' the houses, direct expressions of a substantial portion of Middle Virginians were rescued from the historical oblivion to which these people had been consigned by scholars relying exclusively on documents. The principle weakness of *Folkhousing*, which does not detract from its importance, is Glassie's failure to develop a set of questions which link the documents and artefacts. His handling of the two sorts of evidence is stratified, so that various kinds of evidence are called upon successively to amplify, complement or confirm what has come before. In his words:

> It is not that literary commentary is valueless, but rather that its use is corroborative. Old writing can not be used to construct the epistemologically essential synchronic record that will account for most people (writing is a rarity, making artifacts is universal); but once the synchronic account has been developed, the written record can return to utility as a qualifying supplement. (1975, 11–12)

Glassie seems here to be accepting as legitimate the existence of a dissonance between the past as recorded in documents and in artefacts, but has at least avoided the literate prejudices. In emphasising the artefact he has mitigated the ethnocentric literate bias, and provided a more valid, 'democratic' (as he terms it) history; he has not, however, sought to question the usefulness of the document/artefact opposition. In fact, he exploits it; the purely documentary perspective provides a foil for his approach. The degree of synthesis that Glassie achieves with documents and artefacts is a result of his thick descriptive style, and as a result it is only incidental to his main concern with interpreting the houses.

Both Glassie and Deetz demonstrate by example that, 'the only sound way to ground the importance of [archaeological] research is to know the history of the area and to array one's hypothesis against the documents and work of established historians' (Leone 1982b, 755). Indeed, archaeologists who fail to use the documents to construct a context for their artefacts are little better than antiquarians. Without wishing to promote a formulaic methodology, it is reasonable to suggest that archaeologists should develop specific methods of interrogating documents and artefacts simultaneously:

> What is needed is a set of questions linking the archaeological and documentary records in complementary fashion. Their absence is the major weakness in conventionally practiced historical archaeology. (Leone 1983, 3)

In this respect Glassie and Deetz are conventional.

I have emphasised the work of Deetz and Glassie in order to show their achievements and limitations. Many of the limitations have been remarked upon by Mark Leone (1982b, 1983), who has sought to resolve the principal difficulty of the cognitive or structuralist approach: the inability to explain *why* a specific pattern, competence or mindset was adopted. For Leone, the answer is to link the mental structures shaping material culture with the realities of power via a Marxist concept of ideology. As I noted earlier, Giddens makes a similar suggestion when he argues that human action necessarily concerns power, but he would not accept the concept of ideology used by Leone and neither should we.

Leone's belief in the importance of ideology betrays his materialist perspective, and also explains his dissatisfaction with the concept as it is normally used by archaeologists. The weakness of conventional notions of ideology, which understand it as synonymous with religious and philosophical codes, is their isolation from the material world. In other words, if ideology is only a passive reflection of society, not directly related to the *material* conditions of life, it is not recoverable, and therefore not of interest to the archaeologist. This summarises the rationale behind the 'ladder of inference' associated with Smith (1956) and Hawkes (1954) as well as Binford's view that ideology is epiphenomenal. In contradistinction, Leone presents his concept in two points:

> The first is that ideology, being neither world view nor belief, is ideas about nature, cause, time, person, or those things that are taken by society as given. Second, these ideas serve to neutralize and thus to mask inequalities in the social order; ideas such as the notion of person, when accepted uncritically, serve to reproduce the social order. Ideology's function is to disguise the arbitrariness of the social order, including the uneven distribution of resources, and it reproduces rather than transforms society. (1984, 26)

This concept of ideology, while useful for gaining a critical understanding of an instant in time, a particular institution or even the design of formal gardens (Leone 1984) can be subjected to two criticisms.

First, Leone assumes that there is a single dominant ideology in a society, or that the dominant one is so successful as to be unassailable. If this is so, then it leaves no mechanism for competing ideological formations to develop and closes off the possibility of internally instigated change:

One can put the problem generally by saying that, if we believe in the
social determination of concepts . . . this leaves the actors with no
language to talk *about* their society and so change it, since they can only
talk *within* it. (Bloch 1977, 281)

This implies that when the dominant ideology is working, social reproduction
is perfect, since there exists no vocabulary for criticism. Leone's work has
focused on capitalist societies with notoriously efficient ideologies; however,
this special (capitalist) case may be modified into a more general concept of
ideology which is both more pluralistic and more fluid. The second criticism
is that it appears that social reproduction occurs only if the social actors are
completely mystified. This forces us to imagine people as passengers of historical processes rather than makers of history. It is precisely this sort of
attitude that E. P. Thompson has criticised because it denies historic actors the
ability to act knowledgeably and meaningfully (1978, 173–6, 185). The notion
of ideology and the understanding of the way it works can be retained only if
first we recognise that the dominant ideology is not alone, but is competing
with others; and second, if we treat the mystification as a kind of haze or mist,
not a brick wall. In short, if we treat ideology as 'discourse'.

The position I am proposing is materialist in that the creation of documents
and artefacts is treated as discursive practice which is ultimately grounded in
the reality of power. It follows from ideas already introduced; people are
constantly involved with the creation of their world; material objects and
conceptual schemes are both the means and the results of the constructive
process; and it is possible to read both documents and artefacts because they
are the expressions of knowledgeable social actors. In the final section I
illustrate the value of this approach for studying the archaeology of the Early
Historic period.

IV. Artefacts and power: Pictish symbol stones

What follows are notes towards an analysis of the monumental sculpture
tradition as it relates to the development of the Pictish kingdom. The notes are
inspired by the techniques of reading the expressions embodied in artefacts
discussed in Part III, and follow my belief that those expressions are best
interpreted as social discourse. There are four general assertions about the
stones which serve as the armature for the analysis. Supporting arguments for
these assertions are revealed below; here they are simply stated.

1. The stones are conscious expressions about the state of the Pictish world.
They constitute a discursive practice which seeks to connect the social order to
the cosmic order and has as its goal the reproduction of that social order.

2. The technical properties of the carved stones and their context of use are
the starting point of the analysis. Interpretation of the carved expressions
reveal implicit references to power relations and suggest how the monuments
contributed to the maintenance and legitimation of those relations. The location in the landscape and the resources drawn upon suggest that the monuments are expressions of the elite.

3. Changing standards of authority in social and political discourses are represented in the development and transformation of the monuments over time. The monumental expressions are not static but evolve to accommodate shifting political circumstances, thus charting the development of the kingdom.

4. The stones record fairly radical transitions in Pictish intellectual and social history. Not the least of these are political centralisation, the conversion to Christianity and the end of mytho-praxis. The stones act like documents to fix persons and events firmly in time and space, contradicting reversible time.

Pictish symbol stones have a long history of antiquarian and archaeological study and I have no intention of reviewing the scholarship here. Stevenson's pioneering archaeological analysis of the stones (1955b) and his more recent survey (1970) serve as useful introductions. Unlike most recent discussions they are relatively free of problems associated with art historical perspectives and existing social explanations. The art historical approaches are preoccupied with tracing 'influences' and confuse our aesthetic values with those of the Picts. The symbols are seen as mere decoration, exquisitely executed but inaccessibly remote. When social meanings have been sought in the stones, functionalist explanations have been favoured; for example as boundary markers (Henderson 1971), commemorations of marriage alliances (Jackson 1971, 1984), or burial monuments (C. Thomas 1963, 1984). Because all these explanations treat artefacts as socially inert or passive none of them are able to suggest how the stones might have been effective as social discourse. A failing common to all literature on the stones is that external forces are given priority over internal social dynamics, despite the widely acknowledged indigenous origin of the symbols themselves. This dependence on external influences reflects the failure to treat the stones as expressive media and to recognise that the symbols (whether of local invention, like the crescent and V-rod; or borrowed, like the cross) were not arbitrary, but had referents which were meaningful to Picts. For example, Charles Thomas' proposal that the stones were a local manifestation of Early Christian Celtic burial rites (1963, 1984) neither explains why the Picts should have copied their neighbours nor the specific form of the practice. Similarly, there is as yet no explanation for the incorporation of the cross into the local stone carving tradition which adequately examines it from an internal Pictish perspective.

In the discussion which follows, the details of artistic motif and chronology are omitted for the sake of brevity. Both issues are, to my mind, hopelessly mired in art historical wrangling. The relative chronology is secure enough, even if it does float in absolute terms. Of far more importance here are the questions of context, both historical and social. It is essential to recall that the stones were developed and flourished during the period which saw the growth and expansion of a strong Pictish monarchy (sixth to eighth centuries); a monarchy which was, however, eventually subjected to Scottish rule (during the ninth and tenth centuries). When considering the early stones, which I believe have a funerary context, it is well to bear in mind that the dead do not

Plate 1. The contrast between the rough hewn boulder and the carefully incised symbols of the Dunnichen stone is typical of Class I monuments. The stone's recent history may also be typical; a large proportion of the symbol stones like this one are known to have been moved from their original location since medieval times.

bury themselves. Among other things, burial rites serve to re-establish the social order in the wake of the chaotic intrusion of death. Such rites as accompany death may be seen as statements by the living about the social position of the dead as it relates to the surviving community, and to the status of the newly dead in the world of the ancestors. The later monuments are crosses, so their Christian inspiration is self-evident, but ought not to be seen as purely ecclesiastical or as lacking in secular importance or inspiration. There is much still to be learned about the social fabric of Pictish society from these ostensibly religious monuments. It is generally believed that religious establishments (i.e. churches and monasteries) were scarce when the crosses were erected. We must imagine therefore that the crosses were among the central paraphernalia of the faith and neither peripheral nor incidental to the practice of the religion. Not only were they the most eloquent statements of devotion accessible to the illiterate, but they were the essential technical apparatus of Christian worship.

For this discussion I am following the established classification of the stones because it is well known, it accommodates most of the complete stones, and it orders them chronologically. Class I is earliest, Class III is latest. Class I stones are natural or rough-hewn boulders incised with one or more symbols drawn from a small and strictly observed repertory (plate 1). The case for regarding Class I stones as burial monuments has recently been reviewed, and is strong (Close-Brooks 1980, 1984). The symbols themselves may be abstract designs, representations of objects (e.g. mirrors) or animals (e.g. bulls), and they are not confined to the stones; occasionally they are found on pieces of fine metal and bone objects. Our ignorance of the precise meaning of the symbolic expressions does not prevent us from examining how the system of symbols was used. The choice of symbol and location of the stone (over an ancestor) are not arbitrary, purely decorative or sentimental, but constitute coherent expressions about the living as well as the dead. The ancestors, whom the deceased joins in death, carry a large share of the discursive load. They introduce the supernatural into the discourse and abstract the carved expressions from the mundane world of the living. The animal symbols, for the most part recognisable natural forms, provide their specific cultural referents (be they mythic, tribal, totemic or whatever) with a sense of naturalness. The identification of cultural constructs with nature is one of the ways of protecting assumptions held about the world from question. As representations of material things, some of the remaining symbols indicate familiar and sometimes awesome cultural practices (e.g. hammer and tongs for smithing). The selection of such categories of human activity for representation on the stones must mean they were appropriate also for the society of the dead, implying that these symbols had mythical meanings and the ability to call forth supernatural imagery. The most common symbols are abstract to the point that we can only guess at the material reality they might signify. They may indeed have no material referent but instead refer to purely mental structures, like social relationships or rank. The use in a ritual context of these symbols, which represent Pictish social concepts, extracts them from the ordinary profane world and gives them a sacred sanction through contact with the cosmic order.

The stones fix individuals and, by extension, their kin, firmly in space and time, making their existence less dependent upon memory. The stones, of course, lack the precision or rigidity of documents, while remaining arcane enough to require interpretation. Besides implying the decay of reversible

Plate 2a. The Aberlemno churchyard cross slab is one of the finest executed and best preserved of the Class II monuments. It stands 7.5 feet tall and bears on its west face a cross flanked with interlaced beasts. The closest parallels for the decorative techniques employed here are found in the Lindisfarne Gospel painted in Northumbria around AD 700.

time, Class I stones suggest the illusion of permanence and stability, a hardening of social relationships. One of the motives behind funerary ritual is to ensure that the social void left by the dead is filled, that roles and responsibilities left by the dead are taken up. A strong analogy can be drawn between Viking Age Danish rune stones, which Randsborg (1980) argues were erected by heirs to secure claims to property and social position, and Class I Pictish

Plate 2b. The east side of the Aberlemno churchyard cross slab exhibits two of the symbols over a depiction of a battle sequence which, it has been argued, represents the decisive battle between the Picts and Angles at nearby Nechtansmere in AD 685 (see Alcock, p.30).

stones. Both of these mortuary practices appear at the point of the emergence of kingdoms or early states. In the symbol stones, I think we may be seeing traditional motifs employed as part of the discourse associated with the new social positions engendered by the expanding Pictish monarchy. In terms of religious symbolism, given the inherent dating difficulties, there is no reason why the Class I stones need be seen as pagan (as they are often assumed to be).

Certainly at the time of their erection, however, the Church was external to the system of power.

Class II monuments are cross slabs bearing a relief representation of a cross on one side, usually with figure representations on the reverse (plate 2a, b). The symbols may be found on either or both sides, but only very rarely on the cross side, and are more elaborately decorated than in Class I. This elaboration shows strong stylistic links with the decorative arts of Northumbria and Ireland. The Class II cross slabs introduce the Church into the discourse, while keeping it separate from some of the expressions by expanding the medium to two dimensions – literally and metaphorically. The cross itself, like other Pictish symbols, is an abstract, non-representational design, which embodies numerous meanings, and which in turn requires interpretation. In addition, they introduce an air of the cosmopolitan via the use of decorative styles no longer exclusively Pictish. There is no evidence to suggest that Class II crosses are funerary monuments, nor can they be explained away as evidence of newly converted pagans hedging their bets. I think they mark the point at which the importance of the Church is outstripping that of the ancestors. The prominence of the symbols of Christianity on Class II stones emphasises the adoption of a more powerful discourse, one capable of banishing the animal symbols and their possible regional or tribal associations, one which was supported by a highly centralised, hierarchical, transcendant institution. The Church as a model of institutional organisation or application of power would have justified expansion without regard for temporal or spatial boundaries. Moreover, once installed upon the Church's monuments, the symbols became integrated within a regular ritual cycle which gave the messages controlled, repeated exposure, in contrast to the unpredictable and disruptive association of the Class I stones with death. The Class II stones may also indicate the institutionalisation of the change in the concept of time from a purely cyclical, unprogressive view to a precisely divided, linear, directional view which we associate with writing. The figures on the reverse depict the aristocracy engaged in a variety of worldly activities, such as hunts, which link daily activity and events with the supernatural and serve to justify the social order and the means of maintaining it. The Pictish symbols are less prominent now than before and perhaps have been co-opted and transformed from their original meaning into evocations of authority through the past. Clearly the potency of the expressions carved on Class II slabs derive from the cross slabs as foci of worship, the place at which the Picts encountered God. The sheer monumentality of these crosses would have been a reminder of the relationship between those who could commission such things (presumably those portrayed on the reverse), and the cosmic order symbolised by the cross on the front.

Finally, in the Class III stones, the old symbols find no place on the three-dimensional free-standing cross, and the figural representations are completely subordinated to the symbol of Christianity. While in Class II the human representations were more or less independent of the cross since the two images could not be viewed simultaneously, in Class III the representa-

Plate 3. The outstandingly well preserved Dupplin cross near Forteviot combines Northumbrian styles of interlace and cross shape, and a central boss like those frequently found on Irish and Scottic high crosses with typically Pictish human figures (metric scale).

tions of people are confined within decorative panels which are ordered according to the form and decorative inspiration of the cross (plate 3). The regional distinctiveness of Classes I and II has given way to a variation of Insular art, which implies not so much a loss of identity as an expansion of horizon and a suppression of the local Pictish interests represented by the symbols. The emergence of Class III is frequently linked with the accession of the Dalriadic dynasty of Kenneth mac Alpin (Stevenson 1955b, 122–8). Surely this is a significant political development, and not simply for its contribution to the art history of sculptured crosses. What little we know of the later ninth and tenth centuries suggests that it was a period of relative stability (Duncan 1975, 90–7), one which saw the establishment of an increasingly powerful aristocracy.

Because the symbols are banished and the 'secular' imagery is tightly controlled, it could be thought that Class III stones are expressions devoted to the spiritual, void of political significance. The Church was, of course, far from politically neutral; it had interests to protect and patrons to support (Smyth 1984, 112–5, 131–40; Nieke and Duncan, this volume). This is perhaps best expressed in the Class III decorative style, which clearly mimics fine metal working techniques of the sort adorning both aristocrats and altars (Henderson 1967, 133–4). Thus the authority of the Church as observable in material displays of wealth was unified with that of the elite, and this visual similarity reminds us that the clergy were aristocrats whose interests were those of the dominant social group. So Class III stones, far from expressing the independence of the Church from worldly concerns, enshrined the ornate material symbols of prestige and status that the elite drew upon, and thereby legitimised them.

Inevitably such a quick sketch of the dynamic potential of Pictish stones is bound to be unsatisfactory. Experts will feel that my assertions require more developed arguments, while those unfamiliar with early Scottish history may feel equally sceptical for different reasons. For a more thorough discussion see Driscoll (1988); here, my purpose was only to introduce the concept of discourse as a means of interpreting the political meaning of these monuments. Their prominence and durability are crude measures of aristocratic power, and are adequate indices of the resources available to those in authority for use in social discourse. The formal development of the monuments tells us that the discursive standards were changing over time, as theoretically they should and as we know historically they did. The astonishing variation within types tells us that the makers and their patrons were drawing upon their knowledge of the symbols and stylistic conventions as their needs dictated, thus underscoring the idea that social reproduction is a constantly developing practice undertaken by knowledgeable social actors.

In this chapter I have argued that by approaching the historical record in its broadest sense as an assemblage of cultural expressions, we may improve our ability to understand the past. One specific aim has been to reject the selective approach of discriminating against part of the record on the basis of the presence or absence of writing. It has been argued by linguists and anthropologists interested in symbolic systems that the meaning of an object or concept is dependent upon its relationship within the system. If that is so, then to extract one class of object from the system is to invite misunderstanding. A better alternative is to look at how documents function within the discourse with respect to architectural constructions, with respect to mortuary practice, with respect to jewellery and clothing, and so on.

Clearly, undertaking such comparison entails taking risks by stepping beyond the bounds of one's own speciality. I would hope, however, that mistakes made in such circumstances would be more easily forgiven than those produced by failing to look past one's own doorstep. Most importantly, this more dangerous approach is likely to produce a more socially aware history and books that are more interesting to read.

Acknowledgements

This chapter began life as a ten-minute introduction to the *Early Historical Archaeology* conference. It has grown to this size as a result of a challenge from my brother to develop those ideas which had been mentioned only in passing. An adolescent version was presented at a Glasgow University Archaeology Department seminar. Several friends are particularly responsible for helping to bring it to maturity: Margaret Nieke, Leslie Alcock, David Driscoll and John Barrett. Additional commentary from Andrew Foxon, Ross Samson, Nick Aitchison and Alan Leslie has been most useful. I am all too aware that a number of their criticisms remain unanswered, and I am very grateful for having been saved so many errors.

NOTES

1 I owe this point to John Barrett.
2 Likewise John Barrett clarified this for me.
3 My brother, David, drew this to my attention.

Works referred to in the text

AI : see Bannerman (1974)
HB : see Morris (1980)
HE : see Colgrave and Mynors (1969)
VC : see Anderson, A. O. and M. O. (1961)
VW : see Colgrave (1927)

Abercromby, J., Ross, T. and Anderson, J. (1902) An account of the excavation of the Roman station at Inchtuthill, Perthshire, undertaken by the Society of Antiquaries of Scotland in 1901. *Proc. Soc. Antiq. Scot. 36,* 182-242.

Addyman, P. V. (1976) Archaeology and Anglo-Saxon Society, in Sieveking, Longworth and Wilson (1976), 309-22.

Adomnan: see Anderson, A. O. and M. O. (1961).

Akerman, J. Y. (1855) *Remains of Pagan Saxondom.* London.

— (1860) Report on researches in an Anglo-Saxon cemetery at Long Wittenham, Berkshire in 1859. *Archaeologia 38,* 327-52.

Alcock, L. (1963) *Dinas Powys.* Cardiff.

— (1967) Excavations at Degannwy Castle, Caernarvonshire, 1961-6. *Archaeol. Journ. 124,* 190-201.

— (1971, 1973) *Arthur's Britain. History and Archaeology AD 367-634.* Harmondsworth.

— (1972) *'By South Cadbury is that Camelot . . .': Excavations at Cadbury Castle.* London.

— (1976) A multi-disciplinary chronology for Alt Clut, Castle Rock, Dumbarton. *Proc. Soc. Antiq. Scot. 107,* 103-13.

— (1978) *Her . . . gefeaht wiþ Walas:* aspects of the warfare of Saxons and Britons. *Bull. Board Celtic Stud. 27,* 413-24.

— (1979) The North Britons, the Picts and Scots, in Casey (1979) 134-42.

— (1981a) Early historic fortifications in Scotland, in Guilbert (1981) 150-80.

— (1981b) Early historic fortifications of Scotland. *Current Archaeology, 79,* 230-6.

— (1981c) Quantity or quality: the Anglian graves of Bernicia, in Evison (1981) 168-8.

— (1982a) Cadbury-Camelot, a fifteen-year perspective. *Proc. Brit. Acad. 68,* 355-88.

— (1982b) Forteviot: a Pictish and Scottish royal church and palace, in Pearce (1982) 211-39.

— (1983) Gwŷr y Gogledd: an archaeological appraisal. *Archaeol. Cambrensis 132,* 1-18.

— (1984) A survey of Pictish settlement archaeology, in Friell and Watson (1984) 7-42.

Alcock, L. and E. (1980) Scandinavian settlement in the Inner Hebrides – recent research on placenames and in the field. *Scot. Archaeol. Forum 10,* 61-73.

Allen, J. R. and Anderson, J. (1903) *The Early Christian Monuments of Scotland.* Edinburgh.

Anderson, A. O. (1922) *Early Sources of Scottish History, I: AD 500-1288.* Edinburgh.

Anderson, A. O. and M. O. (1961) *Adomnan's Life of Columba.* London.

Anderson, J. (1883) *Scotland in Pagan Times: The Iron Age.* Edinburgh.

— (1901) Notices of nine Brochs along the Caithness coast from Keiss Bay to Skirza Head, excavated by Sir Francis Tress Barry, Bart., M.P. of Keiss Castle, Caithness. *Proc. Soc. Antiq. Scot. 35,* 112-48.

Anderson, M. O. (1973, 1980) *Kings and Kingship in Early Scotland.* Edinburgh.

— (1982) Dalriada and the creation of the Kingdom of Scotland, in Whitelock, D. *et al.* (1982) *Ireland in Early Medieval Europe.* Cambridge, 106-32.

Anderson, P. (1974) *Passages from Antiquity to Feudalism.* London.

Andrew, C. K. C. (1949) Report of Exeter Conference. *Archaeol. Newsletter 2.*

Andrew, W. J. (1934) The Winchester Anglo-Saxon bowl and bowl-burial. *Proc. Hants Field Club & Archaeol. Soc. 12,* 11-19.

Arnold, C. J. (1980) Wealth and social structure: a matter of life and death, in Rahtz *et al.* (1980) 81-142.

— (1982a) Stress as a stimulus to socio-economic change: Anglo-Saxon England in the seventh century, in Renfrew and Shennan (1982) 124-31.

— (1982b) *The Anglo-Saxon Cemeteries of the Isle of Wight.* London.

— (1982c) The end of Roman Britain: some discussion, in Miles (1982) 451-9.

— (1983) The Sancton Baston potter. *Scot. Archaeolog. Rev. 2(1),* 17-30.

— (1984) Social evolution in post-Roman western Europe, in Bintliff, J. (1984) *European Social Evolution: Archaeological perspectives.* Bradford, 277-94.

Arnold, D. E. (1983) Design structure and community organisation in Quinua, Peru, in Washburn, D. K. (1983) *Structure and cognition in art.* Cambridge.

Arrhenius, B. (1978) review of *The Sutton Hoo Ship Burial I,* by R. Bruce-Mitford, in *Med. Archaeol. 22,* 189-95.

Asad, T. (1979) Anthropology and the analysis of Ideology. *Man 12,* 607-27.

Atkinson, D. (1916) *The Romano-British site at Lowbury Hill in Berkshire.* Reading.

Avery, M. (1976) Hillforts of the British Isles: a students' introduction, in Harding (1976) 1-58.

Bannerman, J. M. W. (1974) *Studies in the History of Dalriada.* Edinburgh.

Barfoot, J. F. and Williams, D. P. (1976) The Saxon barrow at Gally Hills, Banstead Down, Surrey. *Res. Vol. Surrey Archaeol. Soc. 3,* 59-76.

Barley, M. W. (1977) *European Towns, their Archaeology and Early History.* London.

Barrow, G. W. S. (1960) *Regesta Regum Scottorum I: Acts of Malcolm IV.* Edinburgh.

— (1971) *Regesta Regum Scottorum II: Acts of William I.* Edinburgh.

— (1973) *The Kingdom of the Scots.* London.

— (1981) *Kingship and Unity, Scotland 1000-1306.* London.

Bartel, B. (1982) A historical review of ethnological and archaeological analyses of mortuary practice. *J. Anthrop. Archaeol. 1,* 32-58.

Bateman, T. (1861) *Ten Years' Digging in Celtic and Saxon Grave Hills in the Counties of Derby, Stafford and York.* London.

Bateson, J. D. (1981) *Enamel-working in Iron-Age, Roman and Sub-Roman Britain. The products and techniques.* Brit. Archaeol. Rep. Brit. Ser. 93, Oxford.

Bede: see Colgrave and Mynors (1969).

Bersu, G. (1947) The rath in townland Lissue, Co. Antrim. *Ulster J. Archaeol. 10,* 30-58.

Biddle, M. (1975) Excavations at Winchester 1971: Tenth and final interim report. *Antiq. J. 55*, 295-337.
— (1976) Hampshire and the origins of Wessex, in Sieveking, Longworth and Wilson (1976) 323-42.
Binchy, D. (1954) Secular Institutions, in Dillon (1954) 52-65.
— (1958) The fair of Tailtiu and the feast of Tara. *Eriu 18*, 113-38.
— (1970) *Celtic and Anglo-Saxon Kingship*. Oxford.
Binford, L. R. (1962) Archaeology as Anthropology. *American Antiquity 28*, 217-25.
— (1971) Mortuary practices: their study and their potential, in Brown, J. A., Approaches to the social dimensions of mortuary practices, *Mem. Soc. Amer. Archaeol. 25*, 6-29.
— (1982) Meaning, inference and the material record, in Renfrew and Shennan (1982) 160-63.
Blackhouse, I., Turner, D. H. and Webster, L. (1984) *The Golden Age of Anglo-Saxon Art*. London.
Blair, P. H. (1970) *An Introduction to Anglo-Saxon England*. Cambridge.
Bloch, M. (1977) The Past and the Present in the Present. *Man 14*, 278-92.
Bourdieu, P. (1973) The Berber House, in Douglas, M. (1973) *The Anthropology of Everyday Knowledge*. Harmondsworth, 98-110.
Bradley, R. (1984) *The Social Foundations of Prehistoric Britain*. London.
Bradley, R. and Lewis, E. (1968) Excavations at the George Inn, Portsdown. *Proc. Hants Fld Club Archaeol. Soc. 25*, 27-50.
Braithwaite, M. (1982a) *Androcentric Theory and the Wessex Culture*. Fourth Theoretical Archaeology Group Conference, Durham.
— (1982b) Decoration as ritual symbol: a theoretical proposal and an ethnographic study in southern Sudan, in Hodder (1982c) 80-8.
Brandt, R. and Slofstra, J. (1983) *Roman and Native in the Low Countries: Spheres of Interaction*. Brit. Archaeol. Rep. Internat. Ser. 184, Oxford.
Breeze, D. J. and Dobson, B. (1976) *Hadrian's Wall*. Harmondsworth.
Brent, J. (1860) Anglo-Saxon relics, Kent. *Gentleman's Magazine Library*, 533-5.
— (1863) Account of the Society's researches in the Anglo-Saxon cemetery at Sarre. *Archaeol. Cantiana 5*, 305-22.
— (1866) Account of the Society's researches in the Anglo-Saxon cemetery at Sarre. *Archaeol. Cantiana 6*, 157-85.
Briscoe, G. and LeBard, W. E. (1960) An Anglo-Saxon cemetery on Lakenheath airfield: Archaeological Notes. *Proc. Cambridge Antiq. Soc. 53*, 56-7.
Brooks, N. P. (1971) The development of military obligations in eighth and ninth century England, in Clemoes, P. and Hughes, K. (1971) *England before the Conquest*. Cambridge, 69-84.
— (1984) *The Early History of the Church of Canterbury*. Leicester.
Brown, D. (1978) *Anglo-Saxon England*. London.
Bruce-Mitford, R. L. S. (1974) *Aspects of Anglo-Saxon Archaeology*. London.
— (1975a) *The Sutton-Hoo Ship Burial I*. London.
— (1975b) *Recent Archaeological Excavations in Europe*. London.
— (1978) *The Sutton-Hoo Ship Burial, II*. London.
Bullough, D. (1983) Burial, Community and Belief in the Early Medieval West, in Wormald (1983), 177-201.
Burnham, B. C. and Kingsbury, J. (1979) *Space, Hierarchy and Society*. Brit. Archaeol. Rep. Internat. Ser. 59, Oxford.
Burley, E. (1956) Metal-work from Traprain Law. *Proc. Soc. Antiq. Scot. 89*, 118-228.

Burrow, I. (1973) Tintagel – some problems. *Scot. Archaeol. Forum 5*, 99-103.
— (1981) *Hillforts and hilltop settlement in Somerset in the first to eighth centuries A.D.* Brit. Archaeol. Rep. Brit. Ser. 91, Oxford.
Byrne, F. J. (1965) The Ireland of St Columba. *Historical Studies 5*, 37-58.
— (1971) Tribes and Tribalism in Early Ireland. *Eriu 22*, 128-66.
— (1973) *Irish Kings and High Kings.* London.
Callander, J. G. (1932) Earthhouse at Bac Mhic Connain. *Proc. Soc. Antiq. Scot. 66*, 42-64.
Callander, J. G. and Grant, W. (1934) The Broch of Midhowe, Rousay, Orkney. *Proc. Soc. Antiq. Scot. 68*, 444-516.
Campbell, E. (1984) E-Ware and Aquitaine: a reconsideration of the petrological evidence. *Scot. Archaeol. Rev. 3(1)*, 35-8.
Campbell, J. (1979) Bede's words for places, in Sawyer (1979) 34-54.
— (1982) *The Anglo-Saxons.* London.
Carr, E. H. (1961) *What is History?* Harmondsworth.
Casey, P. J. (1979) *The End of Roman Britain.* Brit. Archaeol. Rep. Brit. Ser. 71, Oxford.
Chadwick, H. M. (1940) Who was He? *Antiquity 14*, 76-87.
Chapman, J. C. and Mytum, H. C. (1983) *Settlement in North Britain, 1000 B.C.-A.D. 1000.* Brit. Archaeol. Rep. Brit. Ser. 118, Oxford.
Charles-Edwards, T. M. (1972) Kinship, status and the origins of the hide. *Past and Present 56*, 3-33.
— (1976) The distinction between land and moveable wealth in Anglo-Saxon England, in Sawyer, P. (1976) *Medieval Settlement, continuity and change.* London.
Christison, D. (1905) Report on the Society's excavation of forts on the Poltalloch estate, Argyll in 1904-5. *Proc. Soc. Antiq. Scot. 39*, 259-322.
Clack, P. and Ivy, J. (1983) *The Borders.* Durham.
Clanchy, M. T. (1970) Remembering the Past and the Good Old Law. *History 55*, 165-76.
— (1979) *From Memory to Written Record: England 1066-1307.* London.
Clark, A. (1960) A cross-valley dyke on the Surrey-Kent border. *Surrey Archaeol. Coll. 57*, 72-4.
Cleland, C. E. (1977) *For the Director: Essays in Honor of James B. Griffin.* Museum of Anthropology, University of Michigan, Anthropological Papers 61.
Close-Brooks, J. (1980) Excavations in the Dairy Park, Dunrobin, Sutherland, 1977. *Proc. Soc. Antiq. Scot. 110*, 328-45.
— (1983) Dr Bersu's excavations at Traprain Law, 1947, in O'Connor and Clarke (1983) 206-23.
— (1984) Pictish and other burials, in Friell and Watson (1984) 87-114.
— (1986) Excavations at Clutchord Craig, Fife. *Proc. Soc. Antiq. Scot. 116*, 117-84.
Clough, T. H. M., Dornier, A. and Rutland, R. A. (1975) *Anglo-Saxon and Viking Leicestershire.* Leicester.
Coffin, S. (1976) Linear earthworks in the Froxfield, East Tilsted and Hayling Wood district. *Proc. Hants Fld Club Archaeol. Soc. 32*, 77-81.
Cohen, M. N. (1977) *The Food Crisis in Prehistory.* New Haven, Conn.
Cohn, B. S. (1980) History and anthropology: the state of play. *Comparative Studies in Society and History 12*, 198-221.
— (1981) Towards a Rapproachment. *J. Interdisciplinary Hist. 12*, 227-52.
Colgrave, B. (1927) *Eddius Stephanus, Life of Wilfrid.* Cambridge.
Colgrave, B. and Mynors, R. A. B. (1969) *Bede's Ecclesiastical History of the English People.* Oxford.

Collingwood, R. G. and Myres, J. N. L. (1936) *Roman Britain and the English Settlements*. Oxford.

Conant, K. J. (1978) *Carolingian and Romanesque Architecture* (2nd ed.). Harmondsworth.

Conkey, M. (1978) Style and information in cultural evolution: towards a predictive model for the Palaeolithic, in Redman, C. L. *et al.*, *Social Archaeology: beyond subsistence and dating*. New York, 61-85.

Conkey, M. and Spector, J. D. (1984) Archaeology and the study of Gender. *Advances in Archaeological Method and Theory 7*, 1-38.

Corney, A., Ashbee, P., Evison, V. I. and Brothwell, D. (1967) A prehistoric and Anglo-Saxon burial ground, Portsdown, Portsmouth. *Proc. Hants Fld. Club Archaeol. Soc. 24*, 20-41.

Coulson, C. L. H. (1976) Fortresses and social responsibility in late Carolingian France. *Zeitschrift für Archaeologie des Mittelalters 4*, 29-36.

— (1979) Structural symbolism in medieval castle architecture. *J. Brit. Archaeol. Assoc. 132*, 72-90.

Cousins, M. and Hussain, A. (1984) *Michel Foucault*. London.

Cowan, I. B. (1961) The development of the parochial system in medieval Scotland. *Scot. Hist. Rev. 40*, 43-55.

Cowgill, G. L. (1977) The trouble with significance tests and what we can do about it. *American Antiquity 42*, 350-68.

Cramp, R. J. (1957) Beowulf and Archaeology. *Medieval Archaeol. 1*, 57-77.

— (1977) Schools of Mercian sculpture, in Dornier, A. (1977) *Mercian Studies*. Leicester, 191-234.

— (1978) The Anglian tradition in the ninth century, in Lang, J. T. (1978) *Anglo-Saxon and Viking Age Sculpture and its context*. Brit. Archaeol. Rep. Brit. Ser. 49, Oxford, 1-32.

— (1983) Anglo-Saxon Settlement, in Chapman and Mytum (1983) 263-97.

— (1984) *Corpus of Anglo-Saxon Stone Sculpture I: County Durham and Northumberland*. Oxford.

Craw, J. H. (1930) Excavations at Dunadd and other sites on the Poltalloch estates, Argyll. *Proc. Soc. Antiq. Scot. 64*, 111-27.

Crawford, I. and Switsur, R. (1977) Sandscaping and C-14: the Udal, N. Uist. *Antiquity 51*, 124-36.

Crofts, C. B. (1955) Maen Castle, Sennen: the excavations. *Proc. W. Cornwall Fld. Club 1(3)*, 98-115.

Crowfoot, E. and Hawkes, S. C. (1967) Early Anglo-Saxon gold braids. *Medieval Archaeol. 11*, 42-86.

Cunliffe, B. (1974) *Iron Age Communities in Britain* . London.

Cunnington, W. (1896) *Catalogue of Antiquities in the Museum: Part 1, The Stourhead Collection*. Devizes.

Curle, A. O. (1905) Fortifications on Ruberslaw. *Proc. Soc. Antiq. Scot. 39*, 219-32.

— (1914) Report on the excavation in September 1913 of a vitrified fort at Rockcliffe, Dalbeattie, known as the Mote of Mark. *Proc. Soc. Antiq. Scot. 48*, 125-68.

Curle, C. L. (1982) *Pictish and Norse finds from the Brough of Birsay 1934-74*. Soc. of Antiquaries of Scot. Monograph Series 1, Edinburgh.

Davidson, H. R. E. and Webster, L. (1967) The Anglo-Saxon burial at Coombe (Woodnesborough), Kent. *Medieval Archaeol. 11*, 1-41.

Davies, W. (1973-4) Middle Anglia and the Middle Angles. *Midland History 2*, 18-20.

— (1978) *An Early Welsh Microcosm: Studies in the Llandaff Charters*. London.

— (1979) *The Llandaff Charters*. Aberystwyth.

Davies, W. and Vierck, H. (1974) The contexts of the Tribal Hidage: social aggregates and settlement patterns. *Frühmittelalt. Studien 8*, 223-93.

Davis, N. (1981) The possibilities of the Past. *J. Interdisciplinary Hist. 12*, 267-75.

Deansley, M. (1943) Roman traditionalist influence among the Anglo-Saxons. *Eng. Hist. Rev. 57*, 129-46.

Deetz, J. (1965) The dynamics of stylistic change in Arikara ceramics. *Illinois Studies in Anthropology 4*.

— (1977) *In Small Things Forgotten: The Archaeology of Early American Life*. New York.

de Paor, L. (1961) Some vinescrolls and other patterns in embossed metal from Dumfriesshire. *Proc. Soc. Antiq. Scot. 94*, 184-95.

de Paor, M. and L. (1958) *Early Christian Ireland*. London.

Dickinson, T. M. (1974) *Cuddesdon and Dorchester-on-Thames*, Brit. Archaeol. Rep. Brit. Ser. 1.

— (1983) Anglo-Saxon Archaeology: twenty-five years on, in Hinton (1983) 38-43.

Dickson, W. C. (1928) *The Sherriff Court Book of Fife 1513-22*. Scottish History Society.

Dillon, M. (1954) *Early Irish Society*. Cork.

— (1962) *Lebor na Cert*. Dublin.

Dixon, P. (1979) Towerhouses, pelehouses and Border society. *Archaeol. J. 136*, 240-52.

Dobbs, M. (1947) The site Carrickabraghy. *Ulster J. Archaeol. 10*, 62-5.

Dodwell, C. R. (1982) *Anglo-Saxon Architecture: A new perspective*. Manchester.

Doherty, C. (1980) Exchange and trade in early medieval Ireland. *J. Royal Soc. Antiq. Ireland 110*, 67-89.

Donaldson, G. (1977) *Scottish Kings*, 2nd edition. London.

Drennan, R. D. (1976) Religion and social evolution in formative Mesoamerica, in Flannery, K. V. (1976) *The Early Mesoamerican Village*. New York, 345-68.

Dreyfus, H. L. and Rabinow, P. (1982) *Michel Foucault: Beyond Structuralism and Hermeneutics*. Brighton.

Driscoll, S. T. (1984) The New Medieval Archaeology, Theory vs History. *Scot. Archaeol. Rev. 3*.

— (1988) Power and authority in Early Historic Scotland: Pictish symbol stones and other documents, in Gledhill, J., Bender, B. and Larson, M. *State and Society: the emergence and development of social hierarchy and political centralization*, London.

Dumville, D. N. (1977a) Kingship, Genealogies and Regnal Lists, in Sawyer and Woods (1977) 72-104.

— (1977b) Sub-Roman Britain: history and legend. *History 62*, 173-92.

Duncan, A. A. M. (1975) *Scotland, the Making of the Kingdom*. Edinburgh.

— (1981) Bede, Iona and the Picts, in Davis, R. H. C. and Wallace-Hadrill, J. M. (1981) *The Writing of History in the Middle Ages*. Oxford, 1-42.

Duncan, A. A. M. and Brown, A. L. (1957) Argyll and the Isles in the Earlier Middle Ages. *Proc. Soc. Antiq. Scot. 90*, 192-220.

Duncan, H. B. (1982) *Aspects of the Early Historic Period in South West Scotland: a comparison of the material cultures of Scottish Dal Riada and the British kingdoms of Strathclyde and Rheged*. Unpub. M.Litt. thesis, Univ. of Glasgow.

Dymond, D. P. (1974) *Archaeology and History*. London.

Edel, D. (1983) The catalogue in *Culhwch ac Olwen* and Insular Celtic learning. *Bull. Board Celtic Stud. 30*, 253-67.

Edwards, K. J. and Ralston, I. (1978) New dating and environmental evidence from Burghead fort, Moray. *Proc. Soc. Antiq. Scot. 109*, 202-10.

Emanuel, H. D. (1967) *The Latin Texts of the Welsh Laws*. Cardiff.

Engelbrecht, W. (1974) The Iroquois: archaeological patterning on the tribal level. *World Archaeol. 6*, 52-65.

Eogan, G. (1974) Report on the excavations of a settlement site at Knowth, Co. Meath. *Proc. Royal Irish Acad. 74c*, 11-112.

Evans-Pritchard, E. E. (1940) *The Nuer*. Oxford.

Evison, V. I. (1963) Sugar-loaf shield bosses. *Antiq. J. 43*, 38-96.

— (1975) Pagan Saxon whetstones. *Antiq. J. 55*, 70-85.

— (1981) *Angles, Saxons and Jutes*. Oxford.

Fairhurst, H. (1939) The galleried dun at Kildonan Bay, Kintyre. *Proc. Soc. Antiq. Scot. 73*, 185-228.

— (1956) The stack fort on Ugadale Point, Kintyre. *Proc. Soc. Antiq. Scot. 88*, 15-21.

Farrell, R. T. (1978) *Bede and Anglo-Saxon England*. Brit. Archaeol. Rep. Brit. Ser. 46, Oxford.

Faull, M. (1977) British survival in Anglo-Saxon Northumbria, in Laing (1977) 1-54.

Feachem, R. W. (1960) The palisaded settlement at Harehope, Peeblesshire: excavations 1960. *Proc. Soc. Antiq. Scot. 93*, 174-91.

— (1966) The hill-forts in northern Britain, in Rivet (1966) 59-89.

Fennell, K. R. (1964) *The Anglo-Saxon cemetery at Loveden Hill, Lincs., and its significance in relation to the Dark Age settlement of the East Midlands*. Unpub. Ph.D. thesis, Univ. of Nottingham.

Ferguson, L. (1977) *Historical Archaeology and the Importance of Material Things*. Soc. for Hist. Archaeol. Special Series publication 2, Washington, DC.

Fernie, E. (1983) *The Architecture of the Anglo-Saxons*. London.

Finberg, H. P. R. (1972) *The Agrarian History of England and Wales, AD 43-1042*, Vol. I(ii). Cambridge.

Flanagan, D. (1981) Common elements in Irish place-names: Dun, Rath, Lios. *Bull. Ulster Place-name Soc. 3*, 16-29.

Fortes, M. (1968) Of Installation Ceremonies. *Proc. Royal Anthrop. Inst.* 5-20.

Fowler, P. J., Gardner, K. and Rahtz, P. A. (1970) *Cadbury, Congresbury, Somerset 1968: an introductory report*. Dept. of Extramural Studies, Univ. of Bristol.

Fox, A. and C. (1958) Wansdyke reconsidered. *Archaeol. J. 115*, 1-48.

Foxon, A. (1982) Artefacts in society. *Scot. Archaeol. Rev. 2*, 114-20.

Frere, S. S. (1967, 1974, 1978) *Britannia: a History of Roman Britain*. London.

Frere, S. S. and St Joseph, J. K. (1974) The Roman fort at Longthorpe, *Britannia 5*, 1-126.

Friell, F. G. P. and Watson, W. G. (1984) *Pictish Studies*. Brit. Archaeol. Rep. Brit. Ser. 125, Oxford.

Fry, R. E. and Cox, S. C. (1974) The structure of ceramic change at Tikal, Guatemala. *World Archaeol. 6*, 209-25.

Gerriets, M. (1983) Economy and Society: Clientship according to the Irish Laws. *Camb. Med. Celt. Stud. 6*, 43-62.

Giddens, A. (1979) *Central Problems in Social Theory*. London.

— (1980) *A Contemporary Critique of Historical Materialism*. London.

Gillies, W. (1981) The craftsman in early Celtic literature. *Scot. Archaeol. Forum 11*, 70-85.

Gilmour, B. (1979) The Anglo-Saxon church at St Paul-in-the-Bail, Lincoln. *Medieval Archaeol. 23*, 214-8.

Glassie, H. (1975) *Folkhousing in Middle Virginia*. Knoxville, Tenn.
— (1977) Meaningful things and appropriate myths: the artifact's place in American studies. *Prospects 3*, 1-49.
— (1982) *Passing the Time in Ballymenone*. Philadelphia.
Glazema, P. and Ypey, J. (1956) *Merovingische Ambachtskunst*. Baarn.
Godelier, M. (1975) Modes of production, kinship and demographic structures, in Bloch, M. (1975) *Marxist Analyses and Social Anthropology*. London, 3-28.
— (1977) The concept of 'social and economic formation': the Inca example, in Godelier (1977) *Perspectives in Marxist Anthropology*. Cambridge, 63-9.
Godfrey-Faussett, T. G. (1876) The Saxon cemetery at Bifrons. *Archaeol. Cantiana 10*, 298-3115.
Goffman, E. (1959) *The Presentation of Self in Everyday Life*. New York.
Goody, J. (1968) *Literacy in Traditional Societies*. Cambridge.
— (1977) *The Domestication of the Savage Mind*. Cambridge.
Goody, J. and Watt, I. P. (1963) The consequences of literacy. *Comp. Stud. in Society and History 5*, 304-45.
Graeme, A. (1914) An account of the excavation of the Broch of Ayre, St Mary's Holm, Orkney. *Proc. Soc. Antiq. Scot. 48*, 31-51.
Green, B. and Rogerson, A. (1978) The Anglo-Saxon cemetery at Bergh Apton, Norfolk: catalogue. *East Anglian Archaeol. Rep. 7*.
Gregory, C. (1982) *Gifts and Commodities*. Cambridge.
Gregson, N. (1983) The multiple estate model, in Clack and Ivy (1983) 48-80.
Greig, J. C. (1971) Excavations at Cullykhan, Castle Point, Troup, Banffshire. *Scot. Archaeol. Forum 3*, 15-21.
— (1972) Cullykhan. *Current Archaeol. 3*, 227-31.
Grierson, P. (1959) Commerce in the Dark Ages: a critique of the evidence. *Trans. Royal Hist. Soc. 5th ser. 9*, 123-40.
Griffith, A. F. (1915) An Anglo-Saxon cemetery at Alfriston, Sussex. *Sussex Archaeol. Coll. 57* (Suppl.), 197-208.
Griffith, A. F. and Salzmann, L. F. (1914) An Anglo-Saxon cemetery at Alfriston, Sussex. *Sussex Archaeol. Coll. 56*, 16-51.
Guilbert, G. (1981) *Hillfort Studies: essays for A. H. A. Hogg*. Leicester.
Guthrie, A. (1969) Excavations of a settlement at Goldherring, Sancreed, 1958-61. *Cornish Archaeol. 8*, 5-39.
Hall, E. T. (1966) *The Hidden Dimension. Man's Use of Space in Public and Private*. London.
Hamilton, J. R. C. (1966) Forts, brochs and wheelhouses, in Rivet (1966), 111-30.
— (1968) *Excavations at Clickhimin, Shetland*. Edinburgh.
Hanson, W. S. and Keppie, L. J. F. (1980) *Roman Frontier Studies, 1979*. Brit. Archaeol. Rep. Internat. Ser. 71, Oxford.
Hanson, W. S. and Maxwell, G. (1983) *Rome's Northwest Frontier, The Antonine Wall*. Edinburgh.
Harcourt, R. (1974) The dog in prehistoric and early Britain. *J. Archaeol. Science 1*, 151-75.
Hardin, M. A. (1977) Individual style in San Jose pottery painting: the role of deliberate choice, in Hill and Gunn (1977) 109-36.
Harding, D. W. (1976) *Hillforts: Later Prehistoric Earthworks in Britain and Ireland*. London.
Harris, O. and Young, K. (1981) Engendered structures: some problems in the analysis of reproduction, in Kahn, J. S. and Llobera, J. R. (1981) *The Anthropology of Pre-Capitalist Societies*. London.
Haskins, C. H. (1918) *Norman Institutions*. Harvard.

Hawkes, C. (1954) Archaeological Theory and Method : some suggestions from the Old World. *American Anthropologist 56*, 155-68.

Hawkes, S. C. (1979) Eastry in Anglo-Saxon Kent; its importance, and a newly found grave, in *Anglo-Saxon Studies in Archaeology and History*. Brit. Archaeol. Rep. Brit. Ser. 72, Oxford, 1, 81-114.

Hawkes, S. C., Brown, D. and Campbell, J. (1979) *Anglo-Saxon Studies in Archaeology and History*. Brit. Archaeol. Rep. Brit. Ser. 72, Oxford.

Hayes-McCoy, G. A. (1970) The making of an O'Neill; a view of the ceremony at Tullaghoge, Co. Tyrone. *Ulster J. Archaeol. 33*, 89-94.

Hebidge, D. (1979) *Subculture, The Meaning of Style*. London.

Hedges, J. W. and Bell, B. (1980) That tower of Scottish pre-history, the broch. *Antiquity 54*, 87-94.

Helms, M. (1979) *Ancient Panama : Chiefs in Search of Power*. Austin.

Henderson, I. (1967) *The Picts*. London.

— (1971) The meaning of the Pictish symbol stones, in Meldrum, E. (1971) *The Dark Ages in the Highlands*. Inverness.

— (1975) Inverness, a Pictish capital. *Inverness Field Club*, 91-108.

Hencken, H. (1951) Lagore crannog : an Irish royal residence of the 7th to 10th century A.D. *Proc. Royal Irish Acad. 53c*, 1-248.

Henry, F. (1965) *Irish Art in the Early Christian Period*. London.

— (1967) *Irish Art during the Viking Invasions*. London.

Hensel, W. (1977) The origin of Western and Eastern European Slav Towns, in Barley (1977) 373-89.

Herlihy, D. (1961) Church property on the European continent, 701-1200. *Speculum 36*, 81-105.

Herrmann, J. (1981) *Frühe Kulturen der Westslaven*, 3rd edition. Berlin.

Hewitt, H. J. (1966) *The Organisation of War under Edward III, 1338-62*. Manchester.

Higham, N. J. (1979) *The Changing Past : some recent work in the archaeology of Northern England*. Manchester.

Hill, D. H. (1977) Continuity from Roman to Medieval Britain, in Barley (1977) 293-302.

Hill, J. N. (1970) Broken K Pueblo : prehistoric social organization in the American Southwest. *Anthropological Papers of the Univ. of Arizona 18*.

— (1977) Individual variability in ceramics and the study of prehistoric social organization, in Hill and Gunn (1977) 55-108.

Hill, J. N. and Gunn, J. (1977) *The Individual in Prehistory : Studies of variability in style in prehistoric technologies*. New York.

Hills, C. M. (1977) The Anglo-Saxon cemetery at Spong Hill, North Elmham, Part 1. *East Anglian Archaeol. Rep. 6*.

— (1979) The archaeology of Anglo-Saxon England in the pagan period : a review. *Anglo-Saxon England 8*, 297-329.

— (1980) The Anglo-Saxon settlement of England, in Wilson, D. M. (1980) *The Northern World*. London, 71-94.

Hills, C. M. and Penn, K. (1981) The Anglo-Saxon cemetery at Spong Hill, North Elmham, Part 2. *East Anglian Archaeol. Rep. 11*.

Hills, C. M., Penn, K. and Rickett, R. (1984) The Anglo-Saxon cemetery at Spong Hill, North Elmham, Part 3. *East Anglian Archaeol. Rep. 21*.

Hills, C. M. and Wade-Martins, P. (1976) The Anglo-Saxon cemetery at The Paddocks, Swaffham. *East Anglian Archaeol. Rep. 2*, 1-44.

Hingley, R. (1982) Roman Britain : the structure of Roman imperialism and the consequences of imperialism on the development of a peripheral province, in Miles (1982) 17-52.

Hinton, D. A. (1983) *Twenty-five Years of Medieval Archaeology*. Sheffield.

Hobsbawm, E. J. (1971) From Social History to the History of Society. *Daedalus 100*, 20-45.

— (1979) An historian's Comments, in Burnham and Kingsbury (1979) 247-52.

Hodder, I. (1979) Economic and social stress and material culture. *American Antiquity 44*, 446-54.

— (1982a) *The Present Past: an introduction to anthropology for archaeologists*. London.

— (1982b) *Symbols in Action: ethnoarchaeological studies of material culture*. Cambridge.

— (1982c) *Symbolic and Structural Archaeology*. Cambridge.

Hodges, R. (1978) State formation and the role of trade in Middle Saxon England, in Green, D., Haselgrove, C. and Spriggs, M. (1978) *Social Organization and Settlement*. Brit. Archaeol. Rep. Internat. Ser. 47, Oxford, 439-54.

— (1982) *Dark Age Economics: The Origins of Towns and Trade, A.D. 600-1000*. London.

— (1984) The date and source of E Ware. *Scot. Archaeol. Rev. 3(1)*, 39-40.

— (1986) Peer polity interaction and socio-political change in Anglo-Saxon England, in Renfrew (1986).

Hodges, R. and Whitehouse, D. (1983) *Mohammed, Charlemagne and the Origins of Europe*. London.

Hodges, R., Moreland, J. and Patterson, H. (1985) San Vincenzo al Volturno, the Kingdom of Benevento and the Carolingians, in Malone, C. and Stoddart, S., *Papers in Italian Archaeology 3*. Brit. Archaeol. Rept. Internat. Ser. 245, Oxford.

Hogan, E. (1910) *Onomasticon Goidelicum*. Dublin.

Hogg, A. H. A. (1941) Earthworks in Joydens Wood, Bexley, Kent. *Archaeol. Cantiana 54*, 10-27.

— (1957) A fortified round hut at Carrog y Llam, near Nevin. *Archaeol. Cambrensis 106*, 46-55.

Holmqvist, W. (1975) Helgö, an early trading settlement in central Sweden, in Bruce-Mitford (1975b) 111-32.

Hope-Taylor, B. (1966) Bamburgh. *Univ. Durham Gazette 8*, 11-12.

— (1977) *Yeavering: an Anglo-British centre of Early Northumbria*. London.

— (1980) Balbridie and Doon Hill. *Current Archaeol. 72*, 18-19.

Horn, E. and Born, W. (1979) *The Plan of St Gall*. Berkeley.

Hughes, K. (1966) *The Church in Early Irish Society*. London.

— (1972) *Early Christian Ireland: An introduction to the sources*. New York.

Hutchinson, W. (1794) *A History of the County of Cumberland and some Places Adjacent*. Carlisle.

Hutchison, P. (1966) The Anglo-Saxon cemetery at Little Eriswell, Suffolk. *Proc. Camb. Antiq. Soc. 59*, 1-32.

Innes, C. (1868) *Ancient Laws and Customs of the Burghs of Scotland*. Burgh Record Soc. I, Edinburgh.

Jackson, A. (1971) Pictish social structure and symbol stones. *Scot. Stud. 15*, 121-40.

— (1984) *The Symbol Stones of Scotland*. Orkney.

Jackson, D. A. and Ambrose, T. M. (1978) Excavations at Wakerly, Northants., 1972-75. *Britannia 9*, 115-242.

Jackson, K. H. (1964) *The Oldest Irish Tradition: A window on the Iron Age*. Cambridge.

— (1965) The ogam inscription at Dunadd. *Antiquity 39*, 300-2.

— (1969) *The Gododdin, The Oldest Scottish Poem*. Edinburgh.

— (1972) *The Gaelic Notes in the Book of Deer*. Cambridge.

— (1981) Bede's *Urbs Giudi*: Stirling or Crammond? *Camb. Med. Celtic Stud.* *2*, 1-8.

Jankuhn, H. (1977) New beginnings in Northern Europe and Scandinavia, in Barley (1977) 355-72.

Jobey, G. (1976) Traprain Law: a summary, in Harding (1976), 191-204.

Johnson, N. and Rose, P. (1982) Settlement in Cornwall: an illustrated discussion, in Miles (1982), 151-207.

Jolliffe, J. E. A. (1926) Northumbrian institutions. *Eng. Hist. Rev. 41*, 1-42.

Jones, G. (1973) *A History of the Vikings*. Oxford.

Jones, G. R. J. (1961) Basic patterns of settlement distribution in Northern England. *Brit. Assoc. Adv. Sci. 18*, 192-200.

— (1972) Post-Roman Wales, in Finberg (1972) 283-382.

— (1975) Early territorial organization in Gwynedd and Elmet. *Northern History 10*, 30-41.

— (1979) Multiple estates and early settlement, in Sawyer (1979) 9-34.

Jones, M. K. and W. T. (1975) The crop-mark sites at Mucking, Essex, in Bruce-Mitford (1975b), 133-87.

Kapelle, W. E. (1979) *The Norman Conquest of the North*. London.

Keesing, R. M. (1974) Theories of culture. *Ann. Rev. Anthrop. 3*, 73-97.

Keynes, S. and Lapidge, M. (1983) *Alfred the Great: Asser's Life of King Alfred and other Contemporary Sources*. London.

Kilbride-Jones, H. (1980) *Zoomorphic Pennanular Brooches*. London.

King, D. J. C. (1983) *Castellarium Anglicanum*. London.

— (forthcoming) *The Castle in England and Wales*.

Kinsella, T. (1969) *The Tain*. Oxford.

Knocker, G. M. (1957) Early burials and an Anglo-Saxon cemetery at Snell's Corner near Horndean, Hampshire. *Proc. Hants Fld. Club Archaeol. Soc. 19*, 117-47.

Knowles, D. and St Joseph, J. K. S. (1952) *Monastic Sites from the Air*. Cambridge.

Krautheimer, R. (1971) *Studies in Early Christian, Medieval and Renaissance Art*. London.

— (1980) *Rome: Profile of a City, 312-1308*. Princeton.

— (1983) *Three Christian Capitals*. London.

Kristiansen, K. (1982) The formation of tribal systems in later European prehistory: Northern Europe, 4000-500 B.C., in Renfrew, A. C., Rowlands, M. J. and Segraves, B. A. (1982) *Theory and Explanation in Archaeology: The Southampton Conference*. London, 241-80.

Kuper, H. (1972) The language of sites in the politics of space. *American Anthropologist 74*, 411-25.

Kurtz, D. V. (1984) Strategies of legitimation and the Aztec state. *Ethnology 23*, 301-14.

Laing, L. (1975) *The Archaeology of Late Celtic Britain and Ireland*. London.

— (1977) *Studies in Celtic Survival*. Brit. Archaeol. Rep. Brit. Ser. 37, Oxford.

Laing, L. and J. (1979) *Anglo-Saxon England*. London.

Lane, A. M. (1980) *Excavations at Dunadd, Mid Argyll*. Interim Report, Dept. of Archaeology, Cardiff.

— (1981) *Excavations at Dunadd, Mid Argyll*. Interim Report, Dept. of Archaeology, Cardiff.

— (1984) Some Pictish problems at Dunadd, in Friell and Watson (1984) 43-62.

Lawrie, A. C. (1905) *Early Scottish Charters*. Edinburgh.

Leach, E. R. (1970) *Levi-Strauss*. Glasgow.

— (1973) 'Concluding address', in Renfrew (1973) 761-71.

— (1976) *Culture and Communication*. Cambridge.

— (1979) Summary, in Burnham and Kingsbury (1979) 247-52.

Leeds, E. T. (1912) The distribution of the Anglo-Saxon saucer brooch in relation to the battle of Bedford, AD 571. *Archaeologia 43*, 149-202.

— (1913) *The Archaeology of Anglo-Saxon Settlements*. London.

— (1927) Excavations at Chûn Castle in Penwith, Cornwall. *Archaeologia 76*, 205-40.

— (1931) Excavations at Chûn Castle in Penwith, Cornwall, 2nd Report. *Archaeologia 81*, 33-42.

Leeds, E. T. and Harden, D. B. (1936) *The Anglo-Saxon Cemetery at Abingdon, Berkshire*. Oxford.

Leeds, E. T. and Shortt, H. de S. (1953) *An Anglo-Saxon Cemetery at Petersfinger, near Salisbury, Wilts*. Salisbury.

Leone, M. P. (1978) Time in American Archaeology, in Redman *et al.* (1978) *Social Archaeology: Beyond Subsistence and Dating*. New York, 25-36.

— (1982a) Childe's Offspring, in Hodder (1982c) 179-84.

— (1982b) Some opinions about recovering Mind. *American Antiquity 47*, 742-60.

— (1983) Historical Archaeology and Reshaping the Myths of American origins, in Matthews, J. (1983) *The George Wright Forum*, 1-16.

— (1984) Interpreting Ideology in historical archaeology, in Miller and Tilley (1984) 25-35.

Lethbridge, T. C. (1931) *Recent Excavations in Anglo-Saxon Cemeteries in Cambridgeshire and Suffolk*. Cambridge.

— (1951) *A Cemetery at Lackford, Suffolk: report of the excavation of a cemetery of the pagan Anglo-Saxon period in 1947*. Cambridge.

Levison, W. (1946) *England and the Continent in the Eighth Century*. Oxford.

Li Causi, L. (1975) Anthropology and ideology. *Critique of Anthrop.* 4/5, 90-109.

Longacre, W. A. (1970) Archaeology as anthropology: a case study. *Anthrop. Papers of the Univ. of Arizona 17*.

Longley, D. (1975) *The Anglo-Saxon Connection*. Brit. Archaeol. Rep. Brit. Ser. 22, Oxford.

— (1982) The date of the Mote of Mark. *Antiquity 54*, 132-4.

Loyn, H. R. (1984) *The Governance of Anglo-Saxon England, 500-1087*. London.

Lynn, C. (1983) Some 'early' ring-forts and crannogs. *J. Irish Archaeol. 1*, 47-58.

Macalister, R. A. S. (1945) *Corpus inscriptionum insularum celticarum, I*. Dublin.

McCormick, F. (1983) Dairying and beef production in early Christian Ireland: the faunal evidence, in Reeves-Smyth, T. and Hamond, F. (1983) *Landscape Archaeology in Ireland*. Brit. Archaeol. Rep. Brit. Ser. 116, Oxford, 253-67.

MacGregor, A. (1974) The broch of Burrian, N. Ronaldsay, Orkney. *Proc. Soc. Antiq. Scot. 105*, 63-118.

MacKie, E. W. (1965a) *Excavations on two 'galleried duns' on Skye in 1964 and 1965: interim report*. Glasgow.

— (1965b) Brochs and the Hebridean Iron Age. *Antiquity 39*, 266-78.

MacNeill, E. (1921) *Celtic Ireland* (revised D. Ó Corráin 1981). London.

— (1923) Ancient Irish law: the law of status or franchise. *Proc. Royal Irish Acad. 36c*, 256-316.

MacNeill, M. (1962) *The Festival of Lughnasa*. Oxford.

McNeill, T. (1983) The stone castles of northern Co. Antrim. *Ulster J. Archaeol. 46*, 101-28.

MacNiocaill, G. (1972) *Ireland before the Vikings*. Dublin.
— (1981) Investment in early Irish agriculture, in Scott (1981) 7-9.
Malinowski, B. (1926) *Myth in Primitive Psychology*. London.
Mallory, J. P. (1981) The sword of the Ulster Cycle, in Scott (1981) 99-114.
— (1985) *Navan Fort*. Belfast.
Mann, J. C. (1971) *The Northern Frontiers in Britain from Hadrian to Honorius: Literary and Epigraphic Sources*. Newcastle-upon-Tyne.
Marshall, D. N. (1964) Little Dunagoil. *Trans. Buteshire Nat. Hist. Soc. 16*, 3-61.
Martin, M. (1703) *A Description of the Western Isles of Scotland*. London.
Mauss, M. (1954) Essai sûr le don. Forme et raison d'échange dans les sociétés archaïques. *L'Année Sociologique* (1924) and Cunnison (1954) *The Gift*. London.
Mayes, P. and Dean, M. J. (1976) *An Anglo-Saxon Cemetery at Baston, Lincs., with a report on the pottery by J. N. L. Myres*. Occasional Papers in Lincolnshire Hist. and Archaeol. 3.
Meaney, A. and Hawkes, S. C. (1970) *Two Anglo-Saxon cemeteries at Winnall, Winchester, Hants*. Soc. for Med. Archaeol. Monograph Ser. 4.
Miket, R. (1980) A re-statement of evidence for Bernician Anglo-Saxon burials, in Rahtz, Dickinson and Watts (1980) 289-305.
Miles, D. (1982) *The Romano-British Countryside, studies in rural settlement and economy*. Brit. Archaeol. Rep. Brit. Ser. 103, Oxford.
Miles, H. *et al.* (1977) Excavations at Killibury Hillfort, Egloshayle, 1975-6. *Cornish Archaeol. 16*, 89-121.
Miles, H. and T. (1973) Excavations at Trethurgy, St Austell: interim report. *Cornish Archaeol. 12*, 25-9.
Miller, D. and Tilley, C. (1984) *Ideology, Power and Prehistory*. Cambridge.
Millett, M. with Jones, S. (1983) Excavations at Cowdery's Down. *Archaeol. J. 140*, 151-279.
Morris, J. (1973) *The Age of Arthur*. London.
— (1980) *Nennius: British History and the Welsh Annals*. London.
Muir, R. (1975) Thanages, in Macneill, P. and Nicholson, R. (1975) *An Historical Atlas of Scotland, 400-1600*. St Andrews.
Munro, R. (1882) *Ancient Scottish Lake-Dwellings or Crannogs*. Edinburgh.
Murray, H. (1979) Documentary evidence for domestic buildings in Ireland, c. 400-1200 in the light of archaeology. *Medieval Archaeol. 23*, 81-97.
Musty, J. (1969) The excavation of two barrows, one of Saxon date, at Ford, Laverstock, near Salisbury, Wiltshire. *Antiq. J. 49*, 98-117.
Musty, J. and Stratton, J. E. D. (1964) A Saxon cemetery at Winterbourne Gunner, near Salisbury, Wiltshire. *Wilts. Archaeol. Nat. Hist. Mag. 59*, 86-109.
Myres, J. N. L. (1937) Some Anglo-Saxon potters. *Antiquity 11*, 389-99.
— (1968) The Anglo-Saxon potttery from Mucking. *Antiq. J. 48*, 222-8.
— (1969) *Anglo-Saxon Pottery and the Settlement of England*. London.
— (1970) The Angles, the Saxons, and the Jutes. *Proc. Brit. Acad. 56*, 1-32.
— (1974) The Anglo-Saxon pottery in the Roman fortress at Longthorpe, in Frere and St Joseph (1974) 112-21.
— (1977) *A Corpus of Anglo-Saxon Pottery from the Pagan Period*. Cambridge.
Myres, J. N. L. and Green, B. (1973) *The Anglo-Saxon Cemeteries of Caistor-by-Norwich and Markshall, Norfolk*. Rep. Research Comm. of Soc. of Antiquaries 30.
Myres, J. N. L. and Southern, W. H. (1973) *The Anglo-Saxon Cremation Cemetery at Sancton, East Yorkshire*. Hull.

Mytum, H. C. (1982) Rural settlement of the Roman period in north and east Wales, in Miles (1982), 327-9.

Nash-Williams, V. E. (1950) *The Early Christian Monuments of Wales*. Cardiff.

Nelson, J. L. (1975) Ritual and Reality in the early Medieval 'ordines'. *Stud. Church Hist. 11*, Oxford, 41-51.

— (1976) Symbols in context: rulers' inauguration rituals in Byzantium and the West in the early Medieval Age. *Stud. Church Hist. 13*, 97-119.

— (1977) Inauguration rituals, in Sawyer and Woods (1977) 50-71.

— (1980) The earliest royal *Ordo*: some liturgical and historical aspects, in Tierney and Linehan (1980) 29-48.

Nieke, M. R. (1983) Settlement patterns in the First Millenium A.D.: a case study of the Island of Islay, in Chapman and Mytum (1983) 229-326.

— (1984) *Settlement Patterns in the Atlantic Province of Scotland in the First Millenium A.D.: A Study of Argyll*. Unpub. Ph.D. thesis, Univ. of Glasgow.

O'Connor, A. and Clarke, D. V. (1983) *From the Stone Age to the 'Forty-Five*. Edinburgh.

Ó Corráin, D. (1972) *Ireland Before the Normans*. Dublin.

— (1974) Aspects of early Irish history, in Scott, B. G. (1974) *Perspectives in Irish Archaeology*. Belfast, 64-75.

— (1978) Nationality and Kingship in pre-Norman Ireland, in Moody, T. W. (1978) *Nationality and the Pursuit of National Independence*. Belfast, 1-35.

— (1980) Review of Bannerman (1974). *Celtica 13*, 168-82.

Ó Danachair, C. (1987) An Rí (the King): an example of traditional Social Organisation. *J. Royal Soc. Antiq. Ireland 111*, 14-28.

Ogilvie, R. M. and Richmond, I. A. (1967) *Cornelii Taciti: De Vita Agricolae*. Oxford.

O'Kelly, M. (1962a) Beal Boru, Co. Clare. *J. Cork Hist. Archaeol. Soc. 67*, 1-27.

— (1962b) Two ring-forts at Garryduff, Co. Cork. *Proc. Royal Irish Acad. 63c*, 2-124.

O'Neil, B. H. St J. (1937) Excavations at Breiddin Hill Hill Camp, Mont., 1933-5. *Archaeol. Cambrensis 92*, 86-128.

Ó Ríordáin, S. (1942) The excavation of a large earthen ring-fort at Garranes, Co. Cork. *Proc. Royal Irish Acad. 47c*, 77-150.

— (1953) *Tara, The Monuments on the Hill*. Dundalk.

Ordnance Survey (1966) *Britain in the Dark Ages*. Southampton.

— (1973) *Britain Before the Norman Conquest*. Southampton.

Ortner, S. B. and Whitehead, H. (1981) *The Cultural Construction of Gender and Sexuality*. Cambridge.

O'Shea, J. (1981) Social configuration and the archaeological study of mortuary practices: a case study, in Chapman, R., Kinnes, I. and Randsborg, K. (1981) *The Archaeology of Death*. Cambridge, 39-52.

— (1984) *Mortuary Variability: an archaeological investigation*. Orlando, Florida.

Pader, E-J. (1982) *Symbolism, Social Relations and the Interpretation of Mortuary Remains*. Brit. Archaeol. Rep. Internat. Ser. 130, Oxford.

Parsons, D. (1977) The pre-Romanesque church of St Riquier: the documentary evidence. *J. Brit. Archaeol. Assoc. 130*, 1-51.

Peacock, D. (1984) Comment on Campbell (1984). *Scot. Archaeol. Rev. 3(1)*, 38-9.

Peacock, D. and Thomas, C. (1967) Class E imported post-Roman pottery: a suggested origin. *Cornish Archaeol. 6*, 35-46.

Pearce, S. (1982) *The Early Church in Western Britain and Ireland*. Brit. Archaeol. Rep. Brit. Ser. 102, Oxford.

Peltenburg, E. J. *et al.* (1982) Excavations at Balloch Hill, Argyll. *Proc. Soc. Antiq. Scot. 112*, 142-214.

Pelteret, D. (1981) Slave-raiding and slave-trading in early England. *Anglo-Saxon England 9*, 99-114.

Petrie, G. (1890) Notices of the brochs or large round towers of Orkney. *Archaeol. Scot. 5*, 71-94.

Plog, S. (1980) *Stylistic Variation in Prehistoric Ceramics.* Cambridge.

Pollock, S. (1983) Style and information: an analysis of Susiana ceramics. *J. Anthrop. Archaeol. 2*, 354-90.

Powlesland, D. (1981) *Heslerton Parish Project, 1982-92.* Privately printed.

Proudfoot, V. (1961) The economy of the Irish Rath. *Medieval Archaeol. 5*, 94-122.

Pryde, G. S. (1965) *The Burghs of Scotland, a critical list.* Oxford.

Putnam, G. (1980) Spong Hill cremations, in Rahtz, Dickinson and Watts (1980) 217-19.

Quirk, R. N. (1957) Winchester in the tenth century. *Archaeol. J. 114*, 26-8.

Radford, C. A. R. (1935) Tintagel: the castle and celtic monastery. *Antiq. J. 15*, 401-19.

— (1951) Report on the excavations at Castle Dore. *J. Royal Inst. Cornwall N.S.1*, appendix.

— (1959/78) *The Early Christian and Norse Settlements at Birsay.* Edinburgh.

Raftery, B. (1982) Iron age burials in Ireland, in Ó Corráin, D. (1982) *Irish Antiquity.* Cork, 173-204.

Rahtz, P. A. (1961) An excavation on Bokerley Dyke, 1958. *Archaeol. J. 118*, 65-99.

— (1971) Castle Dore: a re-appraisal of the post-Roman structures. *Cornish Archaeol. 10*, 49-54.

— (1976) Buildings and rural settlement, in Wilson (1976) 49-98, 405-52.

— (1981) *The New Medieval Archaeology.* York.

— (1982) Celtic society in Somerset, A.D. 400-700. *Bull. Board Celt. Stud. 30*, 176-200.

— (1983) New approaches to medieval archaeology, Part 1, in Hinton (1983) 12-23.

Rahtz, P. A., Dickinson, T. and Watts, L. (1980) *Anglo-Saxon Cemeteries, 1979.* Brit. Archaeol. Rep. Brit. Ser. 82, Oxford.

Ralston, I. B. M. (1978) The Green Castle and the promontory forts of North-East Scotland. *Scot. Archaeol. Forum 10*, 27-40.

Randsborg, K. (1980) *The Viking Age in Denmark.* London.

— (1981) Les activités internationales des Vikings: raids ou commercé. *Annales E.S.C. 36*, 862-68.

Rappaport, R. A. (1971a) The sacred in human evolution. *Ann. Rev. of Ecology and Systematics 2*, 23-44.

— (1971b) Ritual, sanctity and cybernetics. *Amer. Anthrop. 73*, 59-76.

RCAHMS (1971) *Inventory of Kintyre.* Edinburgh.

— (1975) *Inventory of Lorn.* Edinburgh.

— (1980) *Inventory of Mull, Coll, Tiree and the Outer Isles.* Edinburgh.

— (1984) *Inventory of Islay, Jura, Colonsay and Oronsay.* Edinburgh.

Read, C. H. (1894) A Saxon grave at Broomfield, Essex. *Proc. Soc. Antiq. 15* (2nd Ser.), 250-5.

Renfrew, A. C. (1973) *The Explanation of Culture Change: models in prehistory.* London.

— (1979) Dialogues of the Deaf, in Burnham and Kingsbury (1979), 253-9.

— (1982) *An Island Polity: The Archaeology of Exploitation in Melos.* Cambridge.

— (1986) *Peer Polity Interaction and Social Change*. Cambridge.

Renfrew, A. C. and Shennan, S. (1982) *Ranking, Resources and Exchange: Aspects of Early European Society*. Cambridge.

Reynolds, N. (1980a) The King's whetstone: a footnote. *Antiquity 54*, 232-7.

— (1980b) Dark Age timber halls and the background to excavation at Balbridie. *Scot. Archaeol. Forum 10*, 41-60.

Reynolds, S. (1977) *English Medieval Towns*. Oxford.

Richards, J. D. (1984) Funerary symbolism in Anglo-Saxon England: further social dimensions of mortuary practices. *Scot. Archaeol. Rev. 3*, 42-55.

— (1987) *An Investigation of the Significance of Form and Decoration in Early Anglo-Saxon Funerary Pottery*. Ph.D. Thesis, North Staffs. Polytechnic.

Richards, M. (1954) *The Laws of Hywel Dda (The Book of Blegwryd)*. Liverpool.

Richardson, J. S. (1948) *The Broch of Gurness, Aikerness, West Mainland, Orkney*. Edinburgh.

Richmond, I. A. (1955, 1963) *Roman Britain*. Harmondsworth.

Rideout, J. S. (1984) *Interim Report: Excavation on the Dunion, Roxburghshire*. Unpub. Scot. Dev. Dept. Ancient Monuments Division.

Ritchie, J. N. G. (1971) Iron Age finds from Dun an Fheuran, Gallanach, Argyll. *Proc. Soc. Antiq. Scot. 103*, 100-12.

Rivet, A. L. F. (1966) *The Iron Age in Northern Britain*. Edinburgh.

Rollason, D. W. (1978) Lists of Saints' resting-places in Anglo-Saxon England. *Anglo-Saxon England 7*, 61-93.

Runciman, W. G. (1984) Accelerating social mobility: the case of Anglo-Saxon England. *Past and Present 104*, 3-30.

Rydh, H. (1929) On symbolism in mortuary ceramics. *Bull. Museum of Far Eastern Antiquities 1*.

Sahlins, M. (1981) *Historical Metaphors and Mythical Realities*. Association for Social Anthropology in Oceania, Special Publication 1, Ann Arbor.

— (1983) Other Times, Other Customs: the Anthropology of History. *Amer. Anthrop. 85*, 517-44.

Saitta, D. J. (1983) The poverty of Philosophy in Archaeology, in Moore, J. A. and Keene, A. S. (1983) *Archaeological Hammers and Theories*. New York, 299-304.

Saunders, A. D. (1978) Excavations in the church of St Augustine's Abbey, Canterbury, 1955-8. *Medieval Archaeol. 22*, 25-63.

Saunders, C. (1972) The excavations at Gramble, Wendron, 1972: interim report. *Cornish Archaeol. 11*, 50-2.

Savory, H. N. (1960) Excavations at Dinas Emrys, Beddgelert, Caernarvonshire, 1954-6. *Archaeol. Cambrensis 109*, 13-77.

Sawyer, P. H. (1978) *From Roman Britain to Norman England*. London.

— (1979) *Names, Words and Graves: Early Medieval Settlement*. Leeds.

— (1983a) The Royal *tun* in pre-Conquest England, in Wormald (1983) 273-99.

— (1983b) English archaeology before the Conquest: a historian's view, in Hinton (1983) 44-7.

Sawyer, P. H. and Woods, I. N. (1977) *Early Medieval Kingship*. Leeds.

Saxe, A. A. (1970) *Social Dimensions of Mortuary Practices*. Unpub. Ph.D. dissertation, Dept. of Anthropology, Univ. of Michigan.

Schuyler, R. L. (1978) *Historical Archaeology: A Guide to Substantive and Theoretical Contributions*. Farmingdale, NJ.

Scott, B. (1978) Iron 'slave-collars' from Lagore Crannog, Co. Meath. *Proc. Royal Irish Acad. 78c*, 213-30.

— (1981) *Studies in Early Ireland*. Belfast.

Scott, J. G. and M. (1960) Loch Glashan Crannog, Argyll. *Discovery and Excavation in Scotland*, 8-9.
— (1961) Loch Glashan Crannog, Argyll. *Archaeol. Newsletter 7*, 2-1.
Shephard, J. F. (1979) The social identity of the individual in isolated barrows and barrow-cemeteries in Anglo-Saxon England, in Burnham and Kingsbury (1979), 47-79.
Shepherd, I. A. G. (1983) Pictish settlements in North-East Scotland, in Chapman and Mytum (1983) 327-56.
Siegel, S. (1956) *Nonparametric Statistics for the Behavioral Sciences.* Tokyo.
Sieveking, G. de G., Longworth, I. H. and Wilson, K. E. (1976) *Problems in Economic and Social Archaeology.* London.
Simpson, W. D. (1954) *Dundarg Castle.* Edinburgh.
Sims-Williams, P. (1983) Gildas and the Anglo-Saxons. *Camb. Med. Celtic Stud. 6*, 1-30.
Skene, W. F. (1871) *Johannis De Fordun, Chronica Gentis Scottorum*, 2 vols. Edinburgh.
— (1890) *Celtic Scotland III, Land and People.* Edinburgh.
Small, A. (1969) Burghead. *Scot. Archaeol. Forum 1*, 61-8.
— (1972) Craig Phadrig vitrified fort. *Discovery and Excavation in Scotland 23.*
Small, A. and Cottam, M. B. (1972) *Craig Phadrig.* Dundee.
Small, A. *et al.* (1973) *St Ninian's Isle and its Treasure.* Aberdeen and Oxford.
Smith, C. (1979) Romano-British place-names in Bede, in Hawkes, Brown and Campbell (1979) 1-19.
Smith, C. A. (1984) Local history in global context: social and economic transition in western Guatemala. *Comp. Stud. in Soc. and Hist. 26*, 193-228.
Smith, C. R. (1856) *Inventorium Sepulchrale.* London.
Smith, I. M. (1983) Brito-Roman and Anglo-Saxon: the unification of the Border, in Clack and Ivy (1983) 9-48.
Smith, J. (1919) Excavation of the forts of Castlehill, Aitnock and Coalhill, Ayrshire. *Proc. Soc. Antiq. Scot. 53*, 123-36.
Smith, M. (1956) The limitations of inference in Archaeology. *Archaeol. Newsletter 6*, 3-7.
Smith, R. A. (1911) Anglo-Saxon remains, in Page (1911) *The Victoria History of the Counties of England: Suffolk.* London, 325-55.
Smyth, A. P. (1971) The earliest Irish annals. *Proc. Royal Irish Acad. 72c*, 1-48.
— (1985) *War Lords and Holy Men: Scotland A.D. 80-1000.* London.
Snedecor, G. W. and Cochran, W. C. (1980) *Statistical Methods*, 7th edn. Ames, Iowa.
Sokal, R. and Sneath, P. (1963) *Principles of Numerical Taxonomy.* San Francisco.
South, S. (1977) *Method and Theory in Historical Archaeology.* New York.
Spalding Club (1841-52) *Miscellany*, Vol.5. Edinburgh.
Spriggs, M. (1984) *Marxist Perspectives in Archaeology.* Cambridge.
Stead, I. M. (1958) An Anglian cemetery on the Mount, York. *Yorks. Archaeol. J. 39*, 427-35.
Steer, K. A. (1964) John Horsely and the Antonine Wall. *Archaeologia Aeliana 42* (4th ser.), 1-39.
Stevens, J. (1884) On the remains found in the Anglo-Saxon tumulus at Taplow, Bucks. *J. Brit. Archaeol. Soc. 40*, 61-71.
Stevenson, R. B. K. (1949) The nuclear fort of Dalmahoy, Midlothian, and other Dark Age capitals. *Proc. Soc. Antiq. Scot. 83*, 186-98.
— (1955a) Pins and the chronology of brochs. *Proc. Prehist. Soc. 21*, 282-94.
— (1955b and 1980) Pictish Art, in Wainwright (1955 and 1980) 97-128.

— (1970) Sculpture in Scotland in the 6th-9th centuries A.D., in *Kolloquium über spätantike u. frühmittelalterliche Skulptur*. Mainz, 65-74.

Stone, L. (1977) History and the social sciences in the twentieth century, in Delzell, C. F. (1977) *The Future of History*. Nashville, 3-42.

— (1979) The Revival of Narrative: reflections on a New Old History. *Past and Present 85*, 3-24.

Sutherland, C. H. V. (1948) *Anglo-Saxon Coinage in the Light of the Crondall Hoard*. London.

Swan, L. (1983) Enclosed ecclesiastical sites and their relevance to settlement patterns of the first millenium AD, in Reeves-Smyth, T. and Hamond, F. (1983) *Landscape Archaeology in Ireland*. Brit. Archaeol. Rep. Brit. Ser. 116, Oxford, 269-94.

Taylor, H. M. (1971) Repton reconsidered, in Clemoes, P. and Hughes, K. (1971) *England Before the Conquest*. Cambridge, 391-408.

— (1975) Tenth century church building in England and on the Continent, in Parsons, D. (1975) *Tenth Century Studies*. Chichester, 140-68.

— (1978) *Anglo-Saxon Architecture*, Vol.3. Cambridge.

— (1979) The Anglo-Saxon church at Wing in Buckinghamshire. *Archaeol. J. 136*, 43-52.

Taylor, H. M. and J. (1965) *Anglo-Saxon Architecture*, Vols 1 & 2. Cambridge.

Tester, P. J. (1968) An Anglo-Saxon cemetery at Orpington. *Archaeol. Cantiana 83*, 125-50.

Thomas, C. (1956) Evidence for post-Roman occupation of Chûn Castle, Cornwall. *Antiq. J. 36*, 75-8.

— (1961) Excavations at Trusty's Hill, Anwoth, Kirkcudbrightshire, 1960. *Trans. Dumfriesshire Galloway Nat. Hist. Antiq. Soc.* 37, 58-70.

— (1963) The interpretation of Pictish symbols. *Archaeol. J. 120*, 31-97.

— (1981) *A provisional list of imported pottery in post-Roman western Britain and Ireland*. Redruth.

— (1982) East and West: Tintagel, Mediterranean imports and the early insular Church, in Pearce (1982), 17-34.

— (1984) Pictish Class I symbol stones, in Friell and Watson (1984) 169-88.

Thomas, F. W. L. (1879) Dunadd, Glassary, Argyllshire: the place of inauguration of the Dalriadic kings. *Proc. Soc. Antiq. Scot. 13*, 28-47.

Thomas, K. (1963) History and Archaeology. *Past and Present 24*, 3-24.

Thompson, E. P. (1978) *The Poverty of Theory*. London.

Tierney, B. and Linehan, P. (1980) *Authority and Power: Studies on Medieval Law and Government*. Cambridge.

Triscott, J. (1980) Aldclune (Blair Atholl parish), Perth and Kinross District, Tayside. *Discovery and Excavation in Scotland 1980*, 82-3.

— (1981) Aldclune, in *Ancient Monuments Board for Scotland, 27th Annual Report*, 6 and facing pl.

Ullmann, W. (1969) *The Carolingian Renaissance and the Idea of Kingship*. London.

Uslar, R. von (1964) *Studien zu frühgeschichtlichen Befestigungen zwischen Nordsee und Alpen*. Köln.

Vatcher, F. de M. and H. L. (1968) Excavations and Fieldwork in Wiltshire, 1967. *Wilts. Archaeol. Nat. Hist. Mag. 63*, 115.

Vierck, H. (1972) Redwald's Asche. *Offa 29*, 20-49.

Wacher, J. (1974) *The Towns of Roman Britain*. London.

Wagner, H. (1974) Der königliche Palast in keltischer Tradition. *Zeitschr. für Celtische Philologie 33*, 6-14.

Wailes, B. (1982) The Irish 'royal sites' in history and archaeology. *Cambridge Medieval Celtic Studies 3*, 1-29.

Wainwright, F. T. (1955 and 1980) *The Problem of the Picts*. Edinburgh.
— (1962) *Archaeology, Place-Names and History: an Essay on Coordination*. London.
Wainwright, G. J. (1967) *Coygan Camp*. Cardiff.
Wallace-Hadrill, J. M. (1971) *Early Germanic Kingship in England and on the Continent*. Oxford.
— (1983) *The Frankish Church*. Oxford.
Wallach, L. (1959) *Alcuin and Charlemagne: Studies in Carolingian History and Literature*. New York.
Wallerstein, I. (1974) *The Modern World System, 1*. London.
— (1979) *The Capitalist World Economy: Essays*. Cambridge.
— (1980) *The Modern World System, 2*. London.
— (1984) *The Politics of the World Economy*. Cambridge.
Warhurst, A. (1955) The Jutish cemetery at Lyminge. *Archaeol. Cantiana 69*, 1-40.
Warner, R. (1973) The excavations at Clogher and their context. *Clogher Record 8*, 5-12.
— (1980) Irish souterrains: later Iron Age refuges. *Archaeol. Atlantica 3*, 81-99.
— (1982) Irish place-names and archaeology. III. A case study: Clochar macc nDaimini. *Bull. Ulster Place-Name Soc. 4* (n.s.), 27-31.
Washburn, D. K. (1978) A symmetry classification of pueblo ceramic design, in Grebinger, P. (1978) *Discovering Past Behavior: Experiments in the Archaeology of the American Southwest*. New York, 101-21.
— (1983) *Structure and Cognition in Art*. Cambridge.
Waterman, D. (1963) Excavations at Duneight, Co. Down. *Ulster J. Archaeol. 26*, 55-78.
Watson, W. J. (1926 and 1973) *The History of Celtic Place-Names of Scotland*. Edinburgh.
Watt, W. G. T. (1882) Notice of the broch known as Burwick or Borwick, in the township of Yescanabee and parish of Sandwick, Orkney. *Proc. Soc. Antiq. Scot. 16*, 442-50.
Webster, G. (1951) An Anglo-Saxon urnfield at South Elkington, Louth, Lincolnshire. *Archaeol. J. 108*, 25-59.
Welbourn, A. (1984) Endo ceramics and power strategies, in Miller and Tilley (1984) 17-24.
Welch, M. (1983) *Anglo-Saxon Sussex*. Brit. Archaeol. Rep. Brit. Ser. 112, Oxford.
West, S. E. (1969a) The Anglo-Saxon village of West Stow. *Medieval Archaeol. 13*, 1-20.
— (1969b) Pagan Saxon pottery from West Stow, Suffolk. *Berichten van de Rijksdienst voor net Oudheidkundig Bodemondersoek 19*, 175-81.
West, S. E. and Owles, E. (1973) Anglo-Saxon cremation burials from Snape. *Proc. Suffolk Inst. of Archaeol. 33*, 47-57.
Wheeler, R. E. M. (1934) London and the Grim's Ditches. *Antiq. J. 14*, 254-63.
White, R. B. (1980) Excavations at Aberffraw, Anglesey, 1973 and 1974. *Bull. Board Celtic Sttud. 28*, 319-42.
Whitelock, D. (1979) *English Historical Documents, Vol.1 : c.500-1042*, 2nd edn. London.
Wiessner, P. (1983) Style and social information in Kalahari San projectile points. *American Antiquity 48*, 253-76.
— (1984) Reconsidering the behavioral basis for style: a case study among the Kalahari San. *J. Anthrop. Archaeol. 3*, 190-234.

— (1985) Style or isocretic variation ? A reply to Sackett. *American Antiquity* *50*, 160-66.

Wightman, E. M. (1978) Peasants and potentates, an investigation of social structure and land tenure in Roman Gaul. *American J. Ancient Hist. 3*, 97-128.

Williams, J. (1971) Tynron Doon, Dumfriesshire: a history of the site with notes on the finds, 1924-67. *Trans. Dumfriesshire Galloway Nat. Hist. Antiq. Soc. 48*, 106-17.

Williams, J. H. and Shaw, M. (1983) Middle-Saxon palaces at Northampton. *Current Archaeol. 85*, 38-41.

Wilson, D. (1960) *The Anglo-Saxons*. London.

— (1964) *Anglo-Saxon Ornamental Metalwork, 700-1100, in the British Museum*. London.

— (1976) *The Archaeology of Anglo-Saxon England*. London.

Winterbottom, M. (1978) *Gildas: The Ruin of Britain and other works*. Chichester.

Wobst, M. (1977) Stylistic behavior and information exchange, in Cleland (1977) 317-42.

Wolf, E. R. (1982) *Europe and the People without History*. Berkeley.

Wood-Martin, W. (1886) *The Lake Dwellings of Ireland*. Dublin.

Wormald, C. P. (1977) The uses of literacy in Anglo-Saxon England and its neighbours. *Trans. Royal Hist. Soc. 27*, 95-114.

— (1978) Bede, Beowulf and the conversion of the Anglo-Saxon aristocracy, in Farrell (1978) 32-95.

— (1983) *Ideal and Reality in Frankish and Anglo-Saxon Society*. London.

— (1986) Celtic and Anglo-Saxon kingship: some further thoughts, in Szarmach, P. E. (1986) *Sources of Anglo-Saxon Culture*. Kalamazoo.

Wormald, C. P., Bullough, D. and Collins, R. (1983) *Ideal and Reality in Frankish and Anglo-Saxon Society*. Oxford.

Yorke, B. (1981) The vocabulary of Anglo-Saxon overlordship, in Brown, D., Campbell J. and Chadwick-Hawkes, S. (1981) *Anglo-Saxon Studies in Archaeology and History 2*. Brit. Archaeol. Rep. Brit. Ser. 92, Oxford, 171-200.

Young, A. (1956) Excavations at Dun Cuier, Isle of Barra. *Proc. Soc. Antiq. Scot. 89*, 290-328.

Youngs, S. M., Clark, J. and Barry, T. B. (1983) Medieval Britain and Ireland in 1982. *Medieval Archaeol. 27*, 172-3.

List of contributors

Elizabeth A. Alcock
Glasgow

Professor Leslie Alcock
Department of Archaeology, University of Glasgow

Dr Christopher J. Arnold
Department of Extra-Mural Studies, University College
of Wales, Powys

Professor Rosemary Cramp
Department of Archaeology, University of Durham

Dr Stephen T. Driscoll
Department of Archaeology, University of Glasgow

Holly B. Duncan
Bedford County Council, Archaeological Field Team

Genevieve Fisher
Department of Anthropology, University of Pennsylvania

Dr Richard Hodges
Department of Archaeology, University of Sheffield

John Moreland
Department of Archaeology, University of Sheffield

Dr Margaret R. Nieke
Historic Buildings and Monuments Commission for
England, London

Dr J. D. Richards
Department of Archaeology, University of York

Michael R. Spearman
Department of Archaeology, Royal Museum of
Scotland, Edinburgh

Richard B. Warner
Department of Antiquities, Ulster Museum, Belfast

Index

Aberdeen, 106, 108
Aberffraw, Anglesey, 29, 40, 41, 43
Aberlemno, Angus, cross-slab, 30
Abernethy, Perthshire, 104
Abingdon, Berks, A-S cemetery, 147-149
Adams, B., 144
Addyman, P., 165
Adomnan's Life of Columba, 6, 31, 33
Aedan, 10
Aelle, 71, 74
Aethelwulf, 88
agricultural produce as revenue in Early
    Medieval Scotland, 105-107
agriculture, evidence for in Celtic Britain,
    25, 26, 100
Aidan, 34
Alba, 9, 102
Alcock, E., 18
    on Enclosed Places AD 500-800,
    catalogue, map and gazeteer of,
    40-46
Alcock, L., 3, 5, 19, 21, 68, 74, 187
    on Potentates in Celtic Britain, AD
    500-800, 22-39
Alcuin, 83, 86
Aldclune, Perthshire, brooch from, 40,
    41, 43
Alexander I, 109
Alfred, 88
Alfriston, Sussex, 115
Anglo-Saxon Chronicle, 124, 125
Anglo-Saxon England, style and socio-
    political organisation in, 129-144
Anglo-Saxon England, stylistic variability
    in 130
Anglo-Saxon period:
    boundaries, 120-124
    buildings, problems of dating, 91
    cemeteries (see under Cemeteries),
    development of political structure,
    112, 113
    graves (see under Graves)
    institutions in Scotland, 103
    integration of archaeological and his-
    torical data, 111-113, 124, 125
    kingdoms, models for development of,
    112, 113
    kings, (see also under kings), 85-87, 69,
    71, 74, 75, 77, 78, 94
    settlement in Northumbria, 69-78

animal bones, 25, 62, 68, 100, 158
annointing of Kings, 85-7, 94
anthropology and historical archaeology,
    173-178
Antonine Wall, 97, 99
arable farming (see under agriculture).
archaeological and historical data, inte-
    gration of in Anglo-Saxon period,
    111-113
archaeology and history in Early historic
    period, 162-187
archaeology, historical and anthropology,
    173-178
Ardanstur Dun, Argyll 18
Ardifuar, Argyll 40, 41, 43
Argyll, (see also individual sites) 6, 7, 8,
    9, 10, 11, 16, 18
Armagh, Co. Armagh, 57
Arnold, C. J, 3, 5, 79, 131, 143, 146
artefacts and documents, integration of,
    162-168
artefacts and power, 178-187
Artefacts,
    arrow heads, 150
    arrows, 116,
    axes, 116,
    balls, crystal, 115
    beads, (see also under beads), 151
    blades, 151, 153, 156, 157, 158,
    160
    brooches, (see under Brooches for
    types), 14, 17-18, 20, 66, 75, 117,
    100, 139-144, 145, 151, 153
    buckles, 116, 117, 151
    chatelaine, 117, 150
    coins, Anglo-Saxon, 26, 115, 125, 150,
    153
    combs, 116, 117, 151, 153, 154, 158
    disc, gilt bronze, 15
    dress fasteners, (see under Brooches for
    types), 132-144
    dress ornaments, 115
    earscoop, 150, 153
    fittings, 151
    glass, (see separate entry),
    hanging Bowls, 27, 100
    helmets, 27, 38, 119
    horn, 116
    keys, 115, 117
    knives, 116, 117, 151, 153

Artefacts—*contd*
mount, gold zoomorphic, 75, 77
nails, 150, 153
neck irons, 39, 65
necklace, 117
pins, 117, 151, 153
playing pieces, 151, 153
razors, 150, 153
rings, 117, 151, 153
sceptres, 119, 125, 126
shears, 116, 151, 151, 153, 156, 157, 158, 160,
shield, 116
spear, 116
spindlewhorl, 151
spoons, 115
standards, 119, 125
swords, 99, 116
thread, gold, 117
torcs, 99
tweezers, 116, 151, 153, 156, 157, 158
weaving batten, 117
whetstone, 125, 146
wristclasp, 151, 153
Asad, T., 172, 173
Athelstan, 101

Bamburgh, Northumberland, 23, 32, 33, 40, 41, 46, 75, 77
Barrett, J., 4, 5, 21, 187
Barrow, G., 102
Baston, Lincs, A-S cemetery, 147-149
Beal Boru, Co. Clare, royal site, 54, 65
Bede: 69, 74, 77, 78, 74, 77, 124, 125
on Dalriada, 9
on fortifications, 32-3, 10
on kingship, 130
on land assessment, 35
on Nechtansmere, 32
on Northumbria, 69, 74, 77, 78
on Paulinus, 34
on origin of Anglo-Saxon tribes, 155
on warfare, 38
Beowulf, 3
Bergh Apton, Norfolk, A-S cemetery, 131, 134, 135, 136, 137
Berisford, F., 160
Bernicia, kingdom of, 33, 35, 70, 72, 74
Berowald the Fleming, 107,
Biddle, M., 91
Binchy, D., 57
Binford, L., 164, 174
Birka, 75
Black Loch Crannog, Wigtownshire, 40, 41, 43
boneworking, 25, 43, 44, 45, 46
Book of Deer, 103, 105,
boundaries, Anglo-Saxon, 120-124
Brechin, Angus, Burgh, 104
Breedon on the Hill, Leics, monastery, 92

Brigantes, 70
Broch of Birsay, Orkney, 40, 41, 43
Broch of Burray, Orkney, 40, 41, 43
Broch of Burrian, Orkney, 23, 25, 40, 41, 43
Broch of Burwick, Orkney, 40, 41, 43
Broch of Gurness, Orkney, 40, 41, 43
Broch of Midhowe, Orkney, 40, 41, 43
Broch of Oxtro, Orkney, 40, 41, 43
Brooches,
Anglo-Saxon, unspecified, 117, 151
annular, 139-141, 143
as status symbols, 14
cruciform, 139, 141
penannular, 14, 17, 18, 20, 66, 139, 143
saucer, 145
small-long, 139, 141
square headed, 75, 139
swastika, 139-141, 143
Brough of Birsay, Orkney, 38
Brunanburgh, Battle of, 102
Bryneuryn, Dinarth, Denbighs, 40, 41, 43
Buiston Crannog, Ayrshire, 24, 26, 28, 40, 41, 43
Bullough, D., 71
Burghead, Moray, Early Historic fort, 26, 40, 41, 43
Burghs:
Aberdeen, 106, 107, 108
Berwick, 107
Burgesses, royal, 107-109
Burgh Status granted to religious centres, 105-108
Charters, 97
Dunfermline, 104, 105, 108
economy of, 105-110
Edinburgh, 108
Glasgow, 106
Haddington, 108
introduction of term, 97
Inveresk, 106, 108
Kelso, 106
Laws of the Four Burghs, 97, 109
Montrose, 109
Perth, 97, 106, 107, 108
St Andrews, 106, 107, 108
Stirling, 107, 108
Burial practice, (*see also under* graves, cemeteries etc)
Anglo-Saxon, in Northumbria, 71, 73, 74
British, in Northumbria, 73,
Germanic, 71, 72, 73
Iron Age, 73
Burnswark, Dumfriesshire, Iron age hillfort, 98
Byrne, F. J, 62

Cadbury-Camelot, Somerset, Early Historic fort, 23, 24, 26, 28, 31, 34, 40, 42, 43
Cadbury-Congresbury, Somerset, Early Historic fort, 23, 24, 34, 40, 41, 43
Cadfan of Venedotia, 29
Caelestis Monedorix, 29
Cains, in Early Medieval Scotland, 105, 106, 107
Caisel, *see* Cashel
Caistor-by-Norwich, Norfolk, A-S cemetery, 147-149, 150, 151, 152, 154
Cambuskenneth, Stirlingshire, Abbey, 106
Canterbury, Kent, 86, 87, 87, 88, 90, 97
Carolingian Empire, 82, 83, 84, 85-7
Carolingian influences on Church architecture, 89-92,
Carr, E., 163
Carreg y Llam, Caernarvs, 40, 41, 43
Carrickabraghy, Co. Donegal, royal site, 54, 60
carvings, in Early Historic sites, 16, 26, 38
Cashel, Co. Tipperary, royal site, 53, 54
Castle Dore, Cornwall, Early Historic fort, 24, 40, 41, 44
Castle Hill, Inverness-shire, Early Historic site, 40, 41, 44
Castlehill, Dalry, Ayrshire, Early Historic site, 40, 41, 46
cattle raiding in Early Historic Ireland, 51
cattle, in Early Historic Ireland, 62-3, 68
Cemeteries: (*see also under* burial practice, graves and site names)
  Anglo-Saxon, 71, 72, 74, 92, 114, 131-144, 145-161
  Anglo-Saxon, mortuary treatment in, 131-144
  Mercian, 92
Cenela, in Dalriada, 6, 7, 10, 16, 17, 32
Cenwulf, 83, 87
Ceolwulf, 86
Charlemagne, 14, 83, 85
Charters, Confirmation, in Early Medieval Scotland, 105-110
Christianity,
  in Dalriada, 10, 11
  in Northumbria, 69, 70, 71
  links with Royal sites in Ireland, 57
Chun Castle, Cornwall, Early Historic site, 24, 40, 41, 44
Church architecture, influences affecting development, 88-92
Church:
  in Middle Saxon England, 83, 85, 85, 86-88, 91, 92
  pictish symbol stones, influence on, 180-186
  role of in Dalriada, 10, 11

role of in Northumbria 77
role of in Carolingian Empire, 83, 84, 85
role of in Middle Saxon England, 94
role of re kingship in Middle Saxon England, 85-7, 94
Churches, siting of in Early Medieval Scotland, 104-5
Clanchy, M., 169, 170
Clatchard Craig, Fife, Early Historic site, 23, 40, 41, 44
Clickhimin, Shetland, Broch, 16
Clogher, Co. Tyrone, royal site, 55, 54, 56-57, 57, 61, 62, 65, 75,
Coldingham, Early Historic site, 101
Collingwood, R. G, 2, 3
Columba, 6, 31, 33
Columbas Chapel, Kintyre, 16
consecration of Kings in England, 85-7
continental connections in Middle Saxon England 79, 80, 83, 84, 85-90
Conveth payments, 105,
Council of Brentford, 86
Council of Chelsea, 86, 87
Coygan Camp, Carmathenshire, Early Historic site, 40, 41, 44
Craftworking, in Early Historic period, 13.14, 25, 66, 75, 77, 98
Craig Phadraig, Inverness-shire, Early Historic fort, 23, 40, 41, 44
Cramp, R., 3
  on Northumbria: the archaeological evidence, 69-78
Crannogs, 17, 24, 26, 50, 55, 59, 61, 65
  as Royal sites in Ireland, 50, 55, 59
cremation urns, Anglo-Saxon, 145-161
cremations, (*see also* cemeteries) 72, 131, 134, 135, 147, 148, 150
Critical theory, 163
crypts, Anglo-Saxon, 90
Cullykhan, Banffshire, Early Historic site, 40, 41, 44
Culross, Fife, Burgh, 104
Cultural considerations in archaeological theory, 167, 168
Cuneglasus, 31
currency, lack of in Celtic Britain (*see also* coins) 26

Dalmahoy, Midlothian, Early Historic fort, 24, 40, 41, 44
Dalriada, 16, 32, 35, 36, 102, 186
  Christian Church in, 10, 11
  Enlargement of Kingdom of, 102
  Irish connections, 8-10
  Kingdom of in Northern Britain 6-21
Damnonii, 98
Darlington, Co.Durham, cemetery, 74
David I, 97, 103, 105, 106, 108, 109, 110

De Paor, M. & L., 68
Deetz, J., 174, 175, 176, 177
Degannwy, Caernarvonshire, Early
    Historic fort, 40, 41, 44
Deira, 70, 72, 73, 74
Dinarth, Denbighshire, 24, 31
Dinas Emrys, Caernarvonshire, Early
    Historic fort, 40, 41, 44
Dinas Powys, Glamorgan, Early Historic
    fort, 3, 23, 24, 27, 34, 40, 41, 44
Documentary evidence: (*see also* Bede,
    Irish Annals, Historical Sources)
  Anglo-Saxon kingship, historical
    setting, 130, 131
  Anglo-Saxon leadership, 113, 114
  Anglo-Saxon settlement in North-
    umbria, 69, 70, 74, 77
  Book of Deer, 103, 105
  Carolingian court and connections
    with England, 85-88
  Consecration of Kings in Saxon Eng-
    land 85-7
  Fortifications 31, 32-6, 101
  Irish Kingship in Early Historic
    period, 48, 53, 57, 58, 60, 61, 62, 63,
    65, 66, 67
  jewellery in Early Historic period, 36
  Potentates, activities of in Early His-
    toric Period, 31-7
  raiding in Early Historic Period, 36
  Tribal Hidage, The, 70, 92, 131
  Welsh Laws, 36, 37
Documentary sources and artefacts,
    integration of, 162-168
dogs, 30, 39, 68
Doon Hill, East Lothian, Early Historic/
    Anglo-Saxon site, 23, 24, 26, 28, 40,
    41, 44
Driscoll, D., 187
Driscoll, S., 21,
  on relationship between history and
    archaeology, 162-187
  on reworking historical archaeology,
    1-5
dress fasteners, (*see also under* Brooches),
    132-144
droveways, in Early Historic Ireland, 62,
    63, 64
Dublin, Viking Town, 102
Dumbarton, Castle Rock, Early Historic
    fort, 23, 28, 31, 33, 40, 41, 44, 101
Dumville, D. N, 23,
Dun Ardtreck, Argyll, Early Historic
    site, 40, 41, 44
Dun Cuier, Barra, Early Historic site, 40,
    41, 44
Dun Fhinn, Argyll, Early Historic site,
    40, 41, 44
Dun Nosbridge, Islay, Early Historic
    site, 12

Dun an Fheurain, Argyll, 40, 41, 44
Dunadd, Early Historic fort, 7, 18, 19,
    24, 25, 26, 29, 31, 32, 40, 41, 44, 75,
    100
  as centre for collection of tribute,
    11-13, 16-17
  as manufacturing centre 13, 14
Dunaverty, Argyll, Early Historic fort, 7,
    11, 40, 41, 44
Dunbar, East Lothian, 23, 32, 33, 40, 41,
    44, 101
  as royal town, 33
Duncan, H., 4, 5
Dundarg, Aberdeenshire, Early Historic
    fort, 40, 41, 44
Dundurn, Perthshire, Early Historic
    fort, 23, 24, 25, 26, 29, 40, 41, 44,
    100
Duneight, Co. Down, royal site, 54,
    61
Dunfermline, Fife, Burgh, 104, 106
Dunion, Roxburghshire, Iron Age hill-
    fort, 99
Dunkeld, King's Seat, Perthshire, Early
    Historic fort, 24, 40, 41, 45
Dunning, Perthshire, church tower, 104
Dunollie, Argyll, Early historic fort, 7,
    11, 28
Dunottar, 31, 40, 41, 44
duns, 17, 24, 37-8
Dunserverick, royal site 54
Dunshaughlin, Co. Meath, royal site, 55
Dunstan, 90
Dupplin cross, Forteviot, 185

Ecgfrith, 30, 32, 33, 34, 71, 85, 86
Eddius, 34
Eddius' Life of Wilfrid, 101
Edinburgh, 31, 40, 41, 45, 107, 108
Edinburgh, Arthur's Seat, 98
Edinburgh, Holyrood Abbey, 106, 107
Edinburgh, Salisbury Crag, 98
Edwin, 69
Egbert, 91
Eildon Hill North, Roxburghshire, Iron
    Age hillfort, 98
Elgin, Moray, Burgh, 107
Elsham, Lincolns., A-S cemetery 147-149
Empingham, Rutland, A-S cemetery, 115
Enclosed Places:
  archaeological evidence, 23-29
  dating evidence for, 42-6
  documentary evidence for, 29, 31-37
  gazeteer, Map and Index of 40-46
  estate management in Early Scotland,
    102-104
Evans-Pritchard, E., 171

Falkland, Fife, thanage of, 103
Faull, M., 73, 74

Fergus Mor, 6, 9, 10
Fernie, E., 91
Finnlach of Moray, 103
Fisher exact test, 136, 139
Fisher, G., 146
  on style and sociopolitical organisation
  in early Anglo-Saxon England,
  128-144
Fisher, V., 3
footprint stones, 16, 26, 38
Forteviot, Early Historic centre, 19
Fortifications:
  as seats of Potentates, 23-4, 25, 26, 27-9
  documentary evidence for, 31, 32-6
  Royal sites in Early Historic Ireland,
  59-61
Franks Casket, 77,
Freswick Links, Caithness, Viking site,
  102
Freswick Sands, Caithness, Viking site,
  40, 41, 45
frontiers, Anglo-Saxon, reconstruction
  of, 120-124

Garranes, Co. Cork, royal site, 54, 55, 58,
  59, 66, 75
Garryduff, Co. Cork, ringfort, 61, 75
gender as cultural construction, 166,
Giddens, A., 169
Gildas, 23, 31
Glasgow, Burgh, 104, 106
Glass, 24, 25, 66,
  Anglo-Saxon, 116, 117, 151, 153, 154
  beads, 14, 15, 151, 154, 157, 158
  cullet 14, 15, 27
Glassie, H., 175, 176, 177
Glastonbury, Somerset, Early Historic
  site, 90
Godfraith, 19
Gododdin, 36
Goldherring, Cornwall, Early Historic
  finds, 40, 41, 45
Goody, J. and Watt, I., 169
Grambla, 40, 41, 45
Graves (*see also* burial practice, cemeteries, inhumations etc)
Graves, Anglo-Saxon: 71, 73
  as territorial indicators, 120-124
  christian practices in 118
  grave goods as cultural indicators,
  130-144, 145-161
  grave goods as indicators of sex, 115-
  118, 126, 155, 156, 158
  grave goods as indicators of status,
  114-120, 125, 126
  grave goods, statistical treatment of,
  136-141, 147-160, 154
  mortuary variability in, 131-144
Green Castle, Banff, Early Historic fort,
  23, 28, 40, 41, 45

Green, B., 144

Hadrian's Wall, 99
Hampshire, Anglo-Saxon boundary
  changes, 121-124
Hamwih, Town and trading centre, 33,
  82, 84, 93
Harehope, Peeblesshire, Early Historic
  site, 40, 41, 45
Hawkes, S. C, 160
Helgo, 75
Helmets as symbols of kingship, 38,
  119
Henken, H. 55
Heworth, York, A-S cemetery, 147-149
hierarchical clustering applied to Anglo-
  Saxon grave goods 154
Hillforts as Towns, 97-100
Hills, C., 160
Historical Sources: (*see also* Docu-
  mentary evidence),
  Irish material, problems with, 48
  Roman for Iron Age society in Scot-
  land, 98-99
historical and archaeological data, inte-
  gration of in Anglo-Saxon period,
  111-113, 124, 125
historical archaeology, reworking of, 1-6
historical archaeology and anthropology,
  172-178
history and archaeology, relationship of,
  164-168
Hodder, I., 6, 82, 128, 129, 146
Hodges, R., 4
  on power and exchange in Middle
  Saxon England, 79-95
Hogback monuments, 104
Holyrood Abbey, Edinburgh, 106, 107
Holywell Row, Suffolk, A-S cemetery,
  115, 131, 136, 137
Hope-Taylor, B., 34, 71
Horndean, Hants, A-S cemetery, 124
hostages in Early Historic Ireland, 65
hostellers, status of in Early Historic
  Ireland, 61
houses, Royal in Early Historic Ireland,
  65-66
Hownam Law, Roxburghshire, 98
Hoywell Row, Suffolk, A-S cemetery,
  134, 135
Hywel Dda, Laws of, 35-6, 37

Ida of Northumberland 71
Ilchester, Roman Town, 34
Illington, Norfolk, A-S cemetery, 147-
  149, 150, 151, 152, 154, 160
inauguration, mounds as places of in
  Ireland, 57, 58
inauguration rituals, Early Historic
  period, 16, 29, 38

inauguration rituals, early Medieval period, 118, 119
Inchtuthil, Roman Fort, 40, 41, 45
inhumations, (*see also* Cemeteries) 72, 73, 131-140
inscriptions, Early Historic, 29
Inveresk, E. Lothian, 101, 106, 108
Iona Annals, references to fortifications in, 31
Iona, 7, 9, 10, 19, 31
Ipswich, Norfolk, A-S cemetery, 33, 84, 93
Ireland:
  cattle in Early historic period, 62-3
  craftworking in Early Historic period, 66
  documents and power, relationship between, 172
  election of 'King' in 18th and 19th cents, 77, 78
  imported pottery in, 63
  kingship in Early Historic period, 47-68
  links with Dalriada, 8, 9-10, 19, 20
  ringforts, 50-1, 58, 59, 61
  royal and ritual sites, 51-67
  society in Early Historic period, 48-50, 55-7
  status of ecclesiastics in Early Historic period, 14
  wine in Early Historic period, 63
Irish Annals, 31
Islay, 12

Jackson, D. A , 133, 144
Jaenbert, Archbishop, 86
Jewellery, (*see also under* specific items), 24, 25, 28, 27, 43-46, 66, 100
  documentary evidence of, 36
Joarre, 89
Johnston, S., 144
Jones, M., 160

Keiss Broch, Caithness, 40, 41, 45
Kellie, Fife, thanage, 103
Kelso, Burgh, 106
Kenneth MacAlpin, 19, 20, 186, 102
Kent, Anglo-Saxon boundary changes, 121-124
Kildonan Bay, Argyll, Early Historic site, 40, 41, 45
Kildonan Dun, Argyll, penannular brooch from, 17, 18
Killdaloig, Argyll, imported pottery from, 40, 41, 45
Killibury, Cornwall, Early Historic site, 40, 41, 45
Kingdoms, Anglo-Saxon, historical setting of, 130, 131
Kinghorn, Fife, Burgh, 104

Kings,
  consecration of in Carolingian Empire, 85-7, 94
  consecration of in England, 85-7
  in Early Historic Ireland, 47-68
  role of in Northumbria, 69, 71, 74, 75, 77, 78
  succession of in Middle Saxon England, 93
Kingship, archaeology of in Early Historic Ireland, 47-68
Kintyre, 16, 17, 28
Kirk Hill, St Abbs, Early Historic site, 23, 28, 40, 41, 45
Kirktoun of Arbuthnot, 105, 106
Kirktouns, origins of, 104-5
Knowth, 55, 54, 58, 58, 61
Krautheimer, R., 88, 89, 92

Lackford, Suffolk, A-S cemetery, 147-149, 150-152, 161
Lagore Crannog, Co Meath, royal site, 3, 55, 54, 57, 58, 65, 66
Lane, A., 16
Laws of the Four Burghs, 97, 109
lawyers, role of in Early Historic Irish Kingship, 62-3
Leach, E. R, 48
leadership, grave goods as indicators of in Anglo-Saxon England, 114-118, 119, 120
leatherworking, 13, 17, 25
Leeds, E. T, 112, 120, 145
Leinster, 63
Leone, M., 177, 178
Levies, in 10th Century Scotland, 101
Levison, W., 83
Lindsay, W., 101
linear earthworks: 70
  Problems of dating in early Anglo-Saxon England, 123, 124
Lissue, Co Antrim, royal site, 54, 65, 66
literacy and power in Early Historic period, 168-173
Little Dunagoil, Bute, Early Historic site, 40, 41, 45
Little Eriswell, Suffolk, A-S cemetery, 131, 133, 134, 136, 137
Longthorpe, A-S cemetery, 147-149
Lorsch, monastery, 89
Lough Ennel, Co Westmeath, royal site, 54, 61
Lough Ooney, Co Monaghan, royal site, 53
Louis, 85

Loveden Hill, A-S cemetery, 147-149, 152

MacNiocaill, G. 62
Maen Castle, Early Historic site, 40, 41, 45
Mair, 104
Malcolm II, 103
Malcolm III, 103
Malcolm IV, 104
Man, Isle of, 9
Markinch, Fife, Burgh, 104
Markshall, A-S cemetery, 147-149
Mausolea, Saxon, 92
McCormick, F., 62, 68
Medhampstede, Huntingtonshire, abbey, 92
Mercia, 83, 92, 93, 124, 125
metalworking, 13, 25, 43, 44, 28, 38, 45, 46, 66, 66, 75, 77, 100-101
Metz, Cathedral, 89
Middle Saxon England;
    interconnections with continent, 79-80, 83, 84, 85-90, 94
    power and exchange in, 79-95
    problems of understanding society in, 79, 80-82, 92-95
Milfield, Northumberland, A-S huts, 76, 77
Monasteries, foundations of in Kent, 87
Monastic architecture, influences on design, 88-92
Monastic communities,
    importance of in Northumbria, 74
    in Dalriada, 10, 11
    in Early Historic Ireland, 63, 66
Moore, R., 144
Moray, 105
Moreland, J., 4,
    on power and exchange in Middle Saxon England, 79-95
mormaers, in Early Medieval Scotland, 103, 104
Mote of Mark, Kirkudbs. Early Historic site, 28, 40, 41, 45, 75, 100-101
moulds, 100-101
    ingot, 98
    penannular brooches, 13, 17, 66
    pins, 98
    ring, 98
    spear-butt, 98
    square-headed brooches, 75
mounds, as places of inauguration in Early Historic Ireland, 57-8,
Mucking, Essex, A-S settlement, 75, 147-149, 150-154
Mull, Isle of, 12,
Munster, 53, 54
Myres, J., 145, 160

Navan, Co Armagh, royal site, 53, 54, 65
Nechtansmere, battle of, 30, 32, 38
Nelson, J., 119
New Pieces, Breiddin, Early Historic site, 40, 41, 45
Newark, Notts, A-S cemetery, 147-149, 150-154, 160
Nieke, M., 4, 5, 187
    on Dalriada, establishment and maintenance of, 6-21
    on reworking historical archaeology, 1-5
Norse infiltration in Dalriada, 19, 20
North Berwick Law, E. Lothian, Early Historic site, 98
North Luffenham, Rutland, A-S cemetery, 115
Northampton, long hall, 92
Northumbria, 12, 33, 34, 35, 83
    burial practice as indicator of change, 72, 73, 74
    consecration of kings in, 86
    early medieval archaeology, 72
    grave goods as indicators of status in, 74
    querns, absence of in, 75
    secular settlement in, 76
    timber buildings in, 75-77
Northumbria, archaeological evidence for the Anglo-Saxon settlement, 69-78
Norton-on Tees, Co. Durham, cemetery, 74
nucleated Forts, 24
Nuer, Kenyan tribe, 171, 173

Ó Corráin, D., 172
Ó Ríordáin, S., 55
Ocklynge Hill, Sussex, A-S cemetery, 124
Offa, 83, 85, 86, 87, 92, 93
Olson, L., 144
Oppida, 98-99
Orpington, Kent, A-S cemetery, 124
Oswald, 71
Oswine, 77
Oswiu, 74, 77
Owles, E., 144
oxen as symbols of Kingship of Clogher, 65

Parisii, 70
Patrick, 23, 57
Paulinus, 34, 69
payments in Early Medieval Scotland, (see also Conveth, Renders etc), 105,
Peer Polity Interaction, 80, 81, 82
Pemble, J., 144
penannular brooches, 14, 17-18, 20, 66, 139, 143
Penda of Mercia, 74

Pepin, 83,

Perth, Burgh, 97

Pictish cross-slabs and symbol stones,
Aberlemno, 29, 30, 182, 183
as symbols of power, 178-187
Christian context and inspiration of,
180-186
context, historical and social, 179
depictions of warfare on, 30
Dunnichen, 180
functionalist explanations of, 179
funerary contexts of, 179-181
hunting scenes on, 30
links with Ireland and Northumbria,
184
symbols as art, 179

Pictland: 28
migrations into from Dalriada, 19, 20

Picts: 8, 9, 30, 32, 101
in Dalriada, 19, 20

Pippin, 85

Pirenne's theory of Town development,
96

politics, theories of development of in
Anglo-Saxon England, 112-113

Pope Hadrian, 85

Portsdown, Hants, 124

Potentates, activities of in Celtic Britain,
22-46

potters, style group re Anglo-Saxon
cremation urns, 147, 158

Pottery,
Anglo-Saxon, 116, 117, 145-160
Anglo-Saxon cremation urns, 145-160
Anglo-Saxon, incised decoration,
156-159
Anglo-Saxon, variability in style as
cultural indicator, 147
A-ware, 25, 43, 44, 45, 63
B-ware, 25, 43, 44, 45, 46, 63
D-ware, 25, 43, 44, 45
E-ware, 14, 15, 17, 25, 43, 44, 45, 63
imported, unclassified, 14, 15, 17,
43-46, 24, 25, 27
wheel-made, collapse of production in,
71

power and artefacts, 178-187

power and literacy in Early Historic
period, 168-173

Ptolomy, on tribes in Scotland, 98

querns, absence of in Northumbria, 75

raiding:
cattle, 51
documentary evidence of, 36

Rathmore, royal site, 54

Ratz, P., 165, 166, 174

regalia, royal in Anglo-Saxon Period,
118, 119, 125, 126

renders in Early Medieval Scotland, (*see
also* Revenues etc), 105-107

Renfrew, C., 47, 70, 71, 80, 81

Repton, Derbs, crypt, 91

revenues, Ecclesiastical in Early Medieval
Scotland, 105-108

revenues, Royal in Early Medieval Scotland, 105-107

Reynolds, N., 146, 160

Richards, J., 3, 146
on style and symbol, variability in
Anglo-Saxon cremations, 145-161

ringforts, 50-51, 54, 55, 58, 59, 61, 62,
67

Roman Towns re development of later
Towns, 96-7

Roman occupation of Scotland, 99-100

Romanist theory of Town development,
96

Royal and ritual sites in Early Historic
Ireland, 51, 52, 53, 54-65, 65-66
fortification of, 59-61
multiple sites, 61, 61
problems of identification, 52-55
site Typology, 58-61

Ruberslaw, Roxburghshire, Early Historic fort, 24, 40, 41, 45

Sahlins, M., 167

San Vincenzo al Volturno, 89, 90

Sancton, Yorks, A-S cemetery, 147-149,
150, 151, 152, 154, 155, 160

Sawyer, P., 1, 165

Scone, Perthshire, abbey, 106

Scotti, 8

Scottish towns, origins and economy of,
96-110

sea transport, 12

Selbach, 32

Selgovae, 98

Selkirk, Tironensians, 106

Senchus Fer nAlban, 6, 12, 13, 35, 36

Sherbourne, abbey, 90

Sheriffdoms, 104

Shires, early in Scotland, 104

skeletal analyses, 147, 149, 155

Slater, E., 101

slave trade, in Early Historic period, 36,
39

smithing, (*see also* metalworking) 26

Snape, Norfolk, A-S cemetery, 147-149

social interaction and stylistic variability
in Anglo-Saxon England, 128-130

social organisation re Iron Age Forts,
99

social role, differentiation of in Anglo-
Saxon pottery style 147, 155, 156-
158

social systems in Middle Saxon England,
79-95

society in Early Historic Ireland, 48-50, 55-7
Sociopolitical organisation, a study of in Anglo-Saxon England, 128-144
South Elkington, Lincolns, A-S cemetery, 147-149, 150-154
South, S., 174
Spearman, M., 3
on Early Scottish Towns, 96-110
spinning, 25
Spong Hill, Norfolk, A-S cemetery, 115, 147-149, 150-152, 154, 155, 157, 158, 159, 160
Sprouston, Northumberland, 77
St Andrews, Fife, 105-6, 108
Stanwick, Yorks, 98
statistical testing of grave goods in Anglo-Saxon cremation cemeteries 147-160
statistical testing of mortuary variability in Anglo-Saxon cemeteries, 136-141
status and wealth in Early Historic Ireland, 61-65
status, grave goods as indicators of, in early Anglo-Saxon England, 114-120
status, grave goods as indicators of in Northumbria, 74
Stirling, Early Historic site, 32, 40, 41, 45, 108
stylistic variability and social interaction in Anglo-Saxon England, 128-140
Sussex, Anglo-Saxon boundary changes, 121-124
Sutton Hoo, Suffolk, royal grave, 65, 71, 92, 115, 118
Swaffham, Norfolk, A-S cemetery, 131, 134, 135, 136, 137
symbol stones, Pictish, as symbols of power, (*see also under* Pictish) 179-187

Talbot, E., 110
Taplow, Bucks, A-S grave, 115
Tara, Co Meath, royal site, 54, 57, 58, 58
Tarbert, Loch Fyne, Early Historic site, 11, 40, 41, 45
Taylor, H., 90, 91
Teinds, 105, 106
Teltown, Co Meath, royal site, 58,
territories, mortuary variability as indicator of, 130-131, 136-144
territories, reconstruction of in early Anglo-Saxon England, 120-124
Thanages, North of the Forth, 102-104, 105
The Mount, York, A-S cemetery 147-149
theory in history, 163, 164
Tintagel, Cornwall, Early Historic site, 34, 23, 40, 41, 45
Tiree, 12
Toisech, 103, 104

Torcs, 99
Towns: (*see also under* Burghs),
Canterbury, 97
creation of in Middle Saxon England, 90
Early Scottish, origins and economy, 96-110
Iron Age Hillforts as, 97-100
Pirenne's theory of development, 96
Roman, 96-7
Romanist theory of development, 96
York, 97
trade connections in 9th and 10th century Scotland, 101-102
Traprain Law, E. Lothian, Early Historic fort, 40, 41, 45, 98
Trethurgy, Cornwall, pottery from, 24, 40, 41, 45
Trevelgue, Cornwall, pottery from, 40, 41, 46
Tribal Hidage, The, 70, 92, 131
Tribute: (*see also* revenues etc)
collection of in Dalriada, 11, 12, 13, 16, 20
collection of in Early Historic Ireland, 49, 62
collection of in Northumbria, 34, 35, 75
Tynron Doon, Dumfriesshire, Early Historic site, 40, 41, 43, 46

Udal, The, North Uist Early Historic site, 40, 41, 46
Ugadale, Argyll, Early Historic Site, 40, 41, 46
Ulaid, federation of, 53
Ulster, 53, 55
Ulster, Annals of, 103
Urquhart Castle, Invernesshire, Early Historic site, 40, 41, 46

variability:
in Anglo-Saxon cremation burials 145-161
mortuary in Anglo-Saxon England, 130
stylistic in Anglo-Saxon England, 128-140
Viking Age sculpture, 74
Viking attacks on England, 88, 90
Viking infiltration in Dalriada, 19, 20,
Vikings, as Traders, 101-102
Votadini, 98
Voteporix, 29

Wailes, B., 51-2, 144
Wakerley, Northants, A-S cemetery, 131, 133, 135, 137, 137
wall paintings, 91, 92
Wallace-Hadrill, J., 89

Wallerstein, I., 80, 84, 82
Walls Hill, Renfrewshire, Iron Age fort, 98
Warner, H., on Dalriada, establishment and maintenance of, 6-21
Warner, R., 3, 5, 55, 68
  on the archaeology of Early Irish kingship 47-68
weaving, 25
Welsh Laws, (*see also* Hywel Dda), 35-7
Wessex, 83, 92, 93
Wiessner, P., 128, 129
Wilfrid, 69
William I., 97, 110
Winchester, Hants, Minster, 88, 90, 91
wine, 15, 28, 63, 100

Winterbourne Gunner, Wilts, A-S cemetery, 115
Wolf, E., 79, 83
wooden objects, Anglo-Saxon, 116, 117
woodworking, 17
World systems models, 80, 81
Worthy Park, Hants, A-S cemetery, 147-149, 152, 160
Wuffingas, 33
Wulfred, 87

Yarrowkirk stone, 30
Yeavering, Northumberland, royal site, 23, 33, 34, 39, 40, 41, 46, 71, 75, 75
York, A-S cemeteries 147-149
York, Roman town, 97